CROFT AND CREEL

Scotland
June, 1991.

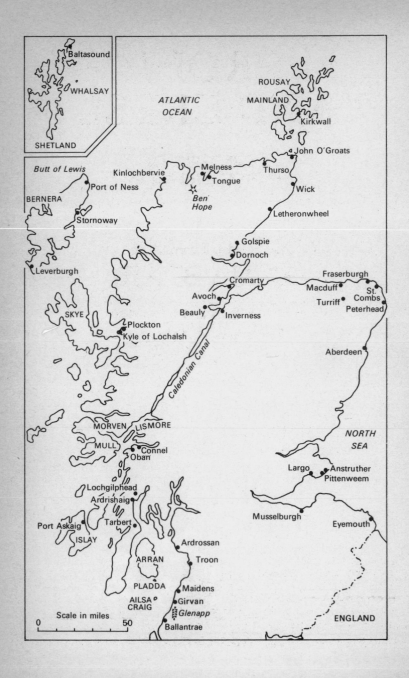

CROFT AND CREEL

A CENTURY OF
COASTAL MEMORIES

Collected and compiled by
ANNA BLAIR

Illustrated by
William B. Taylor

SHEPHEARD-WALWYN

To all those good people in town, hamlet
and croft who have shared their memories
with me, and especially to JOY, for old
friendship and for starting me off on my
first travels for this book.

Also by Anna Blair
A TREE IN THE WEST
THE ROWAN ON THE RIDGE
TALES OF AYRSHIRE
TEA AT MISS CRANSTON'S

ISBN 0 85683 096 8

Printed and bound in Great Britain
for Shepheard-Walwyn (Publishers) Ltd,
26 Charing Cross Road (Suite 34), London WC2H 0DH
by Cox & Wyman Ltd, Reading, Berkshire,
from typesetting by Alacrity Phototypesetters,
Banwell Castle, Weston-super-Mare.

Cover design by Alan Downs
based on an illustration by William B. Taylor.

Contents

Acknowledgements

I am most grateful to the 'rememberers' for this book, who welcomed an inquisitive stranger so warmly. Most are acknowledged by name alongside quotations from our recorded conversations, others prefer to remain anonymous. To all, I offer my thanks.

I acknowledge my debt to Bill Taylor of Troon whose fine illustrations make such a major contribution to the book. Thanks are due also to Shepheard-Walwyn Ltd., for guidance; to Mr. H. G. A. Anderson and Mrs Edith Dykes for help and advice; and to Mrs. Sybille MacKintosh of Inverness for permission to quote from recordings she made in the 1960s with Netta Ross, George Sutherland and Donald MacKintosh of Beauly.

A.B.   Giffnock, 1987

Introduction

This book touches on many aspects of life round the Scottish coast which, if pursued, balanced, and formally arranged by an historian might make a social study of the country. There is something of Education, Crofting, Fishing, Religion, Recreation etc., but the people who 'remembered' for these pages would scarcely recognise under such headings their snippets of reminiscence ... the clogs of Dutch sailors clattering on the cobbles of Peterhead, the Colporteurs, the Temperance Walk at St. Combs behind the flute and drum band ...

They still do the Walk, mind, but there's nae Temperance now.

For these are the random memories of over forty folk who, in recorded interviews, revealed what had once made them laugh and weep, or know fear, joy, embarrassment or discomfort. The book is not about Movements or Theories or Issues of the day, but about what people wore and ate, how they accepted dry closets, trampling their washing in tubs at Beauly harbour, or the killing of the croft pig, or how they sewed oiled sailcloth with a palming needle, a hand-strap with a hard centre to act like a thimble but on the ball of the palm.

And what would the scholar historian have done with the assurance of one proud householder?

It's a verra verra old house this. I'm no' sure whether it's B.C. or A.D. but it's verra old.

The places remembered are widely scattered round the coast or within a few miles of it, and they appear on the accompanying map. Each comes across with its own personality, partly from its location and lifestyle, but more from what lodged in the memories of those who were young there. There was the patronising 'Paraffin City' name given to Connel by its newly electrified Oban neighbours; there was the Girvan Town Crier still announcing the events of the day in the 1920s; the first 'bus in Troon, called 'Stoorie Aggie'; the communal village bull the lads pushed through the doorway of a cantankerous ancient in Plockton; the cows about the streets in Ardrossan, some off the Arran boat and going up to the slaughter-house and some grazed daily on the shore and brought back up the main street every night for milking.

There are no chapters in academic books to tell you that in highland parts there are sometimes two Donalds or Anguses in a family, each called for a separate grandfather.

So the lads would get nicknames . . . maybe Angus Mhor for the bigger one and Angus Rhua for a redhead. There were a lot of nicknames one way and another. The coxwain of the Port Askaig lifeboat now, was called Dougal MacDougall, so they called him Dougie-Twice.

And there are no exam marks for knowing of the Great Cloche-merle-type Schism over the building of public conveniences in Lochgilphead and the controversy about it which raged in the *Argyllshire Advertiser* and *Loch Fyneside Echo* (known locally as The Squeak). And none for being able to relate the story of Donald, who worked at a west highland distillery.

Donald was in cahoots with the excisemen who came with a dip-rod to measure the whisky in the tanks. Now Donald had a couple of sauce bottles fastened inside his trousers and a little sponge and when they'd measured the whisky they drew the sponge up along the rod and squeezed it into Donald's sauce bottles.

The age-range of most of the contributors is from about fifty to ninety-six, but there are three others who, as octogenarians in the 1960s, spoke of old Beauly to Sybille MacKintosh. She has passed their memories on to me and so the period covered is from the 1880s, with a few earlier gleanings from hearsay before that . . . to the 1950s. By then places, for long separate and isolated and with quite individual character, were being drawn into a more homo-geneous likeness. Life became more integrated, more predictable, with the same brands of entertainment, the same chainstores and collectives in main streets. But new and definable identities will come and we can leave the chroniclers of next century to the new eccentricities and humours which they will see in the second half of this one, and record when the time comes.

PARAFFIN CITY AND OTHER PLACES

What were they like, the small places that spawned those who recollect their calf days there with such a mixture of rue and affection? Surely they had as much in common as have the re-memberers themselves, and yet at the same time as much that set each apart from the others.

It's easy to describe each one physically and geographically, but perhaps one tastes the flavour best by seeing them, one by one round the coast, through the eyes of their sons and daughters in recollected incidents or scenes that convey to them the essence of their native haunts.

> Ballantrae's a fresh wee fishing place, quite low along the shore at the mouth of the River Stinchar below the old castle there. And Glenapp opens up a bit to the south. It's a bonnie stretch. When I was young the boats came and went all the time. But it's like most places, you mind it best for the people.

Apart from the steady ebb and flow of summer visitors, Ballantrae played host to a variety of characters.

> In the old days there were always Glasgow orphans fostered here. I badly wanted to be an orphan in a grey jersey and skirt ... quite fancied myself as an orphan. Then th'used to be quite a lot of tramps came about here and up into the glens. Everybody just accepted that ... made up their pieces and boiled their tea-cans for them.

Those were nameless itinerants. But one who took up residence a little way out of the village that was there four hundred years ago, remains a Ballantrae legend.

> Sawney Bean, the cannibal robber, and his family lived in a cave along the shore there ... there would just be a track in those days and he was on the sea side of it. They pounced on passers-by, killed them then hung them up in the cave for their winter food store.

A more genial cave-dweller, remembered by John Mc.Clung from recent years, was Snib Scott, living in another cave above the shore road.

> Snib stayed in that cave with just an old chair, and a pile of newspapers for his bed. I knew him fine because I worked on the roads. He was no harm to anyone and people were good to him. He was quite a likeable sort of chap.

Further along that road lies Girvan, now as in the days of long-yonder a small country town for outlying farming families and local fisherfolk. There's the busy harbour and small boat yard, a street of good shops and a thousand rooms to let for summer.

Used to be full of holiday visitors when I was young. The shore was safe, with good sand, and there was plenty to do and see. When I think back, one of the sights I remember best was the Town Crier going up and down the street making his announcements. One was 'Notice! Notice! The steamer Lady Ailsa will sail for Ailsa Craig today at 2.30 p.m.'

The Town Crier was a colourful and welcome sight. Less welcome to some was Hughie Clark, the Girvan sweep, though what he did to merit his reputation is not revealed.

It was considered unlucky to meet Hughie Clark the sweep. Don't know why. He was good fun really. I remember him making us laugh when he came to sweep our chimney. My mother scolded him for making a mess in the kitchen and he just danced round her, all sooty, chanting 'Mrs. McQuaker, you are, so you are, a most beautiful woman, a most beautiful woman' ... till she couldn't help laughing ... bit of a comic really.

Like Girvan, Troon, twenty-seven miles to the north, has always been a well-ordered pleasant shopping township to the 'Trin', or 'nose', of land snouting a mile or two into the Firth of Clyde ... a Mecca for holiday-makers before the Second War, and a desirable place of residence since, for commuting city business and professional folk. It was self-contained and bien in the early days of the century, with thrift, rather than poverty, the mark of the less well-heeled.

I remember the gentlemen from the big houses being driven by their chauffeurs to the station (that was just after the carriage days when cars were something new). And there was one man that the station porter used to put out wee steps for, to climb up into the train.

The first bus in Troon was nicknamed 'Stoorie Aggie', it threw up so much dust.

Of all the places mentioned in these pages, Ardrossan was probably the nearest to being like part of Glasgow, with its tenements, its accent and its stream of holidaymakers, passing through to go 'doon the watter' from the harbour. But it was small enough for everyone to know everyone, and to be remembered for its own personality and oddities and not as simply a Glasgow satellite.

> Th' was always cows about the streets ... cattle off the Arran boat maybe, going to the slaughter-house; and then next to my grand-mother's house th' was this dairy and they grazed their cows at the shore and brought them back for milking every night.

The Ayrshire sea-board towns are certainly 'lowland' but, even on the same general latitude, the island of Islay far to the west is undisputably 'highland', in place-name, habitant and lifestyle. The southernmost of the Hebrides, its few towns are strung out along three or four roads spoking from Bridgend and running through farming land past distilleries and fishing slips.

Halfway between the Ayrshire coast and Islay, Tarbert is 'of the isles' rather than the lowland mainland, although it lies on the neck of land between Loch Fyne and West Loch Tarbert. John Leitch grew up there ninety years ago.

> Our home was one of a group, a wee hamlet called Cairnbaan near Tarbert. It was a fishing place really and all the fisherfolk spoke Gaelic. My parents did too, to each other all the time even at the tea table. But not to us, and we only paid enough attention to pick up a few words, 'I'm fine', 'How are you?', and so on. There used to be little puffers, wee steam-driven cargo boats ... went to Ayr maybe for cargoes of coal, and brought them back to Tarbert harbour. My father'd buy four or five tons for the winter and stack it behind the byre. We didn't go away much because you'd really to take a boat to go anywhere.

Up Loch Fyne then, past Ardrishaig and we reach Isobel Cameron's Lochgilphead.

> It was a small place then really, in the tiny Loch Gilp that's an inlet in Loch Fyne. Part of the village was at the front with a few guest houses, a hotel and one or two shops. The rest was 'Up the brae' ... the residential part, the Poor House, the Asylum and the Hospital.

At the query (to judge the size and importance of the village) 'Was there a policeman?' there was an indulgent chuckle.

> A policeman! Bless your heart, there was the Chief Constable of Argyll lived at Lochgilphead!

To nourish the minds and souls of the various congregations in the village, there were travelling book and tract salesmen, the Colporteurs.

Everyone just called them the Colpo'chers. They would lay out their leaflets in father's study, him being the minister, take his orders, have dinner or a bed for the night, then go on to the next village or manse ... but mind you, the Colporteurs are still going.

The considerable town of Oban is the next west coast place to be remembered. Oban, the slipway to the western islands, centre for shopping, education, business and Gaelic culture.

It is the metropolis to the likes of Connel, up round the corner into Loch Etive country, the place that in the old days the Oban folk with gas or 'the electric', loftily called Paraffin City. But Connel in Catherine Murray's youth was fast leaping into the twentieth century.

When I first went to the Connel post-office to work, there was a little telephone exchange but too few subscribers to work it, so we had to go round the doors asking people if they would like to put in the telephone. We got eight, and that started the service.

Although it was a tiny place, Connel had an important role as a connection, not only with the Mull of Kintyre, but with Benderloch, Appin and Ballachulish to the north. And the link that was built in 1903 was the huge rail bridge that took the place of the old ferry between South and North Connel.

There was a pedestrian part too. You paid tuppence to walk and about ten bob for a car. The rail line closed twenty years ago and there was a last run that was packed with people. Everybody was really sad to see the last of the Gaelic Express and I remember the fog horns blowing out as it went through.

Across Loch Etive is North Connel and the folk of the twin villages often found 'tuppence', or 'ten bob', too much of an imposition.

So in my young days just about everybody had a boat, so that from one end of the village to the other, people had their own boat lying, and their own wee slipway, to go back and forward across the loch or to go out at night for their wee bit of fishing.

There was small industry in those old days too.

At the turn of the century there was the mill making blankets, and a lot of girls worked there. But that stopped and the village hall's there now.

The lairds here are the Inverary Campbells. The laird's the Captain of Dunstaffnage too. We used to see the old laird about, with his kilt and his crook. There's only the remains of the castle now, but there's

Dunstaffnage House. To keep the title 'Captain of Dunstaffnage', the laird has to spend one night a year there. I remember taking him down once in a wee motor-lorry that I had, and he'd his lamp with him, a bit food and all he needed to keep him for the night.

Looking out to the west, Connel folk see the green hills of the long island of Lismore where Mary Macfadyen lived her girlhood years.

We called it a village but it wasn't really. It was just a crofting community scattered over the island. We were one of nine houses in a row right on the shore with a view to the Morvern hills across Loch Linnhe.

The Oban McCaigs were brought up on a Lismore croft ... made their money through banking, and when they put up their big folly in the town there was s'posed to have been statues of all the family in all the niches. But t'was never done.

North through the Sound of Sleat and Loch Alsh to Plockton. There's maybe a suspicion that the grave face of the Celt marks a humourless man, but Farquhar MacDonald has some less than dour memories of his young days in that village, jutting into Loch Carron, bonnie as its postcards, and lively.

There was a communal bull in the village. It was shared and each one got the use of it for purposes necessary. There was also a man who was as bad-tempered as the bull was docile. The boys used to ride on the beast's back and one night they took it down to the sea front to the old man's house, opened his door, pushed the bull into his hallway and ran.

A known beauty spot, Plockton has always attracted visitors.

When we were young and in the sweetie shop we saw all sorts of visitors. I remember once this man and lady coming in and rooting about for what they wanted. They turned out to be Sir Laurence and Lady Olivier. And big James Robertson Justice was another who used to come about, and in and out of local houses.

North-west next across Skye to the south reaches of Harris ...

I remember a mixture of houses at Leverburgh where I had the bank. Some houses were new and some the old thatched black houses. And there were the white sands not so far away. I remember the early landings of aeroplanes there at varying times depending on the tides. There were a few shops ... a small population just, nothing like the busy fish-station community Lord Leverhulme had thought to make it. It was a ghost township really.

Past the busy fishing and tweed-making town of Stornoway with its famous Nicolson Institute school, its fine harbour and its airport, to the island of Bernera on the west of Lewis.

> It was very much an island community ... still is ... but in my young days everything came by boat and we went everywhere by boat. There was a fair scattering of houses and it was a long walk wherever you went on Bernera itself. Quite hilly. Stornoway was the big town, and you didn't go there often. I was grown-up before ever I visited it.

Near the Butt of Lewis lies Ness ... a handful of settlements at the end of the road, the north-west edge of Scotland. But they had a surprising number of travellers beating a pathway to those faraway doors.

> Yes, a lot of travelling people came round selling from suitcases ... jerseys and cardigans and scarves ... Indians often, and later Pakistanis, (in fact one of the earliest Indian communities in Britain was in Lewis. Some of the children take better to Gaelic than their own tongue). But it was a great treat when they used to come in and open these cases. The aunts I stayed with would maybe buy themselves new cardigans.

None, anywhere, better deserved those new pedlar-case cardigans than those two hard-worked ladies with their croft, their peats, their weaving and two little city evacuees to rear.

Round Cape Wrath and Durness and along the north coast lie the Kyle of Tongue and the village of Tongue ... remote, and sitting on the side of a hill plunging down to the sea loch. The area has been 'a kind of Shangri-la' to John Coghill since he was a lad.

> The hills are beautiful and the climate fine, even for so far north ... and I used to love to watch the movement of the tides. In my young days every plot of it was cultivated with grain and potatoes, turnips and so on. Now it's back to sheep. It's not a big place but there's the church, still with its Laird's Pew ... a fine church.

And the minister of such a parish has to be versatile even yet, for it's not so long since, at a morning service, attended by a holidaymaker, he was seen to act as beadle, lectern-reader, organist and preacher.

Along the Pentland coastline, fretted with the almost deserted, creamy shores of Faar, Kirtomy, Armadale, Melvich and Crosskirk bays, we go round the headland into Scrabster, the fishing village linked to Thurso about a mile away.

The Thurso we knew in the old days was just a small, quite busy town of about 3,000 people, looking out over the Pentland Firth.

The Firth could be sullen and gurly enough to keep the town watchful for danger.

The life-boat station was down at Scrabster. I was in the Lifeboat Guild, and the Thurso folk supported it well because they were so near the need of it.

Across that stretch of water lies Orkney ... another world, where the biggest island of the group, and not Scotland itself, is Mainland, its principal town Kirkwall. For many, in the days remembered here, Kirkwall was the centre of the world. They're sturdy folk in the Orkneys and have survived much 'winter and rough weather'.

There's a tree in Kirkwall ... that's about all the trees in the whole of Orkney. It's very-very bare landscapes and that's why so many household things are made of pleated and woven straw instead of wood. It's rough in winter but you get lovely summers. When I lived in Rousay they were still talking about the Clearances, when folk were pushed east from the west, to make way for sheep. They were given poor wee-bit five-acre crofts of wet sour land between the decent farms. But they worked hard and a lot eventually mastered it and paid their way.

South-east, past Wick about eighteen miles, lies Latheronwheel, cheek-by-jowl with Janetstown, in ungenerous croft country where men and women of the early century had to struggle for a living, and are remembered as doughty fighters who did not craik for what they could not have.

In the city you're always wanting something more. With us you weren't seeing what other people had and needing to get it. You'd the countryside, the birds and the flowers ... and we'd Hogmanay and so on.

No nonsense about commercialised Christmases at Latheronwheel.

We didn't keep Christmas. In fact when I was very young, a lot didn't even keep New Year on January 1st, but on January 12th because of the change in the calendar, (d'you remember the old chant 'Give us back our eleven days?'). A lot of folk resisted British Summer Time too ... left their clocks where they were. They talked about the New Time but they went by the Old.

The local people at Latheronwheel shared their not-very-much with some who had even less.

We'd a lot of tinkers came round selling pegs and pins and thread when I was young early this century. Most of them were MacPhees and Newlandses. There was no compulsory education for the tinkers then, but later they'd to attend school for two or three months of the year, so they settled nearby for that time in their tents and I remember them washing their clo'es in the burn.

Past Golspie and the Dornoch Firth, across the Cromarty Firth are spread the dark soil and rosy sandstone of the Black Isle, with Cromarty at its eastern tip and Beauly just beyond the western end.

Cromarty's just out there on its own, with quaint village streets that lie behind the fisher cots at the shore. When I was young and living at The Cromarty Arms it was a busy wee place with the white tower of the lighthouse and Hugh Miller's cottage (the geologist y'know) and the Big House where Colonel Ross lived. There was a character in Cromarty 't ran a kind of private ferry across the firth to Nigg. He fished, trawled a wee bit as he went along, illegally of course ... then he used to come to the back door of the hotel with a bag of flukies ... very small, but tasty. The cat got half and we fried up the rest.

Round the south shore of the Black Isle, past the odd little village of Avoch with its warrens of narrow streets and its house gables jutting and butting at all angles, its history of smuggling, and of 'lairds" houses bought with fortunes made in foreign parts, the road runs eventually to Beauly. The rememberers of Beauly, Donald MacKintosh, George Sutherland and Netta Ross go back quarter of a century beyond those of other places, for they recorded their mindings in the early 1960s, as octogenarians then, for schoolchildren there who are in early middle-age now.

It was mostly walking everywhere in the 1880s ... a few carts and pony traps or hurlie barrows. A lot of people walked barefoot too, maybe to Inverness, then when they came to the outskirts of the town they'd put on their shoes to be a perfect swell in the town.

I remember market day here with folk down from the glens, and their cattle, horses and flocks of sheep milling around in the square.

There was quite a big shipping trade here in Beauly too. I remember three ships, The Viking, The Baurai and The Hilda. They carried coal and salt and china. And at the side of the harbour there was a place where women tramped their washing in tubs.

At such a crossroads as Beauly there were bound to be characters.

There used to be a wife here they said was a witch and they called her 'The old woman with the pig' because she was always followed by her pig. Then there was Farquhar-w'-the-gun 't he never fired, 'Cripple Granny' that looked after the Priory, and Jimmie Bookie 't sold old magazines to get a penny or tuppence for meal. And there was 'Old Noke 't played the comb and paper and married at eighty-five.

Macduff, one of the fishing towns that barnacle the Moray Firth, is remembered through a blue haze of kippering smoke ... with men emptying fishing-boat holds and hardy creel women trudging from the quay inland to market centres like Turriff. And mingling with the rest, itinerant tinkers shared the small prosperity of hawking round their wares.

Round the humphy back of Scotland the road goes past Fraserburgh and finds St. Combs ... high, windy and clear ... fisher-village and one-time smuggling haunt with a passage from the shore of the Loch of Strathbeg leading up to a trap-door in what John Robertson calls the 'stick bottom' of a cupboard in Haddo House (and hastily translates to 'wooden floor'). Perhaps with the inflow of illicit liquor there was much need of St. Combs' other claim to fame.

St. Combs was a great place for Temperance ... never a pub here, but the Band of Hope and The Temperance Alliance. And every year they'd a Walk w' a flute-and-drum band. We still have the Walk mind, but there's no Temperance now.

South to find the helicopters churning and chopping over the bustling town which is modern Peterhead. But it wasn't always so prosperous.

When I was wee, Peterhead was a town of about eleven thousand people and th' was a lot of poverty. After a rainy day when half the boys hada' turned up at the school it would be 'No boots, Miss'. When they did have them they were great big tackety things and you could hear them clattering about the streets like the Dutch sailors we got in Peterhead in their clogs.

Originally, y'see, the trading in and out Peterhead was with America, and down the street where the sea-captains lived you can see how the gardens are all black earth ... that was the ballast they brought back from Virginia. That street's all dark soil.

Peterhead had its hawkers too.

We'd an Indian pedlar came round every year ... very pop'lar he was.

'Silky Blouses' was his nickname ... never knew his right name, but that's what he sold, so he got 'Silky Blouses'.

Away south now to the tidy harbours, red tiled roofs, fertile hinterland crofts, royal residences and crow-stepped fisher-cot gavels of Fife. In the days remembered there the people were hard-working, well-doing, sometimes hard-pressed but seldom destitute.

They're good folk the Fifers. They dinna talk soft, mind but they wouldna see you stuck.

And that's as gushing a compliment as you'd get from most Fifers. Inland there were rich farms and coal seams and many who laboured there lie now under some of the finest carved gravestones in the country, worked by contemporary craftsmen. But it is his own shore stretches that Alex Archer best recalls.

At these places like Largo, Pittenweem, Crail, Anstruther ... all along the coast here, the life of the places was a' round the harbours, to do w' the fishing. And then th'was lots o' holiday folk.

Across the Firth of Forth lie Leith and Musselburgh, close enough to Edinburgh to be an easy walk. And yet, in Andrew Fairnie's childhood ninety years ago, so separate, that in all his clear unsentimental recollection of those old days he never once mentioned the capital city.

Fisherrow, when I lived there, was just a tiny place pretty well self-contained from Musselburgh. Musselburgh was the 'town' to us ... with carts, pony-traps or wee horse-drawn go-carts. Kirsop's was the big shop. The women all went there ... a well-frequented shop was Kirsop's. And there was the racing too ... Musselburgh's always been known for the racing.

Thirty places ... each of them with so particular a personality that no one of them can properly represent others which are on the same stretch of coast but not noticed in these pages. But perhaps there is just enough likeness between the good folk living within thirty or forty miles of each other in any general area to give a 'feel' to the stranger of how life was there seventy, eighty, ninety years ago.

1

Another Wee Town Out There

The city man can find his way to all the vennels, crannies and
pleasure-domes of his home urbs, and the countryman describe
every burn and moor-path twist in the ten miles all-ways from his
own farm dyke ... more if he's a stout walker. The city man is
sophisticated, street-wise; the country's habitant learnèd in sky-
sign and soil. But the men and women who live and work within
sight and sound of the sea in fishing, crofting and sailing communities are citizens of the world and, even if working the coastlands, look to the sea and the lands beyond it for much of their
livelihood and their philosophy of life.

An Anstruther man who fished the wider seas himself recalls of
his father,

> My father was a deep-sea man ... went out to Australia an' that, on
> sailing ships, oh aye ... in a big four-master called the Bracadale, then
> away up to Los Angeles and San Francisco and back round The Horn.

and of his mother,

> She was employed as a fish gutter and packer, by a Russian company.

His own young experience reads like the opening lines of a travel
adventure.

> I've fished off Rockall and the Faroes ... Klarsvig was interesting too
> ... and Vestmanhav'n ... I've seen all of that. My father being a
> fisherman and my mother a fish worker, they met at Baltasound in
> Shetland. Their fish went to Germany and Holland and up the Baltic.

But in the times of seventy and eighty years ago that this book
remembers, although the fisher-work touched those far places with
the exotic names that trip so familiarly off fisherfolk tongues from
Ballantrae to Thurso and from Eyemouth to Lewis, it all had its

1

first preparations in the small living-rooms of their own shore-side houses ... houses unmistakably belonging to the tight fishing communities which made up the whole of a small village or were a distinct, kenspeckle part of a bigger place.

Early recollections of Rose Baker's childhood are of such houses among the villages beading the south side of the River Forth.

> The fisher houses were on their own, back from the shore, always clean and tidy. I mind their old whitewashed outside stairways, y'ken, and their windows a' shinin'.

And Andrew Fairnie born about 1893 recalls his fishing village home.

> I was born in Fisherrow over there in Musselburgh. My father was a herring fisherman and my mother went out wi' the creel. That's what I was born to. Fisherrow was a wee place by itself in those days.

John Coghill remembers the similar village-within-a-village that was the Fishertown at Golspie.

> It was part of the community certainly, though people at the other end of Golspie wouldn't have wanted the Fishertown folk to come and live beside them, but then neither would the Fishertown folk have liked it the other way round. But my best friends at school, by far, were Fishertown boys ... always in their blue jerseys.

At Anstruther too the fisherfolk were something of a group apart, except for a once weekly meeting-up.

> Here the farmers and fishers kept to theirselves ... met up just at the kirk.

And in the Black Isle,

> There was a wee bit no' mixing at Cromarty with the Fisherton folk. Fisherton was nice ... just wee rows of washed cottages with old-fashioned gardens ... still there ... their gables sideways to the sea ... same as most places.

Another party to the reminiscing puts in a confirmation.

> ... like the higgledy-piggledy fisher-houses at Avoch ... aye, the gavels there were to the sea. At Avoch y'ken, maybe ninety or a hundred years ago the men built their own houses with just stones from the shore, and they'd lofts for mending and storing their nets.

But there were other parts of the shorelands where fishers were not of a wee world apart, but where a man might be part-fisher part-crofter. In Hugh Craigie's early days his Orkney grandfather Marwick was one of these.

> He started from a wee croft away up the top of the hill ... two-three acres just. He went fishing too with his one small boat at first then a bigger boat after, with three hands. ·

And the men of Kilrenny in the East Neuk of Fife had both skills too.

> They came down to their boats in the fishing season and worked in the fields in the summertime.

Whether of set-apart or mingled community, memories like those of Jim Buchan about the fisher-houses he knew, are vivid.

> A' these houses at Peterhead had no more than outside toilets, but the families were proud of their homes. People say fisherfolk are the salt of the earth ... ah well, right enough, Christ chose them, didn't he? Nearly all the houses in the old part of the town were but'n'bens. My grandmother's father built a house for four sons ... just wee ... but it was four different homes, two outside doors to the street and an open stair at the back for th'upstairs houses. Each one had a living room and a tiny bedroom. Some families were five or six bairns and my mother used to say 'twas like a hospital, with beds a' ways.

And one who has spent a long life in a high village that seems at the edge of the world, at St. Combs near Fraserburgh, has no need to carry the picture of her early home in her memory. For it sits not far below on the foreshore, in clear view of her present stone-cottage window.

> We was a' born here at St. Combs, and a' wir bairns was born here ... born in that hint-last hoose doon there where it was a' fishin' ... no rooms up the stair, just the sky light.

The husband of fifty-nine years, a gentle invalid now, but once a laughing St. Combs fisherlad, nods with wry pleasure at the memory of the similar home of his childhood from which a boat crew went out.

So in homes that limpeted the coast from Anstruther and Musselburgh, from Peterhead and St. Combs, and in Oban,

Skigersta, Rousay and Ballantrae, preparations went carefully ahead for the next voyage. And established at the heart of such homes were the staunch women who would presently wait the long wait till their men were safely home again ... well-chosen women, says Jean Buchan, who knew the life and its hazards and accepted them.

> The first thing a fisher-loon did when he was thinking about marrying and lookin' for a hoose was find a wife that wasnae afraid to work, for they'd a hard life the women. My grandfather used to say to a' his sons, 'if you're lookin' for a wife, tak' one 't likes the fill o' her belly and you're sure o' your own meat.'

So much for the right wife. Jim Buchan looks back on a picture of his own mother, bred to the tasks of a fisherman's wife.

> In the livin' room, see, there was the gas bracket this side the wall and two hooks a few feet apart wi' the fishin' net stretched between them and your mother down below in the lamplight mendin' it. Oh aye, I mind fine of her doin' that ... *and* gut and pack.

And Margaret Ritchie looking far back to childhood in Cromarty,

> I remember the women at Fisherton sitting outside their doors with their hands flashing in and out mending the nets. You could hardly see their hands they were so quick.

The nets in good trim, there was each man's small store of vittles to be got ready.

> In the early years that I went out from Anstruther every man had his own kit of food, a bit cheese maybe and a packet of tea.

And in Cromarty,

> The fishermen used to come into the bar of the Cromarty Arms where I was brought up, for their bottle of whisky to take out with them for their wee dram.

Having hooked her man and laid by her marriage lines in the clothes kist, a worthy fisher wife had to learn to be knacky with less romantic baits and lines.

> My mother baited three lines every day wi' the mussels for my father, my brothers and me. My sister, she shelled the mussels ... actually it was my father was the best 't ever I saw shelling mussels ... used a special what they ca'ed a 'shielin' blade' ... a shellin' knife y'ken.

There was a refinement to ordinary baiting that prevented the fankling of lines as they were fed out. Alex Archer of Largo remembers his uncle's way of doing.

> There were four of them and they used to do the baiting of lines putting grass between each row ... used to send us bairns over to Cellardyke for the grass. That was so the lines didnae get tangled as they let them out.

If it wasn't the line fishing they were bound for, the nets had to be dried ready for the setting off.

The fishermen at our place at Lochgilphead joined the boats at Ardrishaig and I can just see yet, the nets up drying along the way between the two places.

The nets dry or the lines baited, the poke of vittles and the bottle safely tucked away, there was one more hurdle before the boats were off ... the ominous portents they might meet on the way to shore or harbour.

A fisherman wouldnae dare meet a minister when he was going to sea ... bad luck that. If they were comin' along wi' their kit on their way out and they met the minister they went away home. There was a minister once came new to Pittenweem, a very nice young city man w' a lot of the fisherman elders in his kirk, so he thought he'd go down and see them away. Someb'dy met him.
   'What are y'ever doin' doon here?' they said. 'Y' best go back home for there's no' a fisherman wants to see you the day.'

It wasn't only the minister, of course. Andrew Fairnie in Musselburgh recalls consternation when men met a cat on the way to the boat. And there were other proscribed creatures.

They never called a *rat* by its name ... always just a 'long-tailed fellow'.

Helen McClung remembers an outrage at Girvan harbour.

A boy threw a rabbit into the hold of a fishing-boat for a prank. But here the men were in a real state. Terrible. And they were awful superstitious about salmon. They never spoke that word on the boats ... just said 'the quare fella'. There was a man went to the other fishing from the salmon and that was such bad luck that the skipper bought him a new set of oilskins that he hadn't touched the salmon in.

Presumably that got rid of the smit and the next catch was heavy. Jim Buchan hadn't heard of the 'quare fella' in Peterhead, but the superstition was there and they called salmon 'cauld iron' or 'red fish' in the north-east.

They never spoke of rabbits here either ... never. Another thing too, of course, you always turned your boat in the direction of the sun. That's the transverse thrust of the propellor does that, mind, but turning the way of the sun was a superstition long before propellors ... in a' fishin' and sailin' places.

Andrew Fairnie in Musselburgh agrees.

Wouldn't take your boat out the harbour against the sun. Never.

All shore hazards jouked, the men got to the boats.

When I was a wee chap about maybe four-years-old, I remember my
father coming out the house and walking down to the harbour, getting
on to the boat wi' the rest of the crew, haulin' up his sail and sailin' away.
Just a wee sail-boat, that was, wi' no shelter on deck.

The creaking Ellen Mays and Lively Ladies were now hives of
activity as the boats prepared to curl sunwise out of harbours all
round the coast, most of them in these remembered times powered
only by sail, their painted names lovingly touched up between
voyages.

One of my grandfather's boats was called the Jeanie Ewing after my
grandmother, the other was the Evergreen. Th'were a big family of sons
and they used to carry the boats down among them.

I mind hearin' about an east coast skipper 't called his boat Ajax, an'
here another skipper took a right fancy to that an' re-named his'n Bjax.

The boats slipped anchor and moved up the west coast, out into
the North Sea, or down into the Irish Sea. Not many boats go out
of Ballantrae now but Mrs. Margaret Kirk of the village carries a
mind picture from her childhood of the armada that used to leave
there in the first years of the 1900s.

When I was walking to school in winter mornings when it was still dark,
the herring boats were going out and it was just like another wee town
out there, with the lights on the boats.

Jenny Stewart remembers these boats going out of Ballantrae too.

They were just sails and oars mind, but this was the main herring-fishing
port for the south-west wi' the BA registration.

And by the time the school-children there were having their lunch
in the school-shed beside the shore, the boats were gone.

On the other side of Scotland another fleet was setting off at
about the same time.

I went out from Anstruther first at fourteen years of age. We went up t'
Aberdeen then on to Shetland and as far's the Faroes. Deep-lining it was
at that time. We went through to the west and fished out of Ayr, then

run wi' the herring across to Belfast and sold them there. It was 'deep sea' at Faroes, that was eighty fathom of string and the hooks hanging down, half of them baited w' herring and half w' mackerel ... fourteen miles of string run out for cod, ling and halibut.

Alex Archer of Largo talks of another way of organising the lines.

There was a way of fishing from what they called sculls. The lines were looped round in circles and attached to the boat so 't as the boat moved off it took the line away.

Perhaps the word 'scull' was from the shallow wicker fish baskets they used at Yarmouth, or perhaps the baskets took the name from the form of the looped lines ... whichever way round, sculls were not just a Fife fad.

They fished from sail-boats here at Peterhead wi' sculls. That was shooting the baited lines from their loops wi' grass in between the coils to let them run out clear.

Earlier than all those memories of fishing grounds and methods are Andrew Fairnie's of his father in the 1890s.

They sailed up to Grangemouth, went through the Forth 'n Clyde canal ... engaged a horse to pull them to Bowling and from there they sailed down to the south of Ireland and fished out of Kinsale at the first of the herring fishing in April. I've known my father five-six weeks out Kinsale then follow the herring as the shoal moved up by the east of Ireland goin' to Mallaig ... took five or six shifts of clo'es wi' them and, if ever they got the chance, slipped through the canal to get home and get them washed. Then it was back and away up north to Stornoway and Shetland. Weeks at a time he was away. It was hard but it was their life and they knew how to work it.

Pittenweem had its own method of line fishing, unique at least among its Fife neighbours.

Pittenweem was always different. They kept the sma' lines and baited the hooks wi' mussels, and they fished here in the Forth. The best mussels came from the River Eden at St. Andrews and the Tay. But if they were scarce there they got them from Wales or Yarmouth. You got a basket o' mussels for baiting for one 'n sixpence.

But fishmonger slabs would have been bleak with only halibut and herring, and George MacGregor, an observer from his tiny bank-hut at Leverburgh, of the Harris scene of half a century ago, remembers the sea-harvest there.

> It was mostly mussels and lobsters. They made their lobster pots on the shore. The lobsters were sent off without delay to Billingsgate to make sure they were fresh at the market.

For some, that was a way of life, for others it was the kind of interesting sideline to the real life-work recalled by John MacRae of the Northern Lighthouse Service.

> The keepers at some stations, like the one we were at on Islay, had maybe fifty or sixty lobster creels. They caught parton crabs too and an agent used to come out from, say, Port Askaig and collect the crabs and lobsters to send to Glasgow.

Still among the upmarket delicacies, James Pryde remembers his grandfather's prey round the Hebridean shores.

> He came to Lewis about 1858 from Sutherland following Sir James Matheson when he became the laird. Sir James was a go-ahead sort of man and the Sutherland men could see that where he was there would be work for them. My grandfather leased fishing rights from him to net salmon, and he built up quite a business.

So netting the salmon, shooting the sculls, following the season's run of herring towards the lands of midnight sun, or simply messing about in in-shore boats we should perhaps leave those sturdy fishers to their caller calling, with their own verdict.

> Aye it wasnae easy, but that was the way it was, and we were thirled to't.

> I'll tell you what ... if you were at the fishin' you'd no hoors, no set times ... no nine-to-five. Forget that. Just work till the work was done.

The bringing home of the catch and its afters we can leave to another chapter and look meantime to how home-life fared while menfolk followed the shoals, and on the crofts behind the shore.

2

Like Crooking an Animal Really

Not far behind the concentration of fishing folk and the small industries that serve them, in rope, net and oilskin making, in boat-building and the maintenance of harbours, either numerically or geographically, are the croft and small farm people of the near hinterland. Sea winds keen their land and they are never far out of earshot of the roar and sigh of waves. But the work traditions of the two communities have always been different.

> Most of the Lismore men went to sea, but the small croft and farm people worked their life a bit differently. The younger brothers and sisters went to the city to study for teachers or ministers or doctors, some of the girls into service. The oldest son usually went into the croft.

Likewise in Thurso.

> A lot of folk were fisher families, but a lot that lived in a bit, off the coast were crofters and farmers, and usually sons followed or went to the city depending if it was a wee or a big farm.

Perhaps more than other groups, apart from the landed gentry, there was a real sense of heritage about those who worked the soil however small the patch. Peter Sinclair of Connel certainly has the aura of being part of a line of patriarchs.

> My father and grandfather were here on this croft. We'd eighty-five acres, but a lot of it was rough. All the work's always been shared ... a family concern, 'though of my generation I was the only one. But I've got two sons following and they've got sons each.

Even his beasts are part of the descending line.

> We've got about sixty sheep, and twelve cows with calves following.

A sense of history hangs about some of the land itself, for a number of crofts and small farms still being worked are either on, or close to, the sites of ones resentfully taken over by those sent there after eviction from their glens at the time of the Clearances.

> My grandfather Craigie started in one of the crofts put on the hillside at Rousay after the Clearances.

There are those who take an objective view of what others call the usurping of crofters by sheep from the south.

> There had been clearances round Tongue, but I think the harshness of it all has been greatly exaggerated. This is something I feel quite strongly about. All right, there was some cruelty, and nob'dy condones that, but it *had* to happen because Sutherland had 25,000 people then. It's only 10,000 now ... but it was just a natural fact of life that the kind of existence they wanted couldn't go on being supported. Every year, before the Clearances in Sutherland, the people had to be subsidised and in wintertime food had to be brought in to keep these big families alive.

But families where the tale of bitterness has been handed down through the generations do not take so sensible and balanced a view of the economics and the emptying of the glens ... David Henderson's for one.

> My great grandfather was evicted from Kildonan by the Sutherlands at Dunrobin Castle at the time of the Clearances. His wife was pregnant and the child (my grandfather) was born in a field at Dunbeath while they were wandering about, trying to find a place to settle. There was a funny or odd thing that was a contradiction in the story of the Clearances. Harriet Beecher Stowe, that kind-of championed the slaves in America, wrote her memories *supporting* the Clearances, from the side of the Duchess of Sutherland. They say she was being entertained at Dunrobin Castle and only heard that view of the story. She got very badly criticised for that up in Sutherland.

But, whatever the family lore, succeeding sons could only get on with life and identify with coast folk whose forebears had never endured eviction. Hugh Craigie, for one, took up his place on the croft at Rousay with right goodwill.

> George, my younger brother, went off after the local school to Inverness Academy, but the real thing I remember about the school was wantin' to get away from it. From my seat in the classroom I could look right across and see the stubble fields and the blackness where the

ploughing was and I just *pined* to get out to it. I just wanted the farm work. It was the sort of expected thing for the oldest son anyway, but it suited me fine.

Down in the south-west the ancestral line bringing Jenny Stewart to her Ayrshire farm-home was on the distaff side.

I was Jenny McCrindle to my maiden name, and going back five generations my great-great-great granny Janet Brown and Robert Burns' mother were sisters. All Ayrshire farming folk mind ... and I was brought up at Merkland farm near Ballantrae.

But back to that grandfather of David Henderson's and his progress to self-sufficiency in spite of his bleak outdoor birth.

My father took over his croft with its twenty-five acres and two horses. A lot had just the one horse, and two crofters would work their horses together for ploughing and so on. But our place had the two.

Most of the small farms in the days remembered were 'mixed'. Jim Still's father's at Forglen, north-west of Turriff and eight miles from the sea, was the furthest inland.

There were sheep, feeding cattle and pigs and we'd a bit of rough ground. The name of the farm 'Ribera' meant that ... Rye Brae.

Some places were worked entirely by the families themselves and had no need of the men on offer at the old feeing fairs. But for the exasperated men who had only tribes of daughters, the markets nearest the twice-yearly term days were an opportunity to size up likely lads for their heavy work. In Argyll, Oban was such a centre.

The term days were 28th May and 28th November and farm workers had the market day off and could go into Oban. Farmers could look for their hands there, and they exchanged the shilling y'know. Maybe a farmer'd have noticed a good worker w' someone else and think, 'Jove, I'll try and get that fellow at the feeing mart.' And the same for a good master. A lot of that went on.

The biggest feeing fair along the south-west coast was at Ayr market. Jenny Stewart (that was Jenny McCrindle to her maiden name),

All the people who want't a situation congregated there and the farmers went too and it was like crookin' an animal really, y'know. A farmer would think, 'that's a likely one there' and would approach the man and they would strike a bargain, clasp each other's hand and the shilling was handed over ... the erling shilling, for a six month engagement, November to May or May to November.

Then there was another day called Dud's Day hiring, after the regular feeing. That was for the ones that didnae get a place the first time. By then they were out their old job and had their duds with them in their bag or tin trunk ... desperate for a place. The farmers maybe got them cheaper on Dud's Day.

Or perhaps it was a second chance for farmers who had been diddled at the real market feeing. Because the erling niffer wasn't always a bond between honest men, and the giving of the coin lent itself to the small but irritating frauds described by Buchan farmer Jim Still.

On occasion one of the lads would take the shilling or half-crown from more than one. But that was a terrible thing to do, and if his mother came to hear of it she'd send him right back.

But 'it' could still leave a farmer woefully short of a much needed hand.

Of all the fairs and markets, the people around Turriff will tell you that from time almost immemorial their Turra' Porter Fair was king of them all, not even excepting the ancient original feeing-meets at the West Port of Edinburgh from which theirs took its name.

They've at least one immortal ballad written of the cantrips there concerning Rob Paterson, a farmer who jibbed at paying the National Insurance for his ploughmen that was new seventy-five years ago, and had his favourite white cow poinded in its place. But the cow broke out ...

Chorus:
Toorie li Toorie loo, Toorie li Toorie loo
The star o' it a' was the fite Turra coo

The coo was got loose and she doon wi' her heid
And up wi' her tail and awa' she did speed
She breenged a' through Turra', tho' whiles fair hard-pressed
Till at last she was catched and placed under arrest
The farmers clubbed in and they bought the coo back
And sine a great hero o' Robbie did mak'

Auld Auchelside said 'twas a rare how-d'y-do
And the star o' it a' was the far-famed fite coo.

But the fair had its serious purposes.

The men were taken on at the Porter Fair at Turriff twice a year, a very busy day, that.

'Are you leavin' your job? ... lookin' for a place?' the farmer would say and when they came to an agreed wage and terms, he would give over the coin to his new man.

And it wasna just the men. Farmers' wives sometimes got their maids that way. But mostly the girls' mothers were more careful than that, and 't was more word-of-mouth how they heard of places that were all right for their daughters. The mothers would do most of the talking at the interview.

Mrs. Hilda Strachan is another who remembers the joys of the Turriff Fair eighty years ago.

Our men got hired half-yearly at the fair. But if they were quite settled they didna bother looking for places. Porter Fair was the taking-on day and they moved in on the term day itself, May or November. It was mostly single men we had and they went into the bothy. It had two double bunks and chaff beds, a lamp too, of course, and a fire in the winter.

When we were small we used to get Porter sweeties. Everyb'dy that came to the house brought a poke of Porter sweeties ... mostly reading sweeties, y'know, 'roses are red, violets are blue, sugar is sweet and so are you', sort' thing. It was traditional.

As essential as the single men now settled in the bothy, or the married ones in the farm cots, were the working animals. Some had but one horse and had to borrow, others were better provided. Hugh Craigie's place in Orkney had a fair complement.

We'd our own horses for ploughing. We'd quite a few and were always bringing on young ones. Some folk shared but most crofts had the pair for ploughing.

And Jim Still's farm home at Forglen had more than enough to manage their work without sharing.

We'd five horses, two pairs and an orra beast. (That's like the orra man. He was the general kind of labourer but actually he was usually good at everything.) Well, our wee highland garron, Dobbin, was like that ...

paid its way. It used to get yoked into a wee float, that was a flat cart you could slot sides into ... and we would take the sheep in it to Turriff about three miles away ... sheep or pigs. When I was about twelve I used to do that. I took them to market, put them off there, then left the garron and the float, still harnessed, and went back to the market to see the animals sold. Then you collected your cash for the sale and took it home to your father. That was just small stuff ... young pigs maybe. I liked doing that. That wee sale was a Thursday. Tuesday was the big market day at Turra ... mostly cattle.

Dobbin was versatile and much in demand.

There was this crofter near us and he used to get the loan of Dobbin to help w' his ploughing. Dobbin always wanted to get going because he was used to the trap or the float. He was clever too, at keeping up front as far's he could, because it's the one furthest back in the yoke gets the hardest work, so he kept well forward to leave the other horse the heavy work.

The animals taken to market by Dobbin and his like had already done their duty in production and reproduction before they ever reached the sale ring. The pigmen, cowmen and shepherds of the crofts had employed their varieties of expertise in their rearing and care, and their use of imagination and knowledge in choice of grazing locations. Sometimes it took a sturdy trudge over moorlands by the herds; like those working inland from Ballantrae.

We'd three score of sheep at Merkland and my mother looked after them. Her father'd been a shepherd and she followed him ... she went on the hill w' them herself.

But sometimes setting the animals on good grazing took, instead, the sea-skills of island or shore-bred ancestors.

One or two of the Leverburgh men had islands where they bred the cattle. Later they brought the yearling calves back over on a fishing boat to send away to sell ... took the boat to Kyle of Lochalsh and sent the beasts from there to Dingwall market. There were two old men lived on one of the islands, just to look after the cattle.

That quiet rural life around Leverburgh was very different from the purposeful bustle dreamed of by Lord Leverhulme when he set up his abortive new town on Harris. For months the shores round the sea-loch had echoed to the sounds of trowel on brick and hammer

on nail, but the model township never quite 'took' in the Hebrides, and, by George MacGregor's time there, it was like an abandoned film set, and life was based again on the steady, timeless round of the seasons ... pretty much as it was on Rousay, although there it was sheep, not cattle that the Craigie family transported from island to island.

We'd our own two boats on Rousay and in the summer we hired a motor boat to tow them and took the ewes that had lambed and been clipped, over to a nearby island and left them there over the summer.

Then we took back the lambs about the end of August and later, in October, we brought the ewes back. We sold the wool clippings to someb'dy in Edinburgh, but there were local women that spun some themselves. My mother used to spin. I remember her working with carders and the wheel.

To city folk who love the country academically, and for holidays, it's surely one of the mysteries of the farming life that those who deliver the young of their animals and rear them up healthy from their endearing, stumbling infancy, can take them coolly to their execution when the economic time is ripe.

If I'd stayed on and become a farmer like all the generations before me I'd just have wanted to keep animals to pat them ... not to see them slaughtered.

Engineering was perhaps a better bet for so squeamish and unlikely a crofter's son. But it wasn't so easy for all farm offspring to escape the trauma of seeing their playfellows quartered and hung ... on the home premises!

We kept hens and sheep and we kept a pig. One of the big days in the year was Pig-killing Day and I remember the man coming in to do that job. The procedure was first the pig was taken from its sty and trailed screamin' up to the barn, duly given a bonk on the head and its throat cut. It ran round and round, the blood flying everywhere, till it died. I was terrified and I tried to run away up the hill but my mother thought I was safer at the pig-killing than away there out of her sight. When it was done and the pig dead, boiling water was poured over the pig and it was scraped with big knives to get the bristles off, then its entrails were taken out and the pig was hung from the rafters. After three or four days it got taken down, then salt and saltpetre and brown sugar was rubbed into it and it lay for ten or twelve days getting turned every second day. Then it was all washed and cut into hams and hung up in the kitchen. It dripped brown stuff on the floor all winter. It was horrible, the pig-killing, but the ham was good.

If the pig-killing was horrible, the sheep killing was worse, for young Jenny herself had to take part in that ritual.

I tried to run off again but they needed me and I was brought back. The sheep was tied up, put on a sheep-stool to get its throat cut and the blood was allowed to run into a bowl under it wi' a handful of salt in the bowl. It was my job to stir the blood and I would be boo-hooin' and

stirrin' . . . and me just a child . . . it was bad, that. But that was your job
and it was for makin' bloody puddin's y'know . . . black puddings. The
skin tube that the entrails were to go in got scraped and scrubbed clean
and steeped in salt water, then cut into lengths, each one tied at one end.
I'd to stand holding the tied end while the blood and suet, the bits and the
oatmeal mixture was stuffed into it and the open end tied up. Then it
was boiled. I've never eaten it since, couldnae face it after all that. Then
the sheep itself was skinned, and hung up for cutting later. You used
some fresh and salted down the rest in a crock for the winter.

More repellent than even that, was the making of broth from the
sheep's head.

That was another big 'thing'. Most of the wool was cut off the head,
then mother got ready a big red fire to get half-a-dozen pokers red-hot
to 'sneister' off the rest of the wool. My! I can hear that sizzling yet
when she ran it along the jaws and ears till the whole thing was bare,
shiny, black skin like ebony, and that was it ready for boiling. I've
detested sheep's head broth all my life, after!

and the answer to the stunned enquirer's comment that she had
some gruesome memories of her childhood was just a shrug, a head
cocking to the side for consideration, and then,

Aye but I've good ones too. It was happy enough . . . no hassle . . . *time*
. . . what is it the poem says?
'What is life if full of care
You have no time to stand and stare?'

Ah, but Jenny, what at?

So it's a relief for us, as it must have been for her, to turn from
that to the 'Cider with Rosie' days of sundrenched fields in harvest,
when mothers and milkmaids left their kitchen swees and byres,
when children took holiday from school and it was all hands
forward to the safe gathering of grain crop and hay while good
weather lasted.

Sometimes, while Orkney crofts like the Craigie's were still
waiting for their crops to be burnished to the right shade of gold,
itinerant workers would go to the warmer south to help with earlier
harvests there.

Sometimes people went away to help with taking in earlier harvests.

They'd set off in quite a crowd and they'd their piper with them. They'd go down into the Mearns and maybe camp on the way. Then after the Harvest there, they'd work their way back north helping in maybe Morayshire and Ross. On these walks they used to take meal w' them and mix it with whisky, if they had any, or water ... in the heel of their shoe or boot. They used th' old drove roads that long ago folk used, to take cattle to the Perth or Crieff trysts.

That droving would have been even before the earliest first-hand recollections in this book which are the ones of 1880s contained in recently unearthed recordings made in 1960 for Miss Sybille Mac-Kintosh of Inverness by three Beauly octogenarians.

Harvest was all with the scythe in Beauly in the days of my childhood in the 1880s. The harvest time was really the most cheerful season of the farm year. There'd be maybe four or five men w' the scythe and behind each man there was a woman tying up a bundle w' the stalks of the corn that they'd knotted into a sort of rope. When they'd bound it into sheaves like that, behind them there was a boy or another woman lifted the sheaves and put them in little stooks. The crops were just like now (the 1960s) but planted a bit more haphazard.

Forty years later in the 1920s there had been little change except that the mechanical reaper had not only arrived but was becoming dated.

A' the women helped wi' the harvest because 't that time it was still the old-fashioned reaper. The reaper came along and dropped the sheaves and if you were following you'd to make a band of twisted straw, lay a sheaf on it, tie 't and put it in a stook w' one or two others. Often you worked in pairs, one made the band and tied, and the other stooked. It was pretty hard work for, as soon as you were finished tying and stooking, the reaper was at your back and you'd to start over again. We were at that and the turnips long before we left the school. It was hard but you didn't think so then because everyb'dy was the same.

Even the very young had their harvest jobs. The small James Still helped with the catering.

We'd all to work when we were young, carrying out the basket wi' their afternoon piece, y'ken. Not the tea ... the big pail of tea was too heavy, and too hot. Maybe the maid would do that ... Polly, in her flowery overall. The workers all just dipped into that bucket for their tea. My mother made up the baskets in the kitchen and if it wasna scones they got, it was two slices of white bread and jam ... great thick slices.

Not far away the same kind of harvest picnic was going on, supervised by Mrs. Hilda Strachan, now far into her eighties but then a young farmer's wife.

We took a piece out to the men in the middle of the forenoon then in the middle of the afternoon. It was a daily job to make the scones for that, on the girdle. Huge, they were, and they got cut in four so they got a quarter each, spread with jam.

It wasn't jam on the Girvan farm of Matt McQuaker.

Our men got cheese on *their* scones and there was a bucket of water with a handful of oatmeal in it ... mealie water. S'posed to give it a wee bit tang and slake their thirst.

And Isobel Craigie remembers a tastier sounding Buchan concoction.

I used to make raspberry vinegar. The berries sat and steeped and got stirred for a day or two, then strained and boiled up w' sugar. The men got a good pail of that to drink from.

After all that socialising in the fields, the grain had to be threshed and winnowed. David Henderson remembers how it was done on crofts around Wick and Lybster and no doubt most other small places in the north-east at that time.

> In my young days (that would be before the First War) they thrashed the corn with a flail. That was just two sticks, hinged with leather thongs. They held the one stick and walloped w' th' other so's the grain fell off. Then when they were to winnow it they made a draught by opening the top half of the hinged door at one end of the barn and the bottom half at the other and they winnowed at the open bottom one and the chaff would separate and fly to the high opening. I liked to watch that when I was wee.

The children were needed too, to help with other crops and products besides the grain and hay ... Hugh Craigie in Orkney ...

> We'd to help w' singling the turnips in July. I learned these jobs like that, thinning the turnips and seeing to the animals pretty early on, long before I was out the school.

And David Henderson did his rounds selling their produce about 1909 or 1910.

> We used to go to Wick with potatoes in the harvest time. You'd to go with a whole day's lifting at one go. You loaded them on to a cart and I used to ride all the way on top of the potatoes. We started about midnight from home and went almost all the way to Wick, then stopped at a stream to give fresh water to the horse. We fed the horse there too and we'd girdle scones for ourselves. Then we went on into Wick and round the streets and I used to get sent to the doors to see if they wanted potatoes ... sold them by the zinc bucket and you were lucky if you got sixpence-a-bucket.

Some living near to a farm but of other occupations, had a more direct way of getting their potatoes. Donald MacKintosh of Beauly remembers how they operated near Beauly.

> If anyone in the village wanted potatoes they could get a drill from the farmer. They provided their own seed potatoes and gave them to the farmer. He planted them and put a marker at the end of the drill. We had a row ourselves and we always asked for a day off the school when they'd to be lifted. They were just put into a creel when the plough threw them up ... often damaged them, the plough. If a family had

several rows, the husband, wife and children all went out to harvest them.

As a youngster, Jenny Stewart had other duties forbye the much lamented feeding of the beasts on a cold Sunday and helping with the 'bloody puddin's'.

> I did the milking too when I was young, and Mother made the butter, then every Monday she went in the pony and trap to the market in Girvan with the butter and eggs to sell. And she brought back flour and oatmeal.

City bairns have to be taught how raw materials turn into goods that may have seemed to them to have no connection with the land, but the youngsters of the natural farming days of over half a century ago knew that being well-fed, warm in bed and clad against the cold, depended on how their family animals and their soil was nourished from year to year.

> As well as the grain to the other mill, the wool of our sheep went to the wool mill. If Father wanted a suit-length of tweed he got it all spun and woven there and Mother got the knitting wool to knit the socks and stockings, the worsted. We got blankets too ... everything was made ... there was very little shop-bought stuff ... just the tailor made my father's suit ... he was just a man in the village worked by lamplight in an end room on to his house. All the women like my mother knitted. They used to wear a belt 't had a sort of bulb on it at their side and they stuck the end of their needle into that.

And so the turn of the seasons has more practical meaning for the bairns of the soil than whether the next fad would be hunch-cuddy or whips-and-peeries.

3
Maggie Linnie had a Mangle

> I sometimes look back and think what a hard life it was for the women
> ... the washing for instance. There was no running water and I'd to
> carry water in wooden stoups from the spring in the field, to put in the
> boiler. Then the hot water was put into big boynes for the washing and
> the girls used to pull up their skirts and tuck them in, then trample the
> clothes in the boynes to get them clean.

That was John Leitch minding how it was, nearly ninety years ago
in Tarbert, Loch Fyne. And Jim Buchan of Peterhead echoes him,
in sixty-year-old memories.

> When the fishermen went away, say to Yarmouth or the north, they
> were away quite a while and brought back a lot of heavy washing.
> Sometimes the women would be two or three days at it.

And that was the way of it from then until forty or fifty years after
John Leitch watched his sisters barefoot among their washing ...
water from rain butts or nearby burns, hand-filled tubs and children
pressed into service to paddle the year's accumulations out of
blankets and plaids. Mrs. MacGregor remembers the routine in
Kishorn.

> When I was in Kishorn I remember my landlady washing her blankets.
> There was a burn flowing down and she used to fill the boiler with
> buckets of water from that. She washed in a wooden tub outside, and
> her children trampled the blankets. I've done it myself for my mother.

In Jenny McCrindle's home in the 1930s the actual vessel for the
washing (after a bit of elbow grease had scoured it) was a multi-
purpose piece of equipment ... and the teamwork method of
ending the process quite ingenious.

> A burn ran down the hill and some of the water ran into a great big tank

at the end of the yard and it was carted in in kettlesful to boil up on the swee. If you'd a big washing you filled up an outside boiler that was usually used to boil up tatties and turnips for the pigs. It was just out in the open there . . . had a chimney that smoked goodstyle. Then after the washing in the tub we did the wringing. One stood at one end of the blanket that was over long sticks and th' other was at th'other end . . . one twisted to the left and the other to the right. Then they were put out to dry on the whins at the side of the farmhouse. We'd a big expanse of whin.

On Lismore, in Miss Mary Macfadyen's early days, instead of bringing the water to the tubs to wash, they took the tubs to the water.

We used lovely soft rainwater from a butt for the washing and we used the burn water as well. We filled a great big pot with burn water and heated it on a fire we'd built against the dyke beside the burn (that bit of dyke's still black, even now). That hot water was timmed into one of the barrels of rain water and the washing got done there and then put into the other barrel of clean rainwater. Doing the blankets was always Mother's job in Maytime and we trampled them.

A busy month was May at Lismore . . . what with the laundering of the blankets and the white-washing of the croft house at five in the morning.

Up in the north-east at Turriff with the Strachan family there was a slight advance on at least the heating of the water,

Part of our range was a small hot water tank with a wee tap. We used to boil up water there, and in the kettles, to get enough for the washing. In the summer it was done outside . . . just in tubs with bungs in the bottom. There was a big zinc cone-thing with a long wooden handle for dumping things like sheets and blankets.

You took the bung out the tub to let the water away into the drain. It was always a big washing we had, because we'd so many beds ourselves and all the single men's bothy bed-clothes too. They'd chaff beds filled fresh every year and it was some job doing all those. But the washing was the real big chore.

Even when there was a shed or wash-house for the operation the water in some places had to be carried in. As late as the 1940s that was one of young Isobel Campbell's duties at Ness.

I used to go to the well for water, with pails on a sort of circular metal girdle. It wasn't a pumping well, it had been a spring that someone had put a pipe in to make a well and the water just ran through it all the time. The water had to be heated on the fire after that then the washing done in wooden tubs in the barn place where the loom was kept. I seem to remember Aunt Kirsty with her skirts held up trampling ... that would be the blankets and bedclothes, the smaller things would be done in a wooden tub with the scrubbing board. It was all a great long chore from the bringing in of the water to the scrubbing drying and ironing.

The most straightforward routine for washing, though not necessarily the least laborious, was to have a purpose-built wash-house. But there were odd chores surrounding that which varied from place to place ... after all a woman had to concentrate ...

So on washing day it was always me or Margaret was kept off the school to watch the baby.
There was always a baby.
You got your turn of the wash-house once a week and when you were done you handed on the key to the next one. If someb'dy finished early, another neighbour with just a wee washing got to use the rest of your time.

The two tubs dried out, the A1 soap powder and the dolly blue packet safely back in the press until next week, the next item on the agenda was the drying of the clothes. Some were hung up on a line stretched between the back-green palings but the heavier things were 'sent out'.

There was this wee shop at the corner, Maggie Linnie's, and she'd a mangle in at a back door. She took in the washing to put through her mangle at thruppence-a-bundle and done it lovely.

And that's how it went in Ardrossan. At Troon, too, the family had its washday duties.

One of our chores was to gather sea-coal that was washed up on the shore ... wee pebbly black things that sent out a great heat. We quite liked that job. Mother lit the boiler fire about six in the morning, then came in and made our breakfast, and left a big pot of stovies on the cooker for our dinner ... just one course on washday. Then she spent the whole day in the wash-house with the A1 powder and lifting yon heavy tubs up and down.

However far they may have removed themselves from the scene

after the coal-gathering the jargon of the whole complex and exact operation was certainly part of the family vocabulary.

> I remember being in a house, where someone was doing a washing when I was young, and coming away with an expression of my mother's that must have made this neighbour laugh, 'My! new wool like that fairly lays the sapple.' ... in the Borders y'know, they call that lather the 'graith'.

And the sweet-smelling finale to the whole day ...

> The ironing was done with flat irons heated at the American stove.

At St. Combs the procedure was much the same, with the additional recollections of XX Pale Soap, Fell's Naphtha and Chloride of Lime followed by a good bleaching, in sun and sea-winds, on the green.

At other homes resourceful women made use of whatever dere-lict dwellings nearby had to offer, to streamline the day's labour.

> In an old bothy across our yard there was still the chimney and an old swee hook, and my granny used to light a fire and boil the washing in there like she had a wash-house.

> I mind my mother lighting a fire against an old broken-down barn wall and boiling kettle after kettle on that, to tim into the half-barrel she did her washing in. Then she dried it all round the yard fence.

Best woollens and starched collars came in for special care by Mary Macfadyen's mother at Lismore.

> My father had heavy woollens for the sea, and when they were washed Mother used to hold them to her face to make sure they were as soft as they'd been when they were new out of Forbes in Oban.
>   And of course she always cleaned her iron on the knife board and put on a white apron to iron my father's collars for wearing with the navy blue suit he'd always on when he was home from the sea.

Biener households delegated the whole chore to well-remembered women who welcomed the wage and seemed often to enjoy the day raising the 'sapple' on someone else's clothes ... often, but not under all circumstances. Catherine Murray recalls their lady.

> This lady came in once a week to do our washing at the big copper boiler

in the wash-house attached to the house. Her name was Penny and she was Irish. I can see her yet at the two big tubs with the Hudson's Washing Powder ... always Hudson's ... then draping the petticoats and nighties and skirts all round the fence to dry. 'Irish Penny' we called her and, before we knew that she just ate fish on a Friday Mother gave her meat. She didn't like to say but afterwards she went away and made herself sick. I always remember that.

Even after all the care taken with steeping and boiling and scrubbing there were curious hazards in some places like David Henderson's home before the washing could be reckoned safely completed.

On good days, instead of going on the wire above the chimney-piece, my mother threw the clothes over the whins to dry. But we'd always to watch the cattle. We'd four cows and if you weren't careful they would eat the washing. That's a fact. And we'd even a certain cow that liked a boot to chew.

Tuesday ... Wednesday ... Friday ... in most recollections washing day could be any of them, subject only to rota where the key to the wash-house was communal. But in Andrew Fairnie's boyhood in Fisherrrow wash day was as fixed as the law of the Medes and Persians.

Every woman did her washing on a Monday, the day th'was no fish, because they were away out with the creel the other days. I remember it all fine ... aye and the kettles of hot water.

And that's the washing over for another week ... the tub dried off, the water drained away, the fire doused and every woman's fluttering line of duds just marginally whiter than the best of any other within sight.

4

Five Herrings for Tuppence

Whether through storm or the eerie limbo of becalm, all having been well, the fishermen and their laden vessels eventually made port, from the Baltic, the Faroes, the south of Ireland or simply from their lobster-pots. Then there were a dozen fates and destinations for their catches, and an army of people with different skills to process and deliver them. Jenny Stewart remembers her father-in-law talk of landings at Ballantrae.

> The farmers had a hand in it here. They used to come down with their horses and carts and drive them right out into the sea. It was who could get a load of fish first off the boats to take by road to Girvan and get the first delivering of it. Then they used to buy a cartload of fertiliser there and bring it back ... two jobs the one trip.

Once the fish were landed the nets were thrown over dunes and dykes and the men went home.

> At one time Cellardyke was called Silver Dykes. And the reason it got that was that when they put their nets over the dykes to dry, the herring-scales stuck to the wall, and shone ... glinted in the sun.

Then it was home and into the blessed warmth and privacy of a bath.

> When the men came off the sea they went right into the washing-house, where the clo'es were washed. There was a big boiler wi' hot water and a clean shift of clo'es waitin' ready in the wash-house, and they washed in the dolly-barrel.

And it was as well to have that fire under the boiler for the unchancy event that a man had brought back more than fish.

> I mind I once came home and before I even went into the house I told my mother, 'that ship t'I was on, there were bugs'. Well, I went down to

the washing-house and *everything* I possessed went up in the fire. That would've been a terrible thing in a fisherman's house. They were so clean.

Meantime back at the quayside the landed fish were ready for the attention of the brave bands of gutters in their long queyts and oilskins, who had been appointed at the beginning of the season.

Before the season started the merchants came round the houses in Peterhead asking if you were for 'erling'. And if you were, you got what they ca'ed erles or arles . . . that's a kind of bargain with money between the employer and someb'dy he was taking on for the season.

That was in the north-east and the gentle west highland voice of Peter Sinclair recalls the scene and certain attendant mischief at Oban.

There was a lot of work on the pier and a lot of ladies employed gutting fish out in the open there . . . a lot of gutting and packing. Och, but they were quick. 'Twas a cold job though. When I was a boy and we'd an hour to spare on the way home from school we used to go down to the pier to watch. Very often we got fish home . . . or maybe pinched it more likely.

There was marketing there too, as there was in the far north.

Scrabster was the fishing village near Thurso. In the old days the

Thurso and Wick boats all came to Scrabster to land their catch. Then it went to the markets ... Thurso itself, of course, then some to Glasgow and some to London.

And there was a general surge of the womenfolk to the quayside at Macduff.

At the time my father was fishing out of Fraserburgh my mother used to work at the sheds at Macduff. We used to look after my young sister to let her go to West's shed. West was the merchant. She left school at eleven to go to the fish at Macduff. The sheds had roofs on them but the doors were open for the men coming in and out with the fish for gutting. It was a' cod at that time, a' the cod laid out on the pier and my mother used to say that you wouldna've got your foot down th'were so many. She told me that sometimes the cod was bigger'n herself. Her mother took her to work at the sheds and she was so tired the first wee while, they'd to take off her oilskin apron she wore for the wet, and her mother lifted her into bed. Then it was up at six o'clock in the morning and away for the whole day at the fish again.

They wore the queyt coat round the Fife villages too and another mother is remembered walking the road from Pittenweem to Anstruther to a shed there.

She wore a pair of leather boots with her oilskin coat. Nae buses then. Wasnae far but it couldna've been comfortable.

Comfortable or not, they were a cheerful lot most of the time, unless of course, Doctor Farquhar MacDonald's memory of the girls up the west coast was of some sort of Celtic wail to keep the spirits up.

I remember them at big troughs of fish, gutting them, and singing ... a kind of Gaelic chanting really. Maybe 't helped with the rhythm of the job ... made their hands move at a great speed anyway.

And one whose breath is still indrawn through her teeth at the remembered tingling of those hands, sees them as if it were yesterday.

You tied up your fingers with bandages for cutting w'the knife, the salt sea'd go into the cuts and chaps, and make them smart. Some of them got awful slashed and hacked, and sore if it was bitter cold. They used to take as many bandage strips as they could find when they went away following the fish. Sometimes a' the fingers were rolled up so thick that it was them that got cut, no' the fingers.

Some of the fish followers went south as far as Lowestoft.

But I liked Yarmouth far the best. At Yarmouth they'd big long baskets of fish they called sculls (the baskets I mean). That was th'only place that ever I saw them. You worked with a crew of two gutters and a packer. Oh it was verra hard work. The herring was poured into a great big box affair called a forelan. The women stood at the side of that and gutted the herring then chucked them back to the packer-woman. She picked them up and packed them into the barrels. Th'was a certain way to lay them, tail by head alternately to the middle. Th'were three sizes of the herring, the smalls, the fulls and the mattie-fulls, so you'd to pack them for size too.

Boats tying up and boats setting off, the thump and clatter of gangways, the salt spray rising off tightening ropes, the silver stream pouring from basket to forelan, and the flash of blade and scale as the fish slithered between gutter and packer on the quay . . . the stir at Yarmouth never ceased. But that was England. Now it was time to go north and ply the knife at Peterhead or beyond, in the same rhythms and methods. Jim Buchan recalls the work there.

You packed them just the same into the barrels. Had to be right, mind, there were inspectors. You left a space at the top of the barrel to let the fish sink overnight, and then you were there about six in the morning to top them up and put in more brine before the next boats came in and you'd to start all over again.

It wasn't all so high-powered, of course. For some, like Alex Archer of Largo, work at the 'fish' was whatever the early century equivalent of moonlighting was called.

I was trying to build up a wee joinery business and I was glad to get evening work at cleaning the fish for the local fishmonger. They used to bring in the fish here and leave it the way it was, for the bidding on the quay. Aye 't was cold work on a winter's night.

That was for the shop, but the late Donald MacKintosh of Beauly, who recorded his memories twenty-five years ago, recalled then, open air selling on the town market days of the 1880s.

I remember there was an old man we called 'Cupach' (the cripple) he used to sit in the square at Beauly sellin' herrin', very cheap it was. You got five for tuppence. And there was a quaint old character call'd Annie May 't sold salmon at the Mercat Cross ... a whole big salmon for sixpence. Servants didn't take places if they were to be given too much salmon.

Sometimes it was a family enterprise after Father brought home the fish, and the spokesman in the group now enjoying their domino days at the Ballantrae Tuesday Club spoke for one of the others.

Mind that dyke yonder? Well, Bob and his brother, before they went to the school in the morning used to line that wall wi' cod to dry when his father and his grandfather brought them in off the boat.

Drying the fish in the sun was one way to keep it eatable, tasty and economical. There were others too that evoke memories of still summer evenings and families at work in fishing villages and small towns round the coast.

When my uncles came back from the fishing into Macduff, they put so much boxes aside and wheeled them up in a barrow and smoked the fish in the sheddie at back. There was an old-fashioned fire with yon sort of ribs, y'know, and a white-washed fireplace round it. They'd a fire there in the winter, for cleanin' the fish at, for it was a cold job. They'd wee hard scrubbing brush things 't the tinkers used to sell them and they scrubbed out the gutted insides with these. After that they hung them up and my granny smoked them. It was all oak she smoked them with, to get the good flavour. That was white fish ... haddock. In the Faroes it was split cod.

Of course it wasn't long after landing that some of the fish found its fresh way to those of the local people who made a less un-comfortable livelihood at some of the town's other trades.

My father worked at the Troon shipyard and was always bringing home fish on a wire. 'Och no, no more', my mother used to say because she didn't like cleaning them. But she would never have wasted them and she'd fry some in oatmeal, then do a big dish of potted herring, and salt down the rest in a stone crock that was kept in the lobby.

In some places local bankers could be woo'd into sweetness too and George MacGregor remembers one of the skippers at Thurso coming into his bank one day.

'Come on down to the harbour with me,' he says, 'I've got a buttie laid
aside for you.'

So we went down to the quay and there's me standing there with no
idea what a 'buttie' was. 'Bring up that buttie!' the skipper shouts and
one of the men came up with this great big halibut.

And a voice from the other armchair in the rememberer's home,
chimes in, full of nostalgic pleasure.

We fried some and it was beautiful ... just beautiful!'

Over on the other side of the country fish were preserved in the
same way as at Macduff, but in Mary Macfadyen's young days there,
there were special Lismore refinements.

When my father had been out with his scringe-net and got a good haul
of fish he'd salt them in a barrel. He did it to per-fec-tion ... put salt on
every round of the layering. Then he made a pickle and put a raw potato
into it to test the density. When he got it right, the potato rose to the
top.

It wasn't all herrings, halibut and haddock though. The Mac-
Gregors did not relish so toothsomely another product of the
Pentland Firth. That memory produced a long-hoarded shudder
even after half a century.

The smell from the crab factory at Thurso was just dreadful! They
brought in the crabs, extracted the meat for making a paste or paté.
Then they crushed the shells for fertiliser. Och what a smell! The wind
wafted it right up to us on the hill above ... just dreadful!'

And for a moment that pungency hung in the air of the 1986 sitting-
room.

Another memory of how his grandfather preserved his Lewis
salmon to keep it fresh for palates served by Billingsgate, is
cherished by James Pryde.

He'd a duck-pond on his small-holding near Stornoway and he built an
artificial pond beside it with a low turf wall, and in wintertime he
flooded it until it was about six inches deep, then waited till 't froze.
Then he collected all the horses and carts he could lay his hands on,
walked the horses on to the pond to break up the ice. Then he filled the
carts with the ice and took them to an ice-house he'd built with very-
very thick walls. He packed the ice all in there solid, and later on when

they'd netted the salmon it was packed in the ice and sent away from
Stornoway to London.

Forbye all that, there were bigger sea-creatures to be dealt with
after catching. Farquhar MacDonald remembers one notable annual delivery from the quayside at Kyle of Lochalsh, and the local
eccentric who received it.

This old man at Kyle was a character. He'd been in his younger days in
the Klondyke ... always wore a Wild West hat ... big man. Now once a
year some of the men carried up through all the village a whole seal on a
luggage barrow to his house. They used to just open his front door and
push it in ... he wouldn't let anybody into his house. And that was it for
the year. He lived on the seal, the meat, the oil and the blubber ... this
yearly seal pushed in his doorway like a parcel.

All the lining, netting and struggling in storm-lashed seas, the
landings and the keening winds in the open sheds, the smoking and
the salting down ... all have one simple purpose in the hinner end
and, although Jim Buchan in his sailing days saw herrings sold for
eating raw from Peterhead barrels that had found their way to the
Baltic, there were, and are, tastier ways to eat them ... and warmer
places.

In the harvest time in Buchan everyone was so busy it was just a case of
eatin' tatties and salt herrin' for quickness.

Nowadays they cannae eat this 'n that, and yet in that days in Orkney
you'd a barrel o' salt herring and that was the staple lunch right through
the harvest, like it or lump it.

The snell sea winds and the smell of fish blow so pervasively
across the shorelands that very little of life for a fair stretch into the
hinterland is not affected by the sea and those who go down there in
ships. Even the crofters look to the horizon when they lift their
heads from the land. And so the tide of it all, as it was in past days,
the creels, the trading, the press-gangs and the disasters must, from
time to time, wash in and out of this book. But while it runs low
there are other matters to occupy the good folk of the sea communities.

5
Toe-plates on your Boots

The school serge and knit ganzies, the Sunday braws and the special-occasion rigouts are the stuff of which most memories of clothes are made for those who were the sea-wind's children. The Sabbath and the high day outfits can be left to their appropriate chapters, but the work-a-day worsteds and cottons are worth a going-over by themselves.

Along cliff-top and shore path, down croft lane and village street, sitting up primly in pony-gigs and skipping cheerfully along the pavements of small coast towns, from the late 1880s well into the new century, came little girls in twos and threes to converge on one to ten-teacher schools in one long memory procession of frilly pinafores.

At Ardrossan the Kanes, Mrs. Jean Durnie's family of seven sisters made one small army of them by itself.

> Th'were eleven of us in our family and all the girls wore yon white starched pinafores to the school.

And further south down the same coast Margaret Kirk recalls,

> When I was wee at the village school here in Ballantrae you wore pinafores with frilly trims, to keep your frocks clean underneath.

So also two hundred miles away in Hilda Strachan's playground days,

> I wore pinafores to school, white frilly pinafores. That's what I remember about my school clothes, that and lacing boots.

And Musselburgh,

> A' the girls at the school wore frilly pinnies ... no' sailor suits or fisherwife costumes ... none of that.

That, it seems, was a conceit of city mammas to make their small girls picturesque and quaint, without having the smallest idea of the rigours of the life where they were a sturdy necessity.

From St. Andrews, Golspie, Beauly and Tongue the pinafore parade goes tripping on. And just to prove the point, should it be doubted,

> Here's my school photo about 1909. Fine I mind that getting taken and what happened. I was all dressed up in my Sunday best, my velvet frock and best bows, the day the photographer was supposed to come. Well, lo and behold, the man didnae turn up! So the next day Mother said, 'You're not getting on your velvet dress another day. You can just go in your ordinary things.' So here's me, just the way I always was at school.

And so she is . . . young Isobel Cameron in the starched pinnie fairly *rippling* with frills, over her jersey, skirt and boots . . . the very picture of Miss 1st Infants of Lochgilphead. And almost every other where across the land.

There wasn't quite blanket submission to fashion though, for Miss Mary Macfadyen remembers sturdier garb at Lismore.

> We wore just plain dresses to school early in the century . . . with heavy coats and boots. The boots were heavy too. Your everyday boots had toe-plates and the boys had tackets on theirs. When you'd new boots in September, och 't was just wonderful.

'Wonderful' was hardly young Jenny McCrindle's feeling about her school gear.

> I remember walking to school, maybe in the autumn, and it would be a hairy jersey up to your neck, and you kept pulling it out to stop it scratching. And then the backs of your legs got all itchy too wi' your stockings. You got wee rashes there and round where your combinations came . . . pure misery. There's an old riddle-me-ree . . .
>
> > 'Hairy oot, hairy in,
> > A' hair and nae skin.'
>
> Well, that was a pair of my black worsted stockin's. Along wi' that I'd a serge skirt and a woolly tammy.

That was just after the First War. But forty years before that, photographed at an upmarket fee-paying Dame School for young ladies in Aberdeen, everyone had a dress buttoned down the front, a lace collar and, except for the peely-wally convalescent in the second row whose hair had been shorn for the fever, they had long flowing hair. The young teacher who, a hundred years later, would have been quite acceptable to her Heidie in jeans and tee-shirt, was wearing a skirt to her ankles and a white mutch-bonnet, tied under the chin. Isobel Cameron, whose mother is one looking coolly out of the sepia, has no doubt that this was no ordinary rag-tag set of pupils.

Och aye, well put-on lassies these at the Dame School.

There was less scope for the imagination to clothe the boys with charm as well as good sense. They were fairly uniform, give or take a shirt under their jerseys or an inch or two in the width of the trouser leg. Peter Sinclair's garb in Connel during the 'twenties were perhaps as near standard as any.

We wore just jerseys and short trousers when I was a boy.

And Alex Archer in Largo much the same but with sourer recollections.

It was short corduroy trousers in wintertime and your legs where they finished got a' chapped and sore.

The jerseys were all hand-knitted. David Henderson of Latheron-wheel remembers his, and the time it took him to graduate to man's estate with regard to the trousers.

I wore a ganzie knitted by my mother, along with trousers to the knees, and wide-wide. (I never got long trousers till I earned them myself).

In the towns where there was a healthy mix of fisherboys and tradesmen's sons there was a little more variety, and if Mammas thought that there was any sort of social caché in Eton collars, one son's recollections soon dispel such snobberies. The late Donald MacKintosh of Beauly in the 1880s was that honest rememberer.

Except for the ones just in ganzies, the boys wore suits and big white collars that were made of celluloid . . . very handy for cleaning just with a spit.

What the best-dressed youths in the cities were duding themselves up in, did not easily percolate to remote clachans on the islands, and lack of such style did not disturb the boys in Orkney, certainly not the young Hugh Craigie in the 1920s.

We wore mostly made-down things, shirts and trousers. They were good-wearing Orkney tweed from the weaving at Kirkwall . . . a sort of herring-bone design.

Most mothers who had to hap their offspring against salt spume or headland winds were adept at such making-down, and sturdy cloth that had served a man's back for a year or two, could just as well be made to cover a pair of small buttocks for a few more seasons.

My mother was good wi' clo'es . . . good at 'turning' . . . making maybe a pair of trousers out a jacket. She knitted all our stockin's too.

Not everyone admired these efforts at countering the cold blasts of coastal winters.

When I first came to Scotland from Orkney I thought folk were affa stuffy, the bairns in mufflers, balaclava helmets and cotton wool on their chests. We never had that things in Orkney . . . and yet it was cold and windy, but we were never all stuffed up like yon.

If he had known what went on underneath, next to the chest gamgee, his contempt would have been unbounded. Even in a North Sea outpost like Peterhead, Jean Buchan remembers.

The women all did their knitting, the men's and boys' jerseys . . . even underpants.

And her husband adds a heartfelt post-script to that.

My mother belonged originally to St. Monance and when I went down there to my grandmother's, here I was wearing green dra'ers y'see, and they found out and I got the nickname *green drawers* there.

Maybe that wool was a cheap job-lot, but it *was* probably new. But there's a twinkle in the eye of a Troon lady who minds the raw material for some of her undergarments.

I remember you had a vest or combinations, then yon liberty bodice and navy blue breeks. And then Mother used to get flour bags from the baker and wash them and bleach them, bleach them and wash them, over and over, bleaching them on the green till all yon flouriness was out them, *and* the name and weight-lettering off them. Out of that she made the bodices of your blue and white petticoat skirts.

Sometimes there was the luxury of *chosen* materials and not quite home-made garments.

When I was wee the draper used to come round maybe twice a year, with the 'bus. Then he would hire someone to take him round the farms with a pony and trap. He used to show his swatches of cloth for maybe a skirt or suit and take orders. Then he would sleep at the house overnight and go on somewhere else in the morning. There were dressmakers and tailors in the village to make the things up . . . and there were folk that made hats too.

In the 1900s Mary Macfadyen's mother made their clothes herself but she sent away from Lismore for the material.

We'd books you see. Catalogues. Ogg Brothers was one, and then we got J. D. Williams' catalogue from Manchester . . . it came regularly, and my mother would send away for patterns and material.

But perhaps the real mistress of home economics was the widowed mother who bartered a seaside holiday 'doon the watter' for cladding for the seven children she had been left to rear with neither pay-poke nor pension.

We'd a dressmaker came from Paisley and stayed for a week and did the sewing for Mother in return. I remember she used to enjoy her holiday first and leave the sewing till the last minute.

Another saving that not all mothers welcomed was the summer joy of shedding boots and stockings. They did that, James Pryde remembers, in Stornoway in the twenties.

We went to school barefoot in the summer. We didn't have to but we liked it. And when we went camping in the holidays with the Scouts we never wore shoes or boots or stockings there. It was good in the heather like that.

They did it in Beauly too, and Golspie, Arbroath, Skye, Girvan and Plockton and doubtless every other town and hamlet in the land. They did it in Ardrossan.

We always wanted to go wi' our bare feet come the summertime but my mother wouldnae let us. Mind as soon's we got round the corner off they came. We liked that because in the sun the pavements were lovely and warm to the soles of your feet. If she caught you, mind, she rattled your ears.

It may have been warm to the soles of the feet on smooth town slabs but there were hazards in the rougher crofting countryside . . . and

ancient antidotes. David Henderson's senses still smart from his
barefoot days.

> We went without stockings and boots from the first good days in April
> at Latheronwheel. The only thing was, when you were running along
> you hit your toes on stones and made them sore. I remember wee sharp
> cuts that opened like lids. And you used to get your feet cut wi' the grass
> ... and d'you know what my mother used to do? She wound a piece of
> worsted thread round your toe into the cut and left it there. And it
> healed. Aye, old cures. Then we got hacks on our feet. And d'you know
> what we did for that? Stuck them in cow dung. S'posed to cure them.
> You didn't get into the house like that, mind ... wi' your feet a' messy.
> Aye, that was your bare feet for you.

Perhaps some staw at that for foot care led to the profession of
chiropodist for his daughter in later years. Anyway, think on that
next time you've chapped hands or feet ... a wee run into the
country, a dabble in some friendly byre and you can throw away
your Elderflower and Almond Blossom skin lotions.

And that, for the moment, is the clouting and casting of clout on
ordinary days. Tomorrow is the Sabbath when the lid of the kist is
opened, the Sunday bests come out and the folk of the coastlands
go to kirk.

6
Giving out the Line

It was never called Sunday in Fisherrow ... always the Lord's Day. And there was the Lord's Nicht. That phrase always makes me think on a chap that told a story to my brother Jim. I don't mind what the tale was about, but this is the way he began it. 'Jeemie, it was the Lord's Nicht, the boat was lyin' in Ireland, the min was shinin' bold and high in the sky, and the Skipper was a Christian man.'

There's many a worse beginning to a best-seller, for this one has stuck in Andrew Fairnie's memory from his youth until he speaks it now at ninety-four.

Aye, it was the Lord's Day in Fisherrow and everybody went to church.

And so they did, almost all of them, in every village and hamlet round the coast and on the islands. But they didn't arrive in their pews willy-nilly without strenuous preparations. The first essential was to see themselves properly dressed ... from the minister down.

Father was the minister and he wore a frock-coat and a lum hat, always, to church.

Our minister was a long lean man about six feet six and in his frock-coat and tile hat, he was just like a long black pole.

His elders and faithful menfolk were, to a man, in dark blue suits, whatever their trade or calling.

Oh aye. My father had his hard hat and his dark suit.

That with a white starched shirt was universal for fathers from Glenapp to Rousay, Janetstown to Musselburgh, Lismore to Pittenweem. Mothers and grandmothers in Beauly in the 1880s favoured dresses down to their feet, hems trailing the dust, sweeping the ground.

Then if it was wet they'd to hold them up out the puddles.

But skirts crept up a little in the next fifteen or twenty years, at least above the ankles, though the ladies were never frivolous with colours.

When she was dressed up my mother wore a long dark dress and big puffy sleeves (like Princess Diana). That would be on a summer Sunday.

It is, of course, their own clothes that are best pictured by the rememberers.

We'd special Sunday clo'es, oh dear me yes? You'd just the two sets, your everyday clo'es and your Sunday clo'es.

My Sunday clothes were a dress and coat and a wee felt hat.

When I was wee in Glenapp we'd always our Sunday clo'es. My mother and the gamekeeper's wife were friends and she used to help machine them for us and we were always nice for the church.

We attended the U.F. church in Connell . . . I remember my nice coat, and my hat with the flowers round it.

That was in the summer, but Jenny McCrindle, not many miles from Glenapp, has darker thoughts about her winter attire.

What we wore on Sundays to go in the machine from the farm to church was a coat, long hairy stockings and boots . . . and a tight hat. That's the way I remember it . . . always tight! And I had combinations that were the bane of my life. They were knitted in thick pink wool. You pulled them on whole and they'd wee bits of legs that were tight under your stockings, so when you were hot they got hairy and jaggy.

Between 1898 and 1910 whatever kind of lacing boots were considered right for the walk to school and the a-leeries in the playground, button-boots were *de rigeur* almost from Bernera to Eyemouth, for the doucer kirk deportment required on Sundays. Little button hooks are still treasured and Hilda Strachan recalls that she used hers too for the chic little footwear variations among her braws.

I had leather spats separate from my shoes, and you pulled the buttons of them through, too, with your hook. I suppose they were gaiters really.

More suitable surely for worship with the Piskeys than among sober Presbyterians.

But flippancy has no place in Andrew Fairnie's memories and his summing-up is a just rebuke.

> It was the Lord's Day, so it was different. We'd all special Sunday clothes. That was one thing everybody was awful partic'lar about, their dress on the Lord's Day. I had a suit, a jacket and trousers y'know, rather than the jersey that did me through the week.

So that was the Sunday best, bought, made up, made down, or handed on, and the family decently provided for the Sabbath. But before they actually set out for worship there were preparations to be made at home to induce the right state of mind for worship. There was no unholy scramble to get the chores done before setting off for the church. Those had all been attended to long before Sunday dawned at all. Jean Durnie remembers how it was on the Clyde coast.

> A very sacred day was Sunday, the Lord's Day. Everything was done on Saturday, the coals in, the cooking done, father's dark suit ready and his collar starched.

The only modification and addition to that, around Stornoway, was that it was peats that were 'in' and that Father was shaved. At Latheronwheel David Henderson recalls another task.

> At Latheronwheel we'd to carry all our water from the well, two days' supply on Saturday to be ready for the Sabbath ... and the extra day's peats were brought in. Some folks wouldnae wash dishes. We never went that far, Mother wouldn't have liked that.

So it seems that in the Henderson house at least, if Cleanliness was next to Godliness, it was not next-down, but next-up.

The dispensation in Mary Macfadyen's Lismore home was only the heating of the broth.

> We called Sunday the Gaelic name for Sabbath 'Sabaid'. There was no work on that day ... just the soup in the pot.

That was the community not only clothed but in its right mind for the kirk, secure in the knowledge that the minister, ordained, called and inducted, however short or long ago, would be there

waiting to take the service when they arrived. John Coghill remembers hearing of his grandfather's settling as minister at Kinloch-
bervie.

> His first charge was at St. Andrews. Then he had a call to Kinloch-
> bervie. That must have been in December 1879. Well, just at that time
> there was the Tay Bridge disaster when so many were killed. But some of
> the mail was recovered and one letter was the one carrying this call. It
> had been soaked but it was readable (I've seen that old dried-out letter).
> Anyway, my grandfather felt that because of that manner of getting the
> call he should accept it and go to Kinlochbervie.

As the flock gathered for worship they might in most places have
expected the minister, living close by, to be there first, resplendent
in frockcoat and lum-hat, but the setting off places for the pastors
were not always part of the kirktown hamlet. John Coghill recalls
his grandfather again.

> After a few years my grandfather became minister at Tongue and that
> left a vacancy for a time at Kinlochbervie. So sometimes he had to go
> back and take services there and I've known of him *walk* from Tongue
> over the shoulder of Ben Hope to get there. And I've known him, at
> seventy-four or seventy-five, walk to Melness to preach, in fact some-
> times he took me with him.

Tongue and Kinlockbervie and the like, in the heartlands of the
long rough walk had, no doubt studied with care the *curriculum
vitae* of such a man before issuing his call.

> My grandfather was heavyweight champion and hammer-thrower for
> the Scottish universities in his time.

Now the people were well on their way to kirk.

> In droves they walked, starting away down at port of Ness and
> gathering as they came up from Skigersta, meeting and shaking hands,
> linking up into ranks four or five abreast, hearing all the local clash. The
> men were in their dark suits and some with bowlers or, later, even
> Anthony Edens, and a lot had watch-chains and fobs.

That was Isobel Wales's vision of the church progress in Lewis.
Further south Helen McClung remembers a similar procession
wending its way down Glenapp long ago.

> We were at the top of the glen and we walked down through it the two

miles to the church. The folk from all the different cottages joined the walk, and it was nice, all talking and hearing the week's news. We walked, rain or shine (unless for a blizzard). A wee bit rain didnae stop us.

Not everyone thought it was 'nice' even if they had the luxury of being wheel-conveyed to Morning Worship.

Sunday was very quiet and *very* boring. We went to church in Barr three miles away, in the pony and machine. There was no cover so if it rained you got soaked to the skin. And you sat there in the church w'the boots or shoes that were wet and tight, and the wee wet hat that was too tight, and you were miserable-frozen-cold.

What a martyr that little disciple, Jenny McCrindle, was to tight clothes!

The arrangements for the Kane tribe at Ardrossan are well-remembered as being by a kind of rota system.

I always mind my mother trailing five or six of us at a time from the top to the bottom of Glasgow Street to the kirk. There was aye someb'dy left at home to look after the baby. There was always a baby ... always.

That was the congregation then, pleased or resentful, sitting in its pews ready for the entry of the pastor.

Our minister was a very reverent person, preached about hell-fire and damnation ... brimstone and sulphur and all that.

If that good shepherd ever preached a gentler sermon, this remember-berer cannot call it to mind. There were diversions certainly, if the order of service was above or beyond the capacity of the young, or too ferocious to be borne. Farquhar MacDonald tells of one riveting paddy during a morning service of his young days.

There was an old beadle in our church and regular as clockwork he used to loll over the end of the pew and have a sleep ... away below the minister's high-up pulpit. Many a time the minister put up with the beadle snoring, and then one day he got his own back. He was a Bible thumper and he used to start quiet and gradually work himself up. Well, one day he was reading the passage about Kindling Fire and setting the Mountains on Fire, and he rose to big heights and shouted the words 'Fire!' and 'Fire!' The beadle jumped in fright into the aisle. 'Fire!' he shouts, 'Where?' The minister with his big shock of white hair leans over and wags his finger, 'In Hell, man, for them that don't listen to the Word of God.'

The small Isobel Cameron too, before the First War, found much
to entertain her while her father expounded from the pulpit.

Sir Ian Malcolm from the big house at Kilmartin came to our church in
his big Inverness cape. He was deaf and he used to sit in the front seat

cupping his hand round his ear, and I used to look at the rings he wore on every finger of his hands. He wore silk shirts too. My! he was a character was Sir Ian.

But no more so than the lady who remembers him. And her small self had other distractions when the proceedings were wearisome.

The great thing I paid attention to, was the Precentor, Mr Carmichael ... we'd no instrument y'see, no organ or piano ... just Mr. Carmichael, the Precentor. He had a tuning fork and he used to go Ping-ng-ng like this (and she flicks an imaginary fork) and hold it up to his ear to get the note and start us off ... sometimes he got the wrong note and we'd to start all over again.

Outside he was even more entertaining, was Mr. Carmichael.

Och, he was a great man. After the service (we'd be about five or six) my sister and I used to get out quick and run round the back and Mr. Carmichael would be waiting for us with his arms outstretched and swing us up and turn round. Then he used to give us an Extra Strong peppermint. Actually Mr Carmichael spent pretty well the whole of the Saturday evening in the pub and was probably none the waur of camouflaging his breath on the Sunday with the peppermints. Anyway we got one each and it was a game on the way home to see which of us could sook hers longest. They were terrible hot and we hated them. But we loved Mr Carmichael.

Precentors were the rule rather than the exception in Ness, Oban and Cromarty kirks as well as a dozen others remembered.

There was no music, no instrument, just the Precentor. The Parish church (as distinct from the Free) did have a wee harmonium. But th'were an awful lot of people against that ... kist o' whistles sort o' thing, y'know.

The walk home after church was quietly sociable too among the adults while the children were finding their own interest on the way.

We'd to pass the Wee Free kirk, and one of the joys of life was standing outside there and listening to the Precentor *giving out the line* ... that was him saying each line before the congregation sang it. That was a rare treat!'

The irony of the Wee Frees providing such entertainment on the

Sabbath may have been lost on the child, but the grown lady could not help smiling.

Not all the services were in English, by no means! In his various parishes Minister Cameron had to serve the Gaelic-speaking communities also by holding alternative or additional services, and at these 'the line was given out'.

> My father was Gaelic speaking (his parents in the Black Isle spoke it all the time). He took an afternoon service in Gaelic. It was the 'line' at that service ... only the Psalms, mind.

And in Harris, in George MacGregor's young days there ...

> Everyone who wasn't at the ordinary service went to the Wee Free or the Gaelic.

Some worthy souls like Catherine Murray's mother took on both.

> There was a Gaelic service once a month and my mother went to it. She had the Gaelic and enjoyed that. She went to the English and the Gaelic, one after the other.

If parents had two kirk attendances, the young fry often had more ... many more. Alex Archer of Largo had a full Sunday.

> When I was a boy a friend of mine was a Baptist and we used to go to the Baptist Sunday School, then go to the Baptist church ... come out at half past twelve and go t'the Free church.

Perhaps that was the usual way of it in Fife, for further along the coast there are similar memories.

> Our Sundays were verra verra strict. We went to church and then to the Sunday School after the church. Then there was the Baptist Kirk. They started about half-past twelve and we went there as well ... aye we did! And then there was the kirk at night at six. We didn't have much time to get into mischief.

Whatever services the young attended, almost without exception they went to Sunday School.

> After the Foundry Boys at ten o'clock we went to the church and Sunday School. We'd to do the Catechism and we got Golden Texts to learn. You just chanted these out at the time. But they often come back to me now and I know what they mean.

Isobel Cameron too had her Golden Texts but that little

daughter-of-the-manse had, as ever, less pious memories of Sunday School than her efforts to memorise her texts.

> My teacher was Miss MacTavish, the fishmonger's daughter, and we always thought she smelled of kippers.

Gena Robertson of St Combs was another who remembers more than her texts.

> We had Sunday School at ten-thirty, then we came out at the back door and had a drink of water out a cuppie w'a lid, filled from a jug, then it was church, and that was all we had to eat or drink until we got home after two.

These were the mainstream churches with their services and Sunday Schools, but other denominations, and ways of doing, had their devotees.

> There were the usual Parish and United Free and Wee Free kirks in Lochgilphead, but there were the Episcopals and the Seceders too, and the Catholics and the *Mission*.

There didn't seem much need for the Mission in so well-kirked a village.

> Aye but you know what the Mission was ... it was for the ones that couldn'ae find anything they agreed wi' in any other church. They had their own wee show.

On Lismore it was difficult for everyone in the Macfadyen household to make the long journey to the conventional service.

> My father always went to the church, in the blue suit, starched collar and bowler hat. But my mother went to a wee meeting in some house. There were a lot of cottage meetings in each other's kitchens.

For one little group of workers in Troon, too, there was a stern inquisition to be faced if they had done no better than attend three or four diets in their own family pews.

> The lady in the baker's shop where I was a junior, belonged to the Bethany Hall and she saw to it that all the juniors went there in the evenings. You couldn't have faced her on the Monday morning if you hadn't been to the Bethany Hall on the Sunday night.

And yet in the midst of all this dedicated beating-of-tracks to

kirks and halls there were some few for whom church-going at all
was a treat reserved for holiday times or retirement.

> Sundays at the lighthouses had to be pretty much like other days
> because you still had to see to the light. But it depended on the people
> what they made of it themselves. I remember one station where there
> was a Wee Free man, the other keeper. So was my father a great man for
> the church, and I can just picture us at the change of watch on a Sunday
> night, round the coal fire and my father reading a passage from the
> Bible, then you all said the Lord's Prayer . . . the next week the Wee Free
> would read. That created an atmosphere I've remembered all my life . . .
> to hear that going on and the gales and sea lashing outside . . . made a
> deep impression on me that.

And so did the odd occasion when the keeper's family got to
church.

> While we were at Turnberry lighthouse we sometimes went to an
> evening service at the Maidens and it was wonderful to hear the
> fishermen singing there on these evenings before they set off the next
> day.

With that memory of the men of the boats and two others of the
fisherfolk Sunday we can close this chapter, at least, on the Sabbath
in shore communities.

> The fisherwomen, no matter where they were for the gutting and
> packing, following the fish, they always went t' the kirk on a Sunday
> night, whichever church they could find.

And Jim Buchan looks back on the first discipline of the week's
fishing.

> Sundays were very strict. If you were going to the sea the beginning of
> the week, no one moved a muscle till the midnight after Sunday. They
> called it 'going away at the *back* of Sunday'.

There are still the hours at home, however few, between services
and the festive eternity of Communion week-ends to hear about.
But we are not made in the same dogged mould as these rememberers of seventy and eighty years ago and perhaps it's best to
leaven the diet of worship with a look at some other aspects of their
lives, before another Sabbath comes round again.

7
I Worked on the Glen Sannox

While the fishing from the waterfronts of the coast, and the crofting in the near hinterland, were perhaps the main occupations in most places, there was also a variety of other work, essential to one or other of those, and to the general supporting of the community life and the running of homes.

Take the jobs that arose from the sea-work itself.

> There were quite a few oilskin and net-making factories about Leven and Anstruther. My first job was at Willie Carstairs' place. We made oilskin clothes, of course, but I was on the 'pallet' making ... they were floats for keeping up the fishing nets ... made with canvas, and oiled all over with several layers of oil, then filled with hot tar to make them waterproof. Then they were rolled up ready for sending out. Quite a dirty job it was.

Young Jean Kane's first job was cleaner

> Oh I loved it. I went straight from school to work in the tea-room in the 'Glen Sannox'. She was a paddle-steamer wi' red funnels. (I still go and see the model of her sometimes in the Glasgow Art Galleries). We went from Ardrossan to Brodick, Lamlash, Whiting Bay, and back again. The 'Atlanta' did the runs sometimes and I didnae like that at all. She was like a cork in the water, bobbin' about wild ... made you feel that squeamish!

She was like most Ardrossan folk.

> Apart from the I.C.I. 'Dinnamite' at Ardeer, everyone worked to do wi' the sea ... on the boats or at the harbour. I mind once there was a boatful of grain went aground at the harbour and the grain got wet and sent off fumes that killed one or two of the men. After that they'd to put on special masks and throw all the rest of the grain into the sea.

Some locals were on night duty.

You always knew when a boatload of sailors came in ... the street-walkers that hadn't seen to their rent for ages, got all paid up. We used to make a joke of it (no' my Mother, mind, but us). We used to say 'Oh my! That's a boat in, so-and-so's rent'll be paid this week!

Those who worked on shipping facilities at Peterhead harbour were not always local.

There wasn't much work ashore for boys in my young days. The thing 't kept Peterhead going was the prison needing warders and storekeepers and cleaners. Then there was the work on the breakwater ... two stretches of that. The locals built one and the prisoners the other.

One of the most expert and dedicated of all coastal tasks was, and is, that of the Lighthouse Service ... remote and mysterious to all except the close-knit breed of keepers.

Working time was precisely divided, as John MacRae, retired from the service now, recalls.

Four hour watches. Say I was coming off duty at midnight, I'd ring down the buzzer at 11.40 to warn the man coming on. His buzzer would be as far as possible from his bed so he *had* to get up to answer. We'd a lot of different duties ... flying the cone to signal a gale ... like a jelly-bag sort' thing, y'know. And we'd to look out for small ships in trouble.

The core of the work though was looking after and working the light itself, from its daily cleaning and polishing to attending the 'works'.

This big lens, the bull's eye, revolving round and magnifying the light ... weighs between twelve and fifteen tons. And it was a simple grandfather-clock mechanism made it go round. The weight went down the centre of the tower and you'd to wind it up again every twenty minutes of the watch. So you'd to be ready to bring it up after the alarm 'clang' came and then another warning two minutes later. You'd to know your own light, and its speed of turning because every tower was different ... Ailsa Craig six flashes every eleven seconds, Turnberry one every twenty-five seconds. Mariners knew them all.

The towers themselves have to stand out clearly day and night.

Had all to be painted every spring. You'd to sit on a board slung over the side and spiral round, painting your way to the bottom.

A demanding and expensive service.

The money mostly comes from the light dues. That's the money that's paid by ships for every light they pass. The only ships that don't pay dues to Britain are fishing-boats and H.M. ships.

So even the little boat that earned the Macfadyen living on Lismore, would be liable, in its day, if it passed a lighthouse.

It was a puffer sort 'of thing and my father carried cargoes up the west coast and round to Orkney. Mostly building materials and coal. He'd been away at sea as a boy, under sail. He was a Cape Horner ... seven times round the horn. Then in the real winter he stayed at home, painted and repaired the boat and saw t' the croft.

The natural turn of island men is always to the sea, some to continue the fishing tradition of their ancestors, others going to the navy or merchant shipping ... in more modern times as a chosen career, but in the earlier days whether they liked it or not ... a kind of conscription.

A big lot of men went to sea from Orkney. Long ago in fact, the press-gangs came to the islands because they were after good sailing men.

And Orkney abounds in tales of chasings and hidings, and clashes between the press-gangs and the youths they had singled out as quarry.

Sometimes they intercepted whaling ships and took off men to put them in the navy. The whaling men were reckoned great seamen.

A more legitimate form of recruitment came after the press-gang days and is remembered at Plockton by Farquhar MacDonald. Many a lad involved left sea-shore life forever, when he signed up.

The Police used to come up to Plockton and places like that, on recruiting drives, with the full police band from the City of Glasgow force. A lot of the boys got carried away with the show and that's why there are so many highland policemen in Glasgow.

Like policemen, there are post-offices everywhere. However isolated a spot, the long arm of the G.P.O. has always stretched out to keep channels open to the rest of the world, and the folk in makeshift shacks or mahogany-countered, bona fide offices, were always king or queen-pins in the community, like Catherine Murray.

I went to the wee post-office in Connel first, then on to the relieving
staff that went out from Oban. The first place I went to was Iona. I was
a bit nervous of going but I was persuaded and then, just as I was getting
on the boat 'Lochinvar' from Oban, the Head Postmaster who was
sending me, said, 'There's just one thing I didn't tell you ... there's no
telephone on Iona just an A.B.C. clock and there's a lot of telegrams
coming and going.' So I panicked. 'Well I know nothing about working
that. I'm going home!' But I didn't. I mastered it eventually. It was a
face with a needle and when the signal came through, the needle
flickered and pointed to a letter and you wrote down the letters till you
could read the message. Later I relieved in Helensburgh, Easdale and
away up to Glenetive at the head of the loch. I stayed in a shepherd's
cottage there in the summer with a three-mile walk to the post office,
then in the winter I was in Glenetive House, the estate shooting-lodge.
It was eerie there because it got dark about 4 o'clock. Then I was at
Benawe Quarries post office across the bridge, and I came and went
there by van. And then there was Taynuilt, Tyndrum and Dalmally.

The reference point at Connel for giving directions or relating
tales is that bridge, spanning Loch Etive and joining North and
South Connel. It is over eighty years old and for a long time, even
after the building of it, provided constant employment. Mr
McSwan remembers the days of endless painting.

Six or seven painters used to be up there all year round. They'd start at
one end, paint all the way over on one side and back along the other, day
in day out. Now it's only painted every so-many years; but in the old
days it kept six Connel families going.

There was 'the shop' too, in most communities, and places the
size of Troon had even a shopping centre with a selection of shops.

I had my Intermediate Certificate at the school and would've liked to go
on, but the nine shillings-a-week I was to get in Kirkwood the Baker's
was needed for the family coffers ... I would leave, of course, when
something better turned up. But I never did, and I was in charge of the
shop by the 1920s.
    It was hard work. The juniors started at seven in the morning,
washing down the white and black tiles. Then you went home for your
breakfast and your dinner and after that you were there till about seven
at night.

As well as out-front assistants, the business employed skilled
bakers and confectioners ... not only skilled, but conscientious
well above and beyond the call of duty!

Our bakers worked with yeast, and sometimes if there was a hard frost at night the baker had to get out his bed and come down to the bakehouses to see if what they called the 'sponge' (that was the dough) was rising ... used to say he could tell by his elbow when the dough was just right. If the frost was very hard he'd sometimes to put extra covers on the dough and if the cookies were a bit 'cheuch' the next day, he used to say 'Oh, the spon'ying's got caught!'

Sales psychology is nothing new, and it was a well-satisfied baker who used to hurry his warm Coburg cakes from oven to front shop, 'get these out there quick, for the smell'.

Here's a weekly wages sheet for 1939. I was in charge of the shop and quite a few assistants, and I got £2.10s., the baker got £3.7s. and the confectioner £3.17s.

And apart from the bagging of goodies and their delivery along with urns of tea and cans of milk in the correct orders for perhaps a dozen different Sunday School picnics each summer Saturday, there was wedding catering and the eventual opening of a handsome tea-room.

... with daffodil china and dark wood lattice-back chairs. It was beautiful.

In remote places, or those with small prospect of direct employment, there were often cottage industries.

There was what they called 'the Ayrshire floo'erin' here. That was white hand embroidery, something like broderie anglaise.

Tissue paper rustles in a press and an exquisite piece is brought out richly embroidered with flowers, sprays and leaves.

Here's a christening gown sewn by our great-grandmother in Irvine who had a robe on display at one of the big Glasgow exhibitions. There's a picture here too.

And the illustration, carefully put away long ago among the fine cotton and tissue, is unfolded. The picture is of a christening robe similar to one bought by Queen Victoria in one of several orders she gave, to help popularise the craft for the Ayshire women.

The work, on the other hand, produced in living rooms and sheds in Lewis and Harris was coarser, but just as much sought after and prized by those who finally bought it. In Isobel Wales's home in Ness ...

We'd a loom, of course. It was in a kind of barn attached to the house. The aunts used to get lengths of wool on a drum from Stornoway, they were called 'tweeds' and Aunt Margaret used to thread the loom with wires that had eyes in them. It was a long skilled job to get it ready for throwing the shuttle. That was your true Harris Tweed. The lengths of cloth were sent back to Stornoway to sell. It was a real cottage industry.

And all over the Hebrides looms were clacking and shifting making the 'stuff' so peculiarly characteristic of the Islands.

Some of the coastal women made their own contribution to

family economics without either going to work locally or pursuing
a craft at home, but by following their men to the fishing grounds
and doing a spot of shrewd bargaining there on their own behalf and
as commission for neighbours at home. Perhaps Mima Buchan
confounded the smooth talkers of Yarmouth with the delightful
curl of her tongue round the rare Buchan-country accent of St.
Combs. She indicates the quiet fisherman at the fireside, her hands
sequined with the scales of fish she is cleaning even now in her
kitchen ... a hand-in from a neighbouring fisherman.

> When I was young I went t' Yarmouth w' *him*. He was fishin' out o'
> there ... stayed maybe eight weeks. Yarmouth was affa fine and verry
> cheap to buy ... the stuff affa low prices ... bought material t' bring
> home and th' was a man there use't keep ends o' sheets to me ... and
> other stuff good for makin' coats to the bairns, at 3s.6d. maybe, and
> 3s.0d. for trousers ... s'posed to be fla's (wee bits no' right) or it was
> 'ends'. I've seen me gettin' a great seersucker bedspread that'd make
> twa-three table cloths. I used t' come home w' a' that in a tea-chest.

Her sister Gena Robertson halts the couthy flow.

> Och she wasna stupid ... used to buy bath towels w' no hems and
> hemmed them up when she got home. Me, I would've been black
> affronted at a' the bargains. She was shoppin' for everyone here. She'd
> the money to spend y'see. *Her* man there never smoked and never drank
> and never ran a car, so he'd plenty. *My* man wasnae like that, he ran a car
> *and* he smoked *and* he drank an' a'. So *she* was the one w' the money to
> spend at the market.

Others, remembered by Netta Ross of Beauly, as having money
to splash out were nevertheless in a different league from those
cheerfully bargaining at open markets, but they added a picturesque cast to old memories of Beauly, and their spending helped
to prosper the stables in the village.

> At the stables, they rented out horses and carriages to the gentry
> coming to the fishing and shooting lodges for the season. As well as
> letting out the horses and machines, they kept hill ponies, garrons, for
> carrying the shot deer back from the hills.

Out of season, there was more mundane bread-and-butter work for
the horses, in carting and farm work.

There's not much history of the 'gentry' having any connection
with the coal-mining work that Andrew Fairnie (reared totally to

the sea) took up instead of fishing ... except perhaps James VI's excursion into the Culross pit, running out under the Forth. He panicked there and is said to have believed he had stumbled into a plot to kill him ... But that is by the way. Andrew Fairnie had no such fears in his pit on the other side of the Firth.

My father discouraged us from the fishing. There were three big mills, cotton, paper and wire rope, and there were coal mines across the River Esk there. I went to the coal and worked underground at 3s.6d. a day as a boy. I was mate or 'drawer' to a collier. I'd to fill the bogies as he worked and drag them back and forward to what they called the 'lie' with a pin marker in his coal with his initials on it so it would be credited to him at the end of the week. Then another man took up six of these bogies at a time and brought down six empty ones to me to take back to the collier ... I worked at that till the 1914-18 war came, and after my years away I went 't the paper mill and was there till I retired.

A post-script ... one industry that belongs in most minds to just one island is recollected by John MacRae. As Harris Tweed to the Hebrides, so too are curling stones to Ailsa Craig, the bun of the Firth of Clyde.

They were still making curling stones there when I was at the light on Ailsa Craig. Folk used to come out on trips on the 'Lady Ailsa' to see them being worked, out of the Craig granite.

They were men and women of many parts, a hundred years ago, with different skills geared to the changing seasons and the needs of the moment. Few had only one and the best of them, a dozen.

It was nothing to see the man who swept your chimney one day, digging a grave the next or lifting tatties for the farmer; or maybe a woman taking off her croft boots to go in to a bit of weaving or carry a baking to the Big House ... maybe mending her man's nets. That was the queer difference I saw, between us on the islands and the city folk. You'd t' turn your hand to so many different things.

8

The Feathers Were Aye Fleein' Aboot

There was a whole monolithic culture in the tenements of cities, still well within living memory. The lay-out and finish of houses was similar from east-end to west-end, give or take a room or two, or wally tiles versus plaster-and-whitewash in the close. And the mechanics of life were common to nearly all, whether these were attended by the hard-pressed mother herself or, in biener residences, worked by a maid or two and a weekly woman for the washing.

But beyond the towns it was different. Houses varied hugely in type, height, length, material and design, and, of those remembered for us here that lay around the coast, no two were much alike. Where better to begin to look at their variety than with the memory of a young girl coming from the sameness of the city for the first time, early in the century, into a scattered community of such houses and the surrounding countryside? Helen McClung recalls her mother's arrival in South Ayrshire.

> My mother used to say she'd never forget coming by train from Glasgow to Pinwherry as a girl of about fourteen, going into service. She got off the train and into the horse-and-cart that went up from Ballantrae in those days to meet the train. It was a stormy, cold night, coming down that road from Pinwherry and the sea that she'd not seen before was wild too. She never forgot that night. But she got that she'd never have moved back to the city.

And she didn't have to, because she married one of Lord Inchcape's gardeners and they set up home in Glenapp ... the home in which Helen McClung had her childhood.

It was quite a nice cottage. We'd our big kitchen w' the range and a wee scullery. Then we'd a sitting room and two bedrooms ... no bathroom of course. In the bedrooms we'd ewers and basins and soap dishes, matching. It was a wash-stand set really.

Our beds were flock I remember, and we'd to take the stuffing out the striped ticking bag at spring-cleaning time. It was sort of grey wadding and you'd to tease it all out.

Jenny Stewart has more critical memories of the home where she was raised, though always with a smile or a chuckle.

Merkland was the farm where I was brought up and it was set right beside the road, but there was more than folk passed it by, for it was the most old-fashioned place w' no modern conveniences at all. It had the open fire, all the water and wood to bring in, and th' outside W.C.

No rose-tinted mindings there.

We'd a 'best' room of course for visitors from neighbouring farms ... and the minister and the elder. My mother would bake for them in her oven-pot, set the fire in the sitting-room and bring out the good china. The minister terrified me, he looked so stern and sober that I used to try and run away, like I did at the pig-killing.

And once back from the fleeing, there were well remembered quarters upstairs where young Jenny and her mother slept.

They were what we called 'caff' beds ... chaff it was really. You got caff from the mill. That was the steam-mill that came round to thresh. Then you emptied out the old caff to go for bedding for the animals and you filled the ticks w' the new caff when you'd dried it. The first night you'd be in that bed it'd be all jaggy, and it was nothing to lie on a thistle. It was a big day the day you changed the bed.

From field to mill, mill to bed and bed to beast-stall, that little exercise in conservation over ... the newly filled bag was upstairs.

It lay on a very-very hard straw pallet on top of wooden planks in the set-in bed. Later we graduated to flock beds but that was harder and lumpier than the caff. Then we'd blankets that had been made before my time, at the old Pitclantie mill ... all hairy and scratchy. But we'd no sheets in my young day.

But surrounding that starkly plenished indoor life at Merkland was a joyful magic that even a stern uncle could not spoil.

You always knew where to find the first snowdrops or primroses and the celandines and windflowers. And th' was an odd fox ... not many though for th' wasn't much cover at Merkland and foxes like cover. We'd a meadow too and in August and September time th' was bogan hay out, and early in the year globe buttercups. I used to take great big bunches to the hotel and get paid for them for pocket-money. Th' was four acres of them ... a sea of gold right down to the river.

Further north up the Ayrshire coast, from the years before the First War comes the memory of a childhood home in the small country and seaside town of Troon. There weren't fields of wild-flowers there to make a lonely child feel with such intensity, but there were other practical pleasures to savour.

My mother and father had taken up house in a two room and kitchen ... bedroom off the lobby, a through-and-through room and kitchen. We had a kitchen bed, the Room had a set-in bed and the wee bedroom had a set-in bed. We'd boards with straw mattresses that were taken out and shaken and beaten at spring-cleaning time and we'd flock mattresses on top of that. We'd to scrub the boards too and that was quite a treat. There were two pulleys in the kitchen and the floor was covered with linoleum and a fireside rug.

We'd neighbours too. There was a lady downstairs with a wooden dresser that she scrubbed white every Friday. I was in her house quite a lot. She used to sit me up at the kitchen sink and teach me rhymes and wee wise sayings, 'Thirty days hath September' kind of thing, and I remember her saying, 'I just look out the window and I thank God for the things I havenae got, I havenae got a drunken man and I havenae got this illness or that problem.'

The social graces also were cultivated in that little Troon home.

My mother taught us poems too, like 'Meddlesome Mattie' and 'The Mouse and the Cake' and we'd to say a 'party piece' when we'd visitors. I remember another neighbour that had just linoleum and rugs on her floor, like us, that she could take out and shake. Then her son brought her a big square carpet. She couldn't get it over the rope and she was all fashed struggling with it and muttering 'My, they're weel-aff that's no' weel-aff'.

Among the memories, the nearest likeness to those of a city tenement home was surely what went on in the bulging Kane establishment at Ardrossan ... the room and kitchen street door flat with its two apartments for thirteen souls.

There were a lot of us to get beds for. Mind, one or two of the oldest ones were away working when the wee ones came along. But there was an inshot bed in the Room *and* a black iron bedstead with brass knobs. So four of us girls slept in the bed, and four or five boys in the inshot.

In the kitchen we'd the big range, of course, and a sink with one of yon brass swan-neck spigots that my mother polished. There was lino on the floor that was that-well scrubbed th' was no pattern left.

The Kanes, like the Troon family, had neighbours too, but without so much time for philosophising or teaching poetry.

Th' was two other houses up the close at the side of our main door. There was Mistress Byers with her big-big family and Mistress Boyle with her big-big family. Th' was maybe thirty children in the three houses, and all of them healthy.

Over to the north-west lies Tarbert where John Leitch was a boy, ninety years ago.

It was a wee croft house, no gas, no running water, no electricity. There was a sitting room with two beds, a bedroom with two beds, a kitchen with two beds, and you went up a ladder to a wee loft with two beds. That was eight beds in that small house. We'd oil lamps that had to be cleaned and trimmed, but not by me. I'd five sisters and I was a sort of spoiled only boy.

And that's maybe why not so much of the inside furbishing and fettling was imprinted on his mind.

But I'd to help my father with the wee croft outside. We'd a quarter acre for potatoes, a quarter acre of corn for the cows, and the garden for all the fruit and the kale.

By the time we cross back and get up to the Firth of Lorn we're touching clan and crofting country, and Peter Sinclair is firmly rooted on the land where he and his sons are still living.

I was born here. It's the croft house and the land itself is up there on the other side of the railway line. My father and grandfather worked the croft before me, then me, and now my sons. They've other work too. One of them's building a new house out there on this plot of land. What we call 'the old byre' there, was my grandfather's house and my father was brought up in it. The roof was thatched with thin rashes. Had to be re-done from time to time. They mostly did it themselves, but there would be thatchers about.

This was our kitchen and the range would've been there . . . and a big table we all sat round.

His neighbour along the lochside, Catherine Murray, also born in
Connel, has more of woman's mind's eye to some of the old
furnishing.

> Our first house, Corriebeg, was right in the village beside the church,
> then when the family got bigger, we moved to Hawthornbank near the
> school. We'd a grandfather clock and wally dugs and I remember a big
> china cat and a wag-at-the-wa'.

Seven or eight miles north-west on Lismore Miss Mary Macfadyen was born on a hogmanay night close to the turn of the
century.

> The men of Lismore had helped to build the Caledonian Canal so they
> were all experienced masons and almost every crofter built his own
> house with stones left over from the Canal. The one where I was born
> would be built like that, but not by my father. They were very old
> houses with thick-thick walls, and then, when my father was at home in
> spells from the sea, he put in two bedrooms upstairs himself. So we'd
> the kitchen (what you'd call a 'living-room' now) with just the open fire
> to cook and then the wee range later. Every Maytime all the houses were
> whitewashed with Lismore lime (it was all limestone the island, no
> peat). My mother would get up at five in the morning to whitewash the
> walls.

Just the walls ... no nonsense there, about early rising to wash the
face in the May-day dew.

Eighty years ago, and even a decade or two later, much that was
north of Oban and Inverness was, to many lowlanders, the un-
charted country of the highlands and islands. Travelling was an
adventure and to go beyond where the train stopped was only for
the explorer or the eccentric. And if Stornoway was just a romantic
Atlantic name to the city man who took his pleasures in Rothesay,
it was just as much a place of mystery to other island families less
than twenty miles away, like the Macleods on Bernera. The
daughter of that house, now Mrs. Pryde, remembers their isolation.

> Stornoway was a long way away. I didn't go there till I was about
> eighteen years of age. Stornoway was the big town.

But behind that misty curtain were lively families in traditional
houses, purpose and situation-built, often from materials found

close at hand. George MacGregor describes the 'black houses', built of strewings of local stone.

> The walls weren't mortared ... it was more like dry-stone dyking and very-very thick and it was thatching ... heather thatching. Some of the older ones had ropes slung across the thatch and ridges, weighted with stones that dangled over the eaves to keep the roof tight in a high wind ... and these old ones had no chimneys so the smoke drifted round the walls before it went up through the hole. The rooms weren't back and front, but side by side in a row, so the more rooms the longer the house.

Further north on the island of Bernera Mrs. Pryde was familiar with 'black houses' there.

> Oh yes, we were in and out of them when we were small, playing y'know. They could be very nice inside ... not the floors, they weren't nice ... just bare cement maybe, or slabs. Thatch, of course, and originally the fire'd been in the middle of the floor and just vents for the smoke ... that's going back a bit though. Later, the fire was built into the wall and some kind of chimney put in.

But Mrs. Pryde did not live in a black house herself and points up the differences ...

> Ours was what they called a 'white house' ... whitewashed on the outside. Black houses were called that because they were dark rough stone on the outside, just laid together dry, and inside the peat smoke made them dark. The roof was dark thatch so there was nothing white about it. There was no social division at all between the black house and the white house people.

The house where she was brought up has stood on Bernera for about eighty years.

> Our father built the house for getting married. He got the stones from round about, from a kind of quarry where everyone found their stones. He was a builder and joiner and everything else.

If young Miss Macleod had left Bernera to make the dizzy journey to Stornoway before she was eighteen she might have been even more awestruck by the sight of streets of sizeable houses forming the town. But she would have been comfortably at home with the bi-lingual conversation in the family of Farquhar MacDonald.

> My first memories are of living in a detached villa in Stornoway with my

parents who were both Gaelic-speaking, though they spoke some English to us in the house.

It was the same in the north-east, up at the Butt of Lewis where young Isobel Campbell spent the summers of the 1930s and all the war years with her two Gaelic-speaking aunts, Margaret who had a smattering of the English, having been in service in Glasgow, and Kirsty, who had only a word or two.

> Ness is really a cluster of villages. Our house was originally just the two rooms downstairs, but after the First War my father put on two upstairs rooms. It was a stone house rendered over, and it was thatched. The bedrooms were upstairs and there was a kitchen downstairs with 'the good room' a step up from the kitchen . . . that was for when people came to visit. And there was a kind of lean-to barn where the loom was kept. The house is mine now but it's in poor condition. The croft's mine too but my cousin Donald grazes his sheep there.

Upstairs, in one of the rooms her father built, she remembers the sleeping arrangements of over forty years ago.

> There was a long board that ran the whole length of the room and slats of wood were laid across it, and on top of that there was a jaggy straw mattress that had to be changed every spring and the old stuffing thrown out to the animals.

The beds and their equipment must have impressed her more than the other furniture, for apart from the meal-kist and that loom in the barn, which belong to other chapters, not much of the other gear there lingered in young Isobel's memory. Not so Hugh Craigie's. His recollections of his croft home in Orkney are sharp and detailed.

> The floor of our house was flagstone for easy washing. That was an improvement on floors in older houses, like where my father was brought up, with a clay floor . . . can you imagine how damp 't must have been
>
> A lot of furniture in the Orkneys was made from straw . . . chairs and stools and so on. There was lots of straw and very little trees for wood. There wasna a lot of furniture and I can remember in our kitchen there were two straw chairs, one each side the fire . . . one my mother's, one my father's. Now nob'dy else ever sat on my father's chair, but we all squabbled to get on my mother's. She'd be maybe washing the dishes y'know and we'd race to sit there. Other than that we'd just wooden joiner-made stools.

Fond as he was of the croft work on their sixty acres and rough grazing, he has no sentimental yearnings for the bedding-down arrangements.

We'd our beds partitioned off and we slept on chaff mats filled new every year. There wasna much frost at Rousay but the wind howled in and you used to waken w' the draughts swerling in and you'd be cold-cold in that beds.

Hugh Craigie has a memory too of conditions in his grandfather's home.

There, the upstairs ceiling was made of the sail off his old fishing boat. He'd nailed that on to the beams and that was the ceiling. He came up the hard way, did my grandfather. The house wasn't important, it was the *land*.

Wheeling round by the north-east corner now, and homing in on the coast-country south of Wick we can take a look through David Henderson's eyes at his old home ... in Clearance country.

My father took over the croft at Latheronwheel eighteen miles south of Wick. We looked out to the North Sea and down to the Moray Firth. And we would see across to Lossiemouth. On clear nights we saw the flashes on Tarbat Ness and Cromarty. Six flashes then a blank, at Tarbat Ness. The croft house was white-washed outside and just a kitchen with a flagstone floor and the Room ... that was the posh place.
    Then th' was the room at the back where we slept. It was free standing box-beds and you could push them into the corner or wherever you wanted them ... no mattresses in the sense we know now ... just our own chaff in thick ticking and you changed it every year.

Perhaps there was something different about the Caithness chaff for, unlike the gripes about jaggy straw and thistles everywhere else he, (no doubt well-cradled nowadays in Dunlopillo and duvet) can say of these old boxes ...

... most comfortable beds ever I slept on, that chaff. When it was new you were away-way high up and we loved that. The old chaff went to the midden.

Those flashes from the lighthouses that had David Henderson dreaming dreams, were part of day-to-day life for John MacRae as a member of the 'keeper' community.

I was born in the Butt of Lewis lighthouse because my grandfather was keeper there and my mother went there to be with her mother when the birth of us twins came due. My own father was keeper at Neist Point on Skye at that time.

There was always a wee community at a lighthouse. There's the tower itself and, alongside it down below, houses for two, or occasionally three, families. Only the work itself goes on in the tower. The houses each have maybe three rooms and so the families would make up the community. Sometimes the houses would be flats one above the other, sometimes side by side like a terrace or semi-detached. You might be ten or twelve miles from any other houses.

In spite of the second sight and superstitious witchery of highland reputation and fey celtic poetry, only one rememberer claimed a household ghost ... none at all in the hard-headed south. Margaret MacKenzie had her own private room-mate but we have to go through the rest of her home before glimpsing that little apartment.

When I went to live with my aunt and uncle at the Cromarty Arms Hotel, you went in at the front door and there was a billiard room on one side and the public bar on the other. The living quarters were through the back and the bedrooms upstairs. There was a lamp-room on the half-stair for cleaning and trimming the oil lamps. There was a great big kitchen with a stone floor and one wall shelved and covered with lots of wee drawers like an old-fashioned chemist's shop. We never touched them but when the navy came in to Cromarty and crowded the public bar the usual fishermen invaded the kitchen out the way, chaffed the maids and opened the wee drawers to see what was inside. It was currants and raisins and rice and barley.

It was a large household with young Margaret, her cousins, uncle and aunt, and the live-in cook and maids.

They slept upstairs and so did I. I had a wee room through a passage and up a wee stone stair ... that was my bedroom. It was supposed to be haunted up there but I didn't mind. I remember my ewer and basin for washing and I remember the visitors' dining-room upstairs. *We* all ate in the nice warm kitchen.

A ghost was easily tolerated in exchange for such comfort.

Jim Buchan's verdict on his early home in Peterhead was succinct and not so kindly.

Dreadful, wi' an outside W.C., though in Peterhead even that was a luxury. I suppose we were lucky we'd our own house at all. A' the fishermen had their own house and they were proud, proud folk.

Of the furnishing, it is the family beds that he recalls.

The beds were in the wall at the Road Heads where I lived in Peterhead. Boxed-in beds wi' a feather mattress. The feathers were aye fleein' aboot. They'd curtains, or maybe some had wooden shutters. That was called a 'bound-in' bed. You'd privacy, right enough but no air, and th' was maybe five or six in the one room.

In retrospect Gena Robertson's early life in St. Combs was an idyll of sweet smells and savours ... of raisin tarts and spices, fruit pies, baked rabbit and smoked fish. And of the furnishing, apart from the shoe rack above the range and the crock in the lobby where the prunes were kept, it was again the beds that came to mind.

They were stuffed w' feathers over a hair mattress. You'd to keep turning it ... affa' soft stuff. Every now and again it was put into the dry boiler w' sulphur to clean it, and then you put new feathers into 't.

Dwellings, of course, were not universally family homes.

Our farm on the Forglen estate was called Meikle Ribera (that meant 'big rye brae'). As well's the house w' the good Room, the kitchen and bedrooms, there was the bothy for the single men, two or three of them at a time. They'd their bunk beds and their fire and lamps. But they ate in the kitchen ... came into the kitchen every morning for their brose.

Down to the shores of the River Forth now for a last glimpse at remembered houses and those odd pieces and ornaments in and about them that have stuck randomly in minds throughout long years.

We'd a three-roomed house in Fisherrow. That was quite big then, built for big families ... and the rents were verra cheap ... paid every half-year. The house was on the main street ... a row of houses. Some of the women pipe-clayed their doorstep and they used to make a nice half-circle in front of the door and draw designs round it. But then when the rain came it was all washed away.

That was surely Art for Art's sake in Andrew Fairnie's greenstick years.

Across the river in Largo was the house where Alex Archer cut his teeth.

They were old cottages here, w' a close through, and you went round the back and up two-three steps to the door. Ours was one of these. Just a kitchen and a nice wee bedroom lit by gas. And the street lights outside were gas too ... lit by the leerie w' his pole. After a while we got the electric.

He doesn't indulge in long descriptions of the unimportant furbishing of that Largo cottage but there was one item that had a hallowed place in the scheme of things.

I remember the first wireless set my father had. He got it for smoking Black Cat cigarettes. It was w' coupons if I dinna forget. A few of the men pooled their coupons and got one wireless first, then another and another till they'd all them. Then they used to take a wee bogie up to Lundin Links on a Saturday for a 'cumulator that did them a week kind o' style ... kept the wireless going ...

They're more uniformly lapped now in divans and wall-to-wall double-glazings and three piece suites. But their young hearts are among the chaff beds and black kettles and who can blame them if they like to believe that those were better days.

9
We've Come to See Poor Janetty

It's easy enough to understand how the skills, arts and philosophies, even the favourite foods, of old civilisations were carried round the world by the likes of Marco Polo or stout Cortez or even round Britain by those who left diaries of their travels like Dr. Johnson in the 18th century or the Waterman Poet John Taylor of the Penniless Pilgrimage of the 17th. But it's more of a puzzle to know how it came about that bools, and chuckies, hopscotch and two-and-out skipping, flourished commonly and concurrently in isolated hamlets miles and mountains apart as far back as living memory and no doubt a good deal earlier. Unless, of course, St. Columba or the Great Cham themselves had their lighter moments and taught the Pictish girls to double-caw or the Hebridean boys how the boys cracked conkers in Lichfield. However ... whatever ... by the 1800s children from Eyemouth to the tip of Lewis and from Stranraer to John O'Groats played, to a fair extent the same games, at least so far as those in their school playgrounds were concerned.

School was, in fact, better remembered for the ongoings in its yards than for its main function.

> There wasnae all the school learnin' there is now. I was three years in the last class and couldnae get any further.

Whether that was because he was so bright that he reached it early, or because he couldn't progress out of it, he wouldn't tell. But the bright eyes and remarkable memory say it all for him. Whatever he may say about those old days in Fife, he certainly qualified in the skills of the playground.

> I was at school in Pittenweem and we played a lot with bats and balls, then th'was the marbles season and the conkers season, the season wi'

your gird and cleek and then the time for leave-o. And in the wintertime
when 't was frost you tried to get up early for school to slide on the great
big puddle 't used to freeze over in front the school.

On Bernera, at Lochgilphead, at St. Combs across the country and
south-west at Ardrossan, the seasons likewise came and went
without announcement.

At school we played peever and skipping and ball.

We played peever and ropes but the *great* game that the *whole* school
played, was leave-o!

Skippin' ropes was the best . . . double caw w' th'enders takin' a rope in
each hand.

There was kick-the-can . . . like hide-and-seek and chases all in one. But
the girls, when they were by themselves, just did peevers and skips and
your one-two-three-a-leeries.

And when the boys weren't muscling in on the girls' ploys they were
dedicated to their own games and their envious pursuit of ex-
cellence . . . and capital. Jim Still can remember his chagrin at his
paltry store of marbles alongside those of some of the other Forglen
experts.

We played marbles and I used to envy the boys that were good at it and
had that great big bags of marbles. We'd all that grey-kind bags like
bank bags, but mine didnae bulge.

From St. Combs the men's memories too are of marbles and of
another universal pastime that would have the 'sussing' policemen
out nowadays.

We played at bools and we played knifey . . . throwing your knife at a
stickie poked in the ground, to see who could get nearest. Oh, y'all had
your knife.

And nary a thought of them as offensive weapons.

Sometimes a game played everywhere had a local name, so that
what they called Scotch Horses or Piggy Backs in other places had a
more romantic and swashbuckling title even when spoken in the
soft Beauly accent. Though how it reached the Moray Firth and
Donald MacKintosh's chums is a mystery.

There was Hussaurs (*sic*) in Beauly. That was a great favourite with the boys ... getting on each other's shoulders and trying to knock one another off.

And when he went on to say, a little patronisingly, how prettily the 'girls' played their singing games, his fellow reminiscer Miss Netta Ross, with just as long a memory, put him sharply in his place.

The girls were just as good's the boys at Hussaurs!

Unlike all these games 'Smuggle the Gegie' was remembered for these pages only in Beauly, and one or two areas of the north-west.

Oh yes, 'Smuggle the Gegie' was another game we played. We stood in two rows and one boy on one side had something hidden in his pocket. His row tried to run to the far end of the playground with the other row trying to catch them and find the boy with gegie in his pocket.

Mary Macfadyen did not remember that from her Lismore playing days but she summed up most of the others in a kind of check-list.

We'd such fun in the playground at the school. We played Het, and Blind Man's Buff, bats and bases, skipping and marbles and ball and chuckies ... all the girls. And the girls' singing games too.

So Donald MacKintosh of Beauly *was* right. The girls did play singing games and not only the hullaracket horse-play of Hussars.

I always remember the girls playing in the playground. There was no yelling or shouting. You just heard them singing or chanting. One game was called Round Apples. It was a circle game.
'Round Apples, Round Apples, by night and by day
   They're coming to steal poor Maggie away
   Maggie's father came out with a knife in his hand
   So turn your back, Maggie, or your life will not stand.'
And Maggie turned her back and they all went round her with their backs to the ring.

And no doubt both rhyme and movement were as easily understood as 'Poor Janetty' whom Mary Macfadyen remembers from Lismore, twenty years later.

It was a game we played in two lines, the one coming up to the other and saying,
   'We've come to see poor Janetty, p'r Janetty, p'r Janetty
   We've come to see p'r Janetty
   And how is she today?'
Then the other row would answer
   'She's up the stairs ir'ning, ir'ning, ir'ning
   She's up the stairs ir'ning
   You can't see her today.'

Poor Janetty had a number of accidents like burning her dress or letting the iron fall on her big toe which prevented her 'being seen today' until the imagined mishaps ran out and the rows changed sides.

We had 'Water Water Wall-flower' too, d'you remember that, with one girl in the middle?

'Water, water wallflower growing up so high
We are all maid-ens and we must all die,
Excepting Mary Macfadyen, the youngest of us all,
She can dance and she can sing
And she can knock us all down.
Fie, fie, fie-fie shame, turn your back to the wall again.'

And in the playground at Ballantrae there was a courting game that Jenny McCrindle and her friends used to play in the twenties...

'There are three Jews new-come from Spain
To call upon your daughter Jane'
'My daughter Jane is far too young
She cannot bear your flattering tongue'
'O then, O then, we'll just away
And call again some other day.'

Up at Turriff there was 'The Farmer's in the Dell' and the song that went with Hilda Strachan's stotting ball.

1, 2, 3 a'leerie
I spy Mrs. Peerie
Sitting on a basket-cheerie
Eating choc-late bis-cuits.

In Girvan a less refined Mrs Peerie sat on her bumbleleerie but no doubt the ball bounced just as truly.

Then there was counting out ...

Eetle Ottle, Black Bottle
Ettle Ottle Out.
I choose you out
For a dirty dish clout!'

And the whole Ballantrae Tuesday Club erupts in a chorus of the oldest remembered favourite of all.

One potottie, two potottie, three potottie, four
Five potottie, six potottie, seven potottie *more*.

Outside the school gates there were other games, if not quite so formal, still played to rules well understood in each community. As with school-yard playing, a child plucked out of Wick and transported to Fife or Oban would find certain of his own familiar games and mischiefs, varying from his home ones only in accent. Hit-the-Stick was one that John Leitch knew as Cat and Bat.

We played Cat and Bat along the road at Tarbert. You'd each a bat and a wee sharp-ended four sided stick called a Cat, with each side marked 1, 2, 3 or 4 and you hit the Cat with the Bat along the road, and depending on the side it landed you got that-many more hits. When it got to its last place you counted back your steps to see who'd won. I played that with my sister; it was a girl's game really.

Andrew Fairnie recalls the mother-of-invention that gave him and his friends their sports equipment of the 1890s.

We played footb'll with a tin can or a bundle of rags. There weren't so many real footb'lls then. We just kicked whatever we could find.

No required Adidas kit for the footie in Fisherrow, Musselburgh. One game would have mystified your lowland lad gone north to Inverness or Argyll and had him wondering if the teuchters had taken to prim lassies' hockey. Peter Sinclair could have told him . . .

Apart from fishing for cuddies, the boys played shinty, oh yes, yes . . . anywhere, all the time. We'd all our shinties. Mine sat at the door there and when you went out you just lifted the shinty and you'd have a ball in your pocket and even when you were on the road to meet your friend you'd be working away with the ball and the shinty. I played in a team when I was young . . . not a grown-up team then. The men played in Oban and later I played there. The Oban team was Oban Camanachd.

It was not all guileless sailor-suited fun in the village or fisher-town streets, of course. There was mischief and the derring-do of what passed for sin in days more innocent than the 1980s.

Not *badness* mind, just naughty things you got up to.

Tenement architecture in Leith made some things all too easy and not really enough of a challenge to high spirits, even in those douce days of Rose Baker's childhood in the early 'twenties.

In Leith all the door bells were at the close-mouth and you could easy ring half-a-dozen and run. Nob'dy could ever catch you.

And still in Leith if you had a lot of barefaced impudence you could have a between meals snack.

There was a fort there and a lot o' soldiers in the streets. We used to ask them for hard-tack biscuits . . . wee square things, hard as bricks.

Then there was the continuing feud between east and west, to be exploited by cheeky Leith bairns who, in spite of walking barefoot

to Portobello, still thought themselves a cut above the holiday
visitors they met there.

> We used to laugh in the street at the Glasgow folk ... mimicked their
> accent and called 'Glasgow keelies!' after them, so we did.

Even in the quiet villages outside Fraserburgh the fishercot children were not above roasting their elders on a dark night.

> We used to dirle the windows, w'a dirler, something to stick it to the
> glass and w'a cotton reel, a string and a slate pencil. You could do the
> likes of that because there was no policeman. So you never got caught.

There *was* a policeman in Turriff though, and he was an integral
part of the on-going tulzie on the street there between lawless
bairns and authority. Hilda Strachan was an important figure in it
all too because hers was the preferred house of refuge in the flight
from the constable.

> When we were small we used to sledge down that hill in Turriff. We
> weren't allowed, of course, and if a policeman came along we used to
> shout to each other 'A.B.C.R.L.' that meant 'A Bobby's Coming, Run
> Loons.' So then we ran to *our* house to where we'd steps down to the
> coal cellar, and we slipped the sledge down there to hide it and then
> came out all innocent.

And firmly believing, no doubt, that the policeman had no idea.

More legitimate on village roads were the bicycles that, one way
or another, most children seemed to acquire at least part-share in,
no matter what their size or suitability.

> Six of us shared the one bike. It was a girl's too. It was maybe all right
> for the wee ones but my feet were aye scraping the road when the pedals
> went round.

Alex Archer had the opposite problem though not with a girl's
bike.

> I learned to go a bike and then you just got shots on other people's. I
> remember when it was too big you just put your leg through under the
> bar and pedalled sideways leaning all to one side.

That was in Largo. Up north in Cromarty one bike served Margaret
Ritchie and her cousins, and surveillance on time-share was strict.

> We'd a craze for bicycles (that would be 't the turn of the century) but
> we didn't have one each. Dear me, no! We'd to share and you just got to

ride two or three lamp posts' distance with somebody running alongside to see you didn't go too far.

But what was a real delight to goggle-eyed children, in these early
20th and late 19th century days, was the arrival of the first cars in
the village. They seemed to come in twos, the first in each case
presumably to the original 'Mr Jones'.

> I remember the first car in Largo. It belonged to Mr Horne the joiner.
> The second was the grocer's (him we used to sell jeely jars to). His had a
> dicky-seat, a Morris Cowley it was. We ran messages for him and
> sometimes on a Sunday afternoon he took us for a run. There was us
> sitting up in the dicky and-here what a speed you were going! Nothing
> really now, maybe 'twenty', but *then* ... my!

Presumably these Sunday outings with Mr Horne, the motor-
owner, were slotted in among the various diets of worship of Alex
Archer's Sundays.

There were two cars in Lochgilphead too, by about 1910.

> Mr Sinclair had an Argyll with great big lamps, and Mr MacBeth ... well
> I don't mind what he had, but you always knew when he was coming up
> the brae in this big noisy car. We used to run down the road to meet Mr
> Sinclair, clamber on to the running-board and ride up home.

Even just watching cars and vans was a fascinating occupation for
small boys like John Coghill.

> The first ones were just coming in when I was a boy. There were maybe
> two in Tongue when I stayed there with my grandfather. And then the
> mail began to come in on a sort of open lorry with a windshield and
> nothing above the man's head.

The new motors were at their most exciting when something went
wrong, of course.

> The first motor that I can remember ... I was standing at a wee shop in
> New Street in Musselburgh and this motor came along from the Races.
> It had solid tyres and it wasna steered by a wheel but a straight handle
> that you turned whatever way you wanted to go ... like a rudder ...
> Well I don't know what happened but we heard some awfie bangs and
> th' was lumps of solid tyre flying up in the air and then he swung right
> round and straight into a shop.

There must have been wet days too when playground and village
streets were deserted and children had to find their amusement at
home.

Nowadays there are whole business empires built on the knick-
knackery considered essential for true indoor play ... toys and kits
to educate this or that faculty: and children who are not dowered
with these are labelled 'deprived'. But it wasn't always so, and, one
after the other, the far-flung rememberers for this book shook their
heads about their playthings, and could really recall only dolls and
the very few other toys which they cherished and guarded as
irreplaceable treasures. Jenny Stewart remembers hers

> I didn't have many toys but I had home-made stuffed dolls ... rag dolls.
> My mother made them ... put waxed paper for a face and drew eyes nose
> and mouth, every one of them special. One of them looked like a girl on
> another farm called Hannah ... so that doll was always Hannah.

Sometimes the getting of a doll involved a long period of planning
and craikings and waiting.

> I remember once there were coupons for a while, on packets of Babbit's
> Powder, coupons for a doll. And there was this picture of a great big
> beautiful doll and oh, but I wanted that doll! I wanted it so much that I
> nearly put the powder down the sink to get the packets emptied and at
> last when I'd enough coupons my mother sent them away in an
> envelope. Oh my! While I waited how I pictured the postman stag-
> gering up the stair with this big parcel; and patience was *not* my middle
> name, I can tell you. But at long last it came, in this wee thin envelope ...
> and it was just a bit of painted cloth. I can see it yet ... with the wee
> dotted line round for cutting it out and stuffing it. Well, after that I'd
> to wait till my mother had time to get the machine out and sew it up.
> Then I'd to go down to the wee grocer's that had a barrel of grapes
> packed in cork or sawdust, and ask for that for the stuffing. Then I'd to
> wait again till he'd sold all the grapes before I got the sawdust. What a
> lesson in patience that was! But the doll was used and loved till there was
> nothing left of the pattern.

So they sang their chants and hopscotched in the playground,
they organised their village dares and shinties and, while it rains
we'll leave them playing impatiently indoors with dolls and dinkies
until the clouds pass and they can be out again. For there's a whole
gamut of country and seaside activity waiting for them there ... the
true heritage of non-city children which we can explore when the
sun shines on them tomorrow.

10
Racing the Linnet

City children of the days around the end of the Victorian era and the early ones of this century had as many indoor ploys as the tigs and hunch-cuddies of playground and street, but most rememberers of sea and coast-land country spoke rather of chores than games inside the house. Board games were for frivolous outlanders and cards a mortal sin ... at least in the Lewis home of the young Isobel Campbell.

> We didn't really have games or toys at Ness when we were young at the beginning of the Second War. Some people had game sets but they were *English*. They were evacuees from Yarmouth and they had things like Snakes and Ladders and Ludo. We'd no playing cards of course. They were 'The Devil's Playthings'.

What such children did have was the endless bounty of the sea, bringing in its own peculiar assortment of things for play ... an ever-changing treasure tide for imaginative children. But they had to be taught to respect its moods and know its dangers, and all round the coast the earliest visits to the sea-shore were with mother. Margaret Kirk of Ballantrae speaks for all of them.

> When you were wee you went wi' your mother and she showed you all about making pies and sandcastles, and gathering shells. And watching for the tide comin' in. The school was near the shore and when I was there, I liked when I got to stay after school and play with th' others... paddling an' that.

The sea-wall, too, served many another purpose beside keeping back the dash of waves and the flying spume.

> The wall was rare for playing wee houses with shells off the shore and sand cakes and yon wee bits of china that the sea had washed smooth. The wee-er kids at four or five were the weans and although you'd

always a 'man', he'd be away working at the fishing. So we didna really
need anyone to *be* him.

The boys too had their own games, like Alex Archer in Fife.

We made sand-cars, of course, and when we'd dinkies we made tracks
for them. But I mind how the best was, we used to get a big chunk of
cardboard, take it to where it was quite steep on the dunes and slide
down the slippery grass sitting on the cardboard.

From 'houses' and shell-gathering, growing youngsters adventured
further, edging towards the sea.

We walked barefoot along yon creamy frill that each wave left and we
gathered flat stones to do skiffing across the water. Some could do nine
or ten jumps.

Others sustained themselves with a little sea-food.

We went along the shore at Macduff gathering winkles ... whelks
y'know, then we made a wee fire and boiled them in tinnies ... like
maybe a syrup tin, aye ... ate them w'a hairpin.

That was up the east coast and Jean Durnie recalls doing just the
same when they were out of sight of home at Ardrossan, but with a
much more complicated drill when Mother was involved.

We gathered whelks along the North Shore (had to be the North Shore
because my father said the Lang Craigs ones were dangerous). Anyway
you looked for an old can and boiled them up on the shore and ate them.
My mother didnae know that. Mostly, mind, we took the whelks home
and she put them in a basin with a good handful of salt and you'd see
them spewing out the sand. Then she used to scrim'le them round, put
the basin under the well and get them washed right clean. Then they
were boiled and there was a great looking round for pins to eat them
with. When they were ready you sat with them in your lap at the front
door-step and ate them.

On lonelier points and headlands, the rocks were the youngsters'
only play places, but the light-housers were a self-sufficient breed,
as John MacRae remembers.

There was nob'dy much to play with but ourselves, if the other keeper
had no bairns our ages. I was lucky with my brother. We guddled in the
rock pools and fished a lot for lobsters and crabs.

But perhaps the strangest fare for young appetites was found at
Macduff.

When I was young there I remember playing at a huge flat rock we called the 'dulsie' rock. Dulse is seaweed and y'know we ate that dulse and we used to suck in the salt water from it. It was good and chewy. We *lived* on it instead of sweeties when we played there.

So let's say that's the younger children pickled and salted down for the winter and look at what the older ones found to do at the shore. By their teens much of the activity in the coastal shallows was either realistic imitation of the work of the adult community or was a kind of apprenticeship to it ... sometimes paid.

We helped the fishermen w' their small boats when they hired them out in the summer to holiday-makers and we got thruppence at the end of the day.

And the great boat-hiring lad turns bairn again as he lays out his wages.

You got a lot for thruppence in those days ... four big sweeties for a ha'penny, or liquorice wheels w' a sweetie in the middle ... and sherbet. Thruppence bought a lot of things.

But there was no such child's play about James Pryde's 'Captain' at Stornoway and what he expected of his crew.

There was a sailor had this boat at a village outside Stornoway. It was just a rowing-boat but he'd once been a gunner on one of the fishery-cruisers. He was an old man that had been on the sailing ships in his early days and he used to get a bunch of us boys together.

'You'll be the first mate', he used to say, 'and you second and you third'. We loved that, so did he, I think ... took him back ... And he'd all sorts of things he showed us like collecting flounders in a net he laid in the shallow water.

Small wonder school palled and you spent three years in the last class when there was real man-stuff fishing to be done.

In the summertime we used to make a line with about a hundred hooks on a bit of m'uncle's old line, and we used to go down, dig bait and bait these hooks and lay them down on the shore at low tide with a big brick at one end and a bottle at t'other. Then the tide would come in and cover the line. When it went back out you'd to hurry down and get what you'd caught before the seagulls picked them all. Then we brought them home to get cooked ... flounders an' that they were, mostly. I wasn't a great fish hand. I liked the fishing not the eating.

The art of true sailing and not simply messing about in oary-boats could be learned if, like John Leitch eighty-five years ago at Tarbert, Loch Fyne, you chose your friends judiciously.

I had a cousin at Tarbert who'd a boat with a wee sail on it and I used to go with him rowing down the West Loch. I remember when we were out once, we came across a big shoal of small fish that clustered all round the boat. We could put our hands in and *lift* them out. They were being devoured by mackerel, so we put small hooks on our rods and took half-a-dozen mackerel without any bother. Took them home and had them lovely and fresh.

There were other useful things a sensible lad could do on the shore, provided he could be trusted not to get up to any capers ... the ferry flag for instance would have lent itself quite easily to that. But John Coghill *was* a sensible lad.

There was the ferry from Melness across the Kyle of Tongue and when

we were young I remember putting up the white flag to signal the
ferryman from the other side, for someone waiting to get across.

Another place besides Tongue in its deep-cut Kyle, which has its
own distinctive feature to delight children with never a thought of
helping anyone or learning how to do grown-up things, was the
Crinan Canal built between Ardrishaig and Crinan; and it held its
own charm for youngsters from these two villages and Lochgilphead.

One of our great things was to walk up the side of the Crinan Canal and
see the bridge being opened to let a boat through. It opened *across* the
way, not *up* and the bridge-man knew us and allowed us to stand on it
while it was swinging open.

Then there were the locks that fascinated us. It was a mystery to us
how the locks worked. And oh! I remember *The Linnet*. It was a wee
pleasure boat that went up the canal ... a wee steamer. The Lochgilphead children used to race it ... which wasn't very difficult ... and the
passengers used to throw pennies to the running weans. But-here, we
weren't allowed to race The Linnet. Our mother wouldnae let us. It was
the pennies, I think, really ... manse weans didn't beg for pennies!

But at Lochgilphead we played up the brae with the Sinclair children
and the Sinclairs had an Uncle Donald and Uncle Donald had a boat ...
a wee puffer like *The Maggie*, d'you remember *The Maggie*? Well, this
puffer would take a wee-bit cargo from here to yonder to deliver and we
used to be allowed on to it and to go below, when it came up the canal.

There were some who dabbled in deeper waters, those round
seaside jetties or in the inshore shallows, and they faced real danger
in a sudden change of wind or weather. Catherine Murray, née
MacSwan lives in South Connel on Loch Etive and a graceful bridge
has leapt the loch to North Connel since 1903. Between the two
villages are the Falls of Lora where the water swirls round an
outcrop of rock in a tidal current. That was the setting of one of her
girlhood adventures.

My father had shops in both villages and he had a rowing boat to go
between them. It was cheaper y'see because there was a toll on the
bridge. Well, my friend and I liked the rowing boat and one day we went
out to bring back the lady book-keeper to South Connel. After we got
to her side it turned very stormy.

'Oh no!' says she, 'I wouldn't dream of going over the loch on the
boat. I'll take the bridge.' But of course *we* weren't going to give in.

Well :.. the water came lashing into the boat and we didn't know
whether to turn back or go on. So there we were, singing hymns and
praying, halfway across Loch Etive. We got back safely but it was quite
an experience.

Being neither the 'fish' of the sea-going folk nor the 'fowl' of the
croft-farm people, she was part of the little business and trade
community in Connel and so her life touched both worlds. Her
home was a villa with a fair spread of garden and rough ground on
which the family reared its collection of animals. Young Catherine
of the Loch Etive prayers and hymns was, by her own admission, 'a
bit wild'.

We'd a Shetland pony among the other animals and we used to get the
big wooden wash-rub and tie it with a rope to the pony's tail. Of course
the pony spilled me out and went racing off round the garden w'the tub
still tied to his tail, and plants flying everywhere. Another time I
remember was taking the wash tub to Loch Etive and getting into it for
a boat.

And there was the MacSwan goat too.

I remember thinking it was a shame to keep it tied up and I let it loose.
Well, it chased me to the top of the garden and back, then out the back
gate and round to the front and through the hedge. I was terrified.

Some other folk milked their goats for family consumption and to
the reasonable question, 'What was the goat for?' her reply came,

It wasn't for anything, my father won it in a raffle.

A more interesting prize, certainly, than the conventional bottle of
whisky.

Those then were the children of foreshore villages whose homes
were cheek-by-jowl with the sea. But behind them, a mile ... two
miles or more, inland, the children of crofts and farms, who could
easily have joined them, had wide countryside of their own to roam
and the pre-occupations of the daily round there, to offer different
pursuits. Like those of their sea-side counterparts, some of their
activities were sheer play, and others an apprenticeship to the life
around them.

They played 'Hoist the green flag' in the long grass at St Combs
and ate their own gathering of hazelnuts on Lismore. In Glenapp

they played houses in dells and picked bluebells from woods, they made dams and filled jam jars with minnows at the App or the Gregg, blissfully regardless of sanitary sanctions.

> In those days when folk had dry closets they got emptied into the river
> ... but we didn't care, we paddled there just the same.

And Helen McClung recalls another sturdy, less-than-wholesome pastime which would have had city bairns cringeing.

> One of the great things we did was ... th' were cow-pats in the field that we'd to cross to get to the River App to play, and you used to see how many you could jump in before you got to the river. We played a lot in our bare feet and doing the cowpat steppie-stones was the favourite.

Others had a fascination with the morbid.

> 'Well what are we going to do today?'
> 'We could go to the cemetery.'
> We liked that especially if there was a funeral. But if there wasn't we liked just walking among the graves reading the stones. There was one there to a man killed at the Battle of Pinkie in 1547 that had been armour-bearer to the Stewarts of Appin.

Jean Durnie, as one of the young Kanes in Ardrossan, perhaps in a dearth of whelks to boil up, turned her attention inland a little, for other seasonal titbits.

> When the Irish potato pickers, that came over every harvest, had finished the fields, we used to go up and collect a' the wee bools of potatoes that were left. When we took them home my mother used to say 'You're sure you werenae stealing these potatoes?' She was strict, my mother ... awful good. We'd our grace before dinner and wouldn't've dared to do anything wrong. She was awful good ... and we'd our prayers before bedtime.

Surely Mother Kane was reassured by the thought that a little gleaning was safely in the Biblical tradition of Ruth. Harvest time is rich in memories like that, and those of Isobel Craigie at Turriff.

> When we were bairns in the harvest-time we used to go down to the stack yard. The horses and carts would be going away up the hill to be re-loaded and we used to hang on to the cart and get a hurl to the top, then run down again to catch the next lift up.

If the sea-shore children knew their whelks, their flukies and their crabs, the croft ones knew the creatures of river and moor and had encounters with them that still 'flash upon the inward eye' eighty or ninety years later. John Leitch remembers his.

One day I was walking alongside a stream they used to call 'the boys' burn'. There were bushes and alders and this day I saw the most beautiful coloured bird sat on one of the branches. It was a kingfisher, bright blue and copper . . . we just stood and looked at each other until he flew away. I never forgot that picture.

He must have been a quiet mover because he recalls another such meeting with a bird, usually too shy to be caught close-up.

I was hiding in the bracken near a fence and all of a sudden I looked up and-here sitting on the top wire was a bird. It gave a sort of gurgle and came out with 'Cuck-ooo' clear as clear. Then it kind of coughed and cleared its throat and flew off.

'Noisy' isn't the first word that comes to mind as a description of river fish but George MacGregor recalls a Harris river orgy that broke the hush of an evening stroll.

One night I was out for a walk with a friend and we heard this noise coming from a narrow burn at the roadside.
'Is it ducks?' says I.
'No' says he, 'I think it's fish.'
That was hard to believe but we went over to the track-side and sure enough, in this wee burn that you could have straddled with your feet apart, there was two salmon spawning in just a wee pool that they'd found. What a noise! Just like ducks.

Up by Fraserburgh Gena Robertson and her sister remember going out nest-hunting.

We looked for nesties in the grass . . . larks', y'ken. You'd to wheesht, then clap your hands and watch where they rose from. But you werena allowed to tell anyone. That was the rule.

Sometimes the most lasting mindings were of mishaps on the way to whatever the play for that day was to be. Farmyards had hazards for the unwary.

I remember when my friend Gertie Norrie was coming through our yard along a path that we called the 'close' and she walked over a heap she didna realise was pig-dung. It looked dry really. Anyway one leg just about disappeared . . . and Gertie was a tall girl!

Older fry in their play began to wander further afield to take
responsibility and to learn skills that would serve them later on the
land and with their animals.

Tongue to me as a boy was heaven on earth. I climbed and went rod-
fishing, and my grandfather had a hatchery to stock the river.

With the answer to the query 'Did he do this commercially?' Grandfather's character was conveyed with a laugh and one sentence.

Commercially? No, I don't think he *ever* did anything commercially.

Much of John Coghill's playing experience was under the benign
eye of that grandfather, for he spent his two-month summer
holiday there, from his house at Golspie, and had interests aroused
on all sides.

He kept bees. That was interesting. And Mr Campbell the blacksmith
kept bees and they used to share their problems and go out together
after swarms.

He had a glebe too, of maybe an acre, that he worked as 't was part of his
stipend. We worked for him at the hay and cleaning out the byre; he
paid us so much for that and I think that's when we first learned to value
money.

I remember walking seven miles with my grandfather to go fishing along
a three-mile stretch of river and then walking back. I couldn't have been
more than twelve and he'd be seventy-five at that time. He was
dedicated to that area. His father'd been a gamekeeper in the
Grampians and I believe he was killed by a poacher. His sister was an
attendant to Queen Victoria at Balmoral.

John Leitch, who sailed Loch Tarbert with his cousin of the wee
sail-boat, had a way of exploring the countryside too, that must
have been the envy of boys who were not so blessed in their friends.

I was friendly with the doctor's son and his father had given him a
donkey and a wee carriage as a present when he was ten or eleven. The
donkey-cart had two wee seats each side and two wheels. We used to
harness the donkey into the shafts and go away down the Campbeltown
road and round the glen about four miles. You got the roads to yourself.
There was a dog at the doctor's place called Tuppence and he and the
donkey were great pals. Tuppence would be jumping about and barking
when he saw the donkey getting harnessed. Then he would run off and

the donkey'd go galloping after him. We used to go for miles on a Saturday and take a picnic.

Down at Glenapp too there were boys learning early the proper care of their animals.

There was the horses. When it came harvest time it was all horse-work of course and at night-time each boy claimed a horse and got riding it back to the stable, feeding it and taking it into the field for the night.

To close these memories of children at play, let's go back to the younger ones, busy on their ploys, careless, heedless and without conscious purpose of learning to grow up.

We played up the mountain at Lochgilphead. (It wasnae a mountain at all really, it was just a heathland brae). We played with Callum and Millie, the Sinclair twins. Both mothers had handbells and when it was time to come in we were summoned by the bells. They rang out across the mountain and we were s'posed to come rushing home. Sometimes we did, but sometimes we dawdled a bit longer and didnae bother.

11
All the Ladies were that Style

The rhythm of life lived with tide and season brings the Sabbath round again and the recollections of quiet ordered Sundays, after or between services, are as vivid as any others in elderly minds. Indeed, among the memories, for every one of toys or school there are half-a-dozen of the day of 'rest', sharp as etchings.

There's a bleak little picture of Jenny McCrindle's arrival home after church for the rest of the day at the farm.

> There'd been no heating in the church and when you came home, the fire was out and you'd to feed the cattle before you got something to eat. And that was *it*. After that you were s'posed to read the Bible the rest of the day.

The Craigie household on Rousay in the twenties allowed a little variety of reading material.

> You weren't supposed to do much on a Sunday. You'd only maybe t' read . . . there wasn't much to read anyway . . . we just had the *Orcadian* and *The Christian Herald*, and oh yes! *The People's Friend* . . . and maybe *The Children's Newspaper*. But you never read really secular papers on a Sunday.

The first duty of Jenny McCrindle might have been feeding the cattle before eating, but for most others it was the doffing of the church braws. In Jean Durnie's Ardrossan home, that was a firm rule.

> When we got home we'd to take off our good clothes and put them away for the next Sunday. We'd a big wardrobe right-enough but it was m'Uncle Willie's big sailor-kist that we used mostly, with the compartment at the side for hats. Everything went in there after the Sunday School.

Andrew Fairnie, looking back not far short of a century, has no

fault to find with a Musselburgh Sunday as the lungs of the week . . .
getting the breath back for the rigours of the next round of work.

> It was very quiet in Fisherrow. The women wouldna even sew on a
> button on the Lord's Day. They kept it perfect . . . absolute rest. That
> was all. The food had all been got ready the day before. It would likely
> enough be flank meat out the kale-pot.

In Lewis too, Sunday was for rest and minding the Ps and Qs to
keep things peaceful. Isobel Wales's maiden aunts saw to that, even
as late as the 1940s.

> At Ness there was no work in the house on Sundays. Nothing. We were
> reprimanded for anything! Like reading what the aunts called 'vain'
> books. And whistling! Well! I remember our next-door neighbour Mrs.
> Monro was terrible if she heard you whistling. There was a Gaelic saying
> 'A hen crowing and a young maiden whistling are the two things God
> hates most to hear'. That's a translation. So doing it on the Sabbath was
> a double abomination.

There were other undetected misdemeanours further south on
Harris, committed carefully by George MacGregor as a young
banking outlander.

> Sunday on Harris . . . very quiet. If you were an incomer you'd to be very
> careful not to offend. But once or twice I slipped out to the back for a
> walk up the hill that they called Rogneval.

They were strict too at Connel in Argyll, but by the time Peter
Sinclair was a small boy after the First War, there were some
families where the reins were loosening a little. But not in his home.
He still lives in the house where he was born and he remembers his
frustration at not being in the vanguard of Sunday liberation.

> I can remember standing at this window wanting to get out when the
> other wee ones were there playing. But we were never allowed.

The father of eleven in a small tenement house in Ardrossan must
surely have been forgiven for allowing himself the dispensation of
sending some of his tribe to take a breath of fresh air, out of his way,
on a Sunday afternoon seventy-five years ago.

> We used to get out for a walk by ourselves on a Sunday afternoon. 'No
> goin' near the harbour, mind.' 'No Daddy, we'll no' go near the
> harbour.' But it was the first place we made for . . . the only interesting
> place in Ardrossan. We used to see the big-masted schooners wi' the

lady at the prow ... figureheads you know. We would have liked to ask our father more about all that but we couldnae very well say we'd been to the harbour.

Orcadians were less generally absolute sticklers about Sabbath observance than the Western Islanders. They were more easily allowed quiet indoor pursuits or perhaps a short walk in the salt air off the Westray Firth. But certainly nobody lifted a hand in the outside labour of the Craigie croft.

We never worked a Sunday. That wasn't done at all. Even in chancy harvest weather. But we always seemed to get the harvest in all right without that. You might get up near the middle of the night to work. But never on Sunday.

And that was it. Sundays were for peaceful reflection and, apart from one pleasing little ritual of a Largo worthy of seventy years ago, almost the whole population observed absolute rest.

I remember my father's uncle used to come in every Sunday morning for his wee nip, before he visited Granny and Grandpa further along the village.

If Sundays were special, Communion Sundays were extra-special. In fact in many places they were the fourth day of a five- or six-day season. Catherine Murray remembers the celebration in Connel and Oban.

There was the Fast Day on the Thursday. It was a school holiday and the shops were shut. There were services all week-end until the Tuesday.

And Isobel Cameron from her manse days in Lochgilphead before the First War remembers the stir in their parish and household.

Communion was always a busy time. The season lasted from Thursday till Tuesday. The Thursday was what we called Fast Day. We'd a school holiday and the shops were shut. There was no real fast, but the old name had hung on. It was just the end of the Communion tokens at that time. That Thursday was just like another Sunday ... a most bewildering day for a child. There were church services and we'd to play very quietly, if at all. Then there was a service on the Friday and one on Saturday, three on Sunday and a thanksgiving service on Monday. I used to wonder if it was a thanksgiving by the maid, Katie, and by my mother, that it was all over. All the visitors left on Tuesday.

Well she might wonder, for there was open-house for the peri-
patetic sermon-tasters who went round all the reachable
Communion seasons, not to mention lodgings for the guest
preachers.

> Och aye, there were these old warriors came to hear the different
> preachers that used to come as visiting ministers to the host Com-
> munion. One preacher would arrive on the Wednesday, on the midday
> boat from Inverness or Glasgow. He would depart on the Friday and
> another arrive on the Saturday. All of them stayed at the manse and
> Mother provided *vast* quantities of food. We'd lots of farmers in the
> church and they'd've brought in fowls. I can see these fowls yet, hanging
> up by their legs in the kitchen. I remember helping to pluck them and
> gathering up the feathers to keep for stuffing pillows and cushions.

They were nothing if not thrifty at the manse, seeing to the stuffing
alike of hungry visitors and parlour upholstery.

Communion seasons were much the same on Bernera island in
Lewis at that time, and twenty years later. The visiting minister and
worshippers were sure of a lodging, if not always at the manse, then
certainly with members of the host congregation, as Mrs. Pryde
recalls.

> They came from other parts of Lewis by boat ... and stayed with
> members of the congregation. There was never anyone left behind after
> a service. Didn't matter whether you knew them or not.

And memories of the 'thirties and 'forties Communions at the Butt
of Lewis recalled by Isobel Wales suggest little change twenty years
after the Bernera celebrations.

> People came together from other parts of the island. It was quite a social
> occasion ... started on Thursday, the Fast Day, and went on till
> Monday or Tuesday. Friday was the men's day when they got up and
> gave their spiel on a set text. The Saturday was just a series of services.
> People came to wherever on the island it was Communion week-end.
> They came to Ness from Shawbost or Stornoway or Point. They would
> go to the first service, then the visitors and home congregation stood
> about in knots outside the church and locals invited the others back to
> eat with them ... even if they didn't know them from Adam or Eve.
> Then at school you'd a kind of head-count, boasting y'know, 'We'd six
> strangers in our house,' 'Och that's nothing, we had eight' or ten ... or
> whatever. It was all very social, a kind of celebratory week-end. There

were several Communion sittings, of course, at the actual Lord's Supper. Communion's still a big occasion in Lewis ... very important in church life ... but cars have changed its character quite a bit because no one has to stay over and there isn't the same need of hospitality.

The sober Sabbath, with mim, stiff-dressed children reading Bible stories, their elders either lost in meditation or taking part in countless services ... the five consecutive days of the Communion season, may seem to flightier generations who need the constant stimulation of activity and pleasure, to have been dreich beyond tholing. But most who remembered it spoke with a sigh for its passing. Let Jean Durnie, now in her eighties, have the last word.

The Kirk was everything to my mother. It was her whole Sunday and her guide for everything. It was her social life as well. She met all her friends at the Prayer Meeting. All the ladies were that style.

12
For Good Writing You Got Paper

'Comprehensive' they called them when the newly dreamed-up phenomenon burst on the nation in the 1960s ... a glossy new conception of togetherness in schools. They must have wrinkled puzzled brows when they heard of it all, in many of the villages on the fringes of Scotland because, since last century, for most of their schooling, lairds' sons and the lads-and-lassies-of-parts had flicked their inky darts in happy exchange with others in their classes whose only dream was to get off into the adventure of domestic service, bait the lines or single their fathers' turnips.

Only in older years and where hamlets were tiny did the older children, destined for college, have to segregate themselves off to attend high schools and academies, sometimes miles from home.

The earliest memory of school at all, among those recorded here, is a second-hand one of David Henderson's father in the days before compulsory education.

> He went to a wee school that was on our croft land. Like in the one I was at myself, there was a stove in the middle of the school room and in his day each pupil carried a peat to the school for the fire.

Another glimpse of an earlier generation came from Peter Sinclair in Connel as he pointed out a building close to the one where he was sitting.

> My father went to a school that was in our old farmhouse.

There *was* an admission of some faint feeling of superiority about Margaret Ritchie's eighty-year-old memories of her schooldays at the turn of the century in the Black Isle.

> The wee school was in the main street near Hugh Millar's cottage (he was the famous geologist y'know). There was just this wee bit of

uppishness between us and the fisher children. Mind we were quite friendly but we did look down our silly noses a bit.

The first thought of schooldays in places far from the city or town for most rememberers, is the long walk to get to school. For the very young, the distance between home and playground could even delay their debut among the Mixed Infants.

We didn't go till we were six because we'd such a long walk. When you did start you'd to be well wrapped up.

That was Mrs. Pryde's memory of the trudge to the single-room school in Bernera where in the same apartment the schoolmaster took the older youngsters and the other teacher took the rest.

The memories leap-frog south over an island or two to Lismore where Mary Macfadyen had her childhood.

It was a long walk to school by road, but we'd a short cut up through the crofts and over a style at a dry-stane dyke.

Further down the west coast Mrs. Margaret Kirk had to step it out to Ballantrae.

The time I was at school th' were no tarmacadam roads ... just rough stones, and we walked the three miles to school wi' our wee piece for dinner-time. On the way home we went into this auntie's house and she gave us a slice of bread wi' syrup on, and by the time we were on the road home it was all sugary and l-luvely!

Sometimes the journey was too difficult to make at all. David Henderson remembers days like that in the bleak wilds of Latheronwheel.

Many a time in the winter we'd be a week absent with the school cut off by the snow.

Three or four miles tramp seems a dour preliminary to the day's lessons for pupils of six and seven, but eighty, sixty, fifty years ago it was widespread from Eyemouth to John o'Groats on the east, along the north coast and down the rugged loch shores of the west. And few resented it ... rather they found diversions that made it even longer and quite entertaining. For Jim Still, Forglen school was three miles away by road,

but we went by a footpath over a little shaky bridge. It was a real bonnie

path along the burnside and you wasted your time and got your feet wet
... we liked that.

That was a summertime dawdle. In winter the young Stills were
indulged with transport and the picture of them setting out is as
attractive as the wander along the burn path.

I can remember us sitting up in the trap with Dobbin, the wee garron,
pulling us. You'd your short trousers to your knees and the handknit
stockings and Fair Isle pullovers that Mother knitted.

So at the sound of the nine o'clock bell winter and summer the
local children who had only louped a wall or run the twenty yards
from a fisher-cot were joined, lining up in twos, by the young
outlanders who had a good hour's trek behind them already. Not all
of them liked it when they got there. Peter Sinclair at Connel was
not keen and Helen McClung couldn't be doing with it at all.

When I was young in Glenapp I started in the wee Glen school. That
was the teacher's sitting room, Mrs. Ross's house. And I cried so much
that she'd to take me to my father in the churchyard. Yes! Y'see he was a
gardener to Lord Inchcape and one of his jobs was to keep the graveyard
tidy. So I waited there with my father till it was time to go home. Funny
that ... me liking the churchyard better than the sitting-room. But after
a while all these wee house-schools like Glenapp and Auchenflower
closed down and we came here to school in Ballantrae.

The schools varied in size and complement of teachers, bigger in
towns like Musselburgh and Peterhead, smaller in hamlets like
Connel.

In the Primary there was the Big End and the Wee End, with a
schoolmaster and a lady teacher. The smaller ones were at the Wee End
and the older ones at the Big End.

So Catherine Murray remembers the village school at Connel.
Peter Sinclair's memory of the same school of about forty children
from outlying crofts as well as the village, is just as clear ... perhaps
not surprisingly, since one of the 'sons following', another Peter,
remarked as he walked by the back door and warmed his hands at
the kitchen fire to add his ha'porth of later memories.

I went to the same school's my father ... same building.

Few people seem to have gone through their schooldays under a succession of utterly faceless teachers and for the most part look back with warmth at the ones they liked and only wry distaste at those they would cheerfully have missed. Some like Catherine Murray's schoolmaster were taken quite seriously at the time but are seen in hindsight as laughable and eccentric.

> When we moved from the Wee end to the Big End we got the schoolmaster for everything, but it's the Nature Study I remember. All the Nature Study we got was weeding the schoolmaster's garden. And when we'd finished I would be sent down to my father's shop for twenty Gold Flake and a bag of Imperials. We all got an Imperial for our hard work and he got the Gold Flake.

Twenty years earlier the schoolmaster at Ballantrae had interesting foibles recalled by Mrs. Margaret Kirk.

> He was a tyrant but he was a good teacher. He was a councillor too and as well as going off to the council meetings he always went to a' the Ballantrae funerals. He used to leave what work we'd to do written up on the board and someone to clipe on the ones that didn't behave. We were glad when someone died and he was away to the funeral.

Mary Macfadyen carries with her, incontrovertible proof that she had a remarkable teacher in the Primary School on Lismore.

> He used to put things on the board and if you were kind of quick, he got you to go over and over it, until you knew it by heart.

Miss Macfadyen must have been 'kind of quick' for sitting at her fireside nearly eighty years on, she recites first the set of sixteen lines from 'The Merchant of Venice' beginning 'Let me play the fool ...' and another wedge from Lorenzo's love passage 'How sweet the moonlight sits upon this bank', with scarcely an indrawn breath and certainly not a mistake.

> He was keen on grammar too ... noun and adjective clauses and adverbial clauses of kind and condition ... d'you remember clauses of kind and condition? If you *wanted* to learn he helped you. If you didn't, he didn't give a rap and just let them puddle on.

And those were the dominies who ruled the village roosts, in the junior schools brought back to mind.

Universally recalled by forty rememberers all round the coast were the little rituals connected with those ubiquitous implements

of ancient schooldays, the slate and slate pencil ... in some places
from as early as 1875 to as late as the 1930s.

> We used them when I was a child and we sharpened our slate pencils on
> a wall or window slab. There was a wooden rim round your slate and
> when you took it home at the holidays you'd to scrub it white.

That was at the turn of the century and thirty years later her
daughter was doing the same, and could recall other slate 'business'.

> I had a wee boxie wi' a cloth for cleaning my slate and I can smell that rag
> yet ... yon sour smell. Then there was a slot in front of your desk for the
> slate to sit in.

Margaret Kirk used the Ballantrae sand to clean her slate and
though the councillor-heidie there demanded that as a more regular
chore than merely every holiday, it was with a real incentive.

> You scrubbed that wood every Friday, and the cleanest one on the
> Monday got three aromatics. D'you mind aromatics? ... well, wee
> brown and pink aromatics. Oh aye, and we used a ha'penny sponge on
> the slate itself and kept it in a wee tin box ... oh, that slate-pencil scree-
> eeved when you wrote with it and made your teeth grit.

Indeed there were teeth 'gritting' for generations all over Scotland
at the sound of that scree-eeve.

And there were other rewards for virtue in that school, forbye
the aromatics.

If you were good you got to clean the blackboard.

The boys had more robust ways of cleaning their slates. Very
robust at Connel.

Oh dear no, no wee sponges for the boys! You just used to spit and rub
your sleeve across.

There was a slight refinement at Latheronwheel over the spit-and-
sleeve.

We spat on a rag and cleaned our slate with that. Oh aye, I remember
the slates for sums and spellings, but for *good* writing you got paper.

'Slates', 'blackboard', 'lines', 'spellings' ... school vocabulary
quickly learned by children come straight to the classroom from
Jack and Jill and Miss Muffet. But for many infants in the north-
west there was an added complication that might have made the
little lady in Glenapp cry even sorer. Mrs. Pryde remembers her
start at school in Bernera.

When I first went to school, tho' we understood a little English, the
home tongue was Gaelic. But at school you were taught everything in
English, and it was difficult for wee ones.

Isobel Wales remembers how it was further north in Lewis twenty
years later.

The children I went to school with were Gaelic-speaking at home but all
the school lessons were in English, so from scratch they had to begin
speaking English. The first teacher would have both tongues herself
just to break them in.

I think there was a positive policy of suppressing Gaelic then, because
English was the language you 'got on' in.

Positive ... or negative?

There were interesting activities besides playing in the yards and
outbuildings of most little academies when numbers of the children
could not get home at lunchtime.

We carried a piece from home and a bottle of milk and had that at

dinnertime ... outside if't was dry ... in the shed if't was raining ...
never *in* the school.

Mostly it was jammy or jeely pieces and there was a wee shop close to the
school that you got a mug of cocoa to go wi' your piece.

Even if you did manage home yourself, like David Henderson at
Latheronwheel, you were sometimes part of the midday picnic
anyway.

We went home, but there were some had three or four miles to walk, so
they brought something to eat and my mother used to take some of
them in and make cocoa for them ... she'd some arrangement with their
mothers.

Even a visit to the school toilets could be a novel experience for
some.

We'd dry closets at home and we saw our first chain-pull at the school
when they were put in. So-here, we were all in and out the whole day
pulling that chain.

But perhaps the most entertaining place to leave the younger half of
the school population is with young Isobel Cameron of the Infants
at Lochgilphead, the hapless victim of her parents' advanced ideas.

I think my mother was unique in her time, for she allowed us to draw on
the kitchen wall that was whitewashed every spring-cleaning. Oh my!
Talk about graffiti. We drew and wrote and counted on that wall. I had
an imaginary family of friends called the Bruces, and *I* drew the Bruces,
Mother, Father, and children, cat and dog ... I drew them all the time.
And it was the Bruces got me into terrible trouble at school.

I was just into the big school ... I'd be seven, and being in the first
class I got out at 3 o'clock and waited until 4 o'clock for my bigger
friends. Well-here, I found that the school shed was newly white-
washed, *so* I got wee chips of charcoal from the school pile and began on
the shed wall. And by four o'clock it was all nicely decorated with
whiggles and diggles and pictures of the Bruces ... squiggles all round.
Next day we were just beginning to say 'Our Father' when in marched
the Headmaster, Mr. Mitchell ... a holy terror him ... and he boomed
out '*Some child* has *defaced* the school shed.'

'Oh that was me,' says I, all innocent (after all what was a blank white
wall for, if not the Bruces?) Well if I hadn't been the minister's offspring
I would likely have got the belt, but instead I got sent out with a bucket
of water and a cloot and I made a bigger mess than ever, till the jannie

came out and looked at it. 'Och, I think you've done plenty now' says he.

And that was the end of me and the graffiti.

They were all Jock Tamson's bairns together, then, in the Wee Schools of the coastlands, and in many places most were still classmates up to the fourteen-year-old leaving date, in what they called the Advanced Division or the Supplementary. After that stage the much-praised old Scottish system should have made it possible for studious boys and girls, whatever their background, to work their way through area academies to university and into one of the professions. That was the theory, but in the real and earnest life of sea and soil, there were often well qualified youngsters who could not take up these opportunities.

I'd no option but to leave school. It was verra difficult times. I remember three different councillors from Pittenweem came to my mother to see if I couldn't get to stay on, but she said she needed me to be working. And that was that. I just went straight to the fishing at fourteen.

That was in Fife. And the meagre expense to take David Henderson to school at Lybster from Latheronwheel would have been out of the question for him. But he did have a taste of one profession which, if times had been easier, he might have followed.

Lybster Higher Grade was seven or eight miles away, and when I was about twelve I was ready for that. But there would have been fares and books, so I didn't go. And for my last year or two I was a sort of pupil-teacher at Latheronwheel. That was quite useful to the school when there was just the one teacher there.

Even in centres of sizeable population, small towns like Troon, family circumstances could dictate the future of an academic youngster.

I loved the school but my father died at forty-four and my mother was left with seven of us. I hadn't wanted to leave the school but Marr College wasn't opened yet and there was only the wee Primary and what we called the Big School, in Barassie Street. For more than that I would've had to go to Irvine or Ayr with fares and all your books.

So in the Higher Grade Schools in many places there was a fair

mixture of disappointed high flyers who didn't get to High Schools
or Grammars, as well as those who were happy enough at the
prospect of being fourteen. One lad that Catherine Murray recalls
is unlikely to have spent his adult life pining for a scholastic future.

> We were all sitting an exam and the teacher said 'Now at the top of the
> page write your *surname* first, before your Christian name, and this boy
> wrote 'Sir Bobby Jones'. We kept that up as a joke on him afterwards.

Nor was David Henderson entirely crushed by disappointment at
the prospect of not 'going on'.

> I remember bicycle lamps were lit with carbide, and it was a great thing
> to put a wee bit in the inkwell and let it all froth up. Another trick we
> had was to put it in a tin, set a match to it, close the lid and then the lid
> would shoot off.

The Kane twins in Ardrossan took these last years at school light-
heartedly too.

> My twin sister was a bit of a tomboy and at school there would maybe be
> fighting, and Margaret would hit someb'dy. But they wouldnae know
> which of us it was and would go into the classroom crying and couldnae
> say who'd hit them.
> 'Was it Jean or was it Margaret?'
> 'Don't know.'
> But I knew fine ... it was always Margaret.'

Whether Margaret was the wild one or not, Jean too was part of the
mild harassment meted out to the unfortunate teacher of the top
class.

> We ca'ed her Hairy Mary because she'd long hair, untidy and straggly.
> She was a skinny wee cratur and she wore big-big high heels that she
> couldnae walk on ... just shoogled along. Och, we took a right rise out
> of her.

It was a fact of life for families in outlying parishes far from
accessible towns that their older children had to leave home to
continue their schooling. John Coghill speaks of the areas he knew
best.

> There was the Primary school at Tongue but the secondary children
> went to Golspie or Thurso.

Jenny McCrindle went locally at Barr in her junior years and even
then, 'locally' meant three miles on foot.

But then at twelve I'd to go to Girvan High School and in the four winters I was there it was too dark to travel and I had to stay in digs in Harbour Street. Oh I liked that, my uncle at home was so strict . . . and in Harbour Street they'd every mod. con., gas lights and hot and cold water . . . bliss!

Although there was a secondary school and lodgings in Kirkwall by the twenties, some families who had relatives in Inverness or Edinburgh elected to send them to kin there and give them a taste of real mainland life. Hugh Craigie saw one of the brothers off like that into the wide world.

My brother George went to Inverness. I remember how these young-sters like him used to go off laden with eggs and farm produce for their aunties.

The Nicolson Institute at Stornoway might have seemed the
logical place for all Hebridean youngsters to go to school, but
Harris was part of Invernessshire so older pupils migrated to
Inverness. From the islands of Mull, Lismore, Coll and Iona and
isolated communities on the mainland, they came to Oban High
where Peter Sinclair and Catherine Murray were two of the nearly-
locals.

> After the Qually some stayed in the Supplementary at Connel waiting
> for the leaving age and some went to Oban High. We went by train and
> all our expenses had to be paid, fares and books and so on. And we took
> flasks and sandwiches. Others used to have to stay all week, or all term,
> in digs.

Young Mary Macfadyen was one of these.

> We'd to take the ferry from Lismore across to Port Appin and then the
> train to Oban. I was in lodgings in Oban and I just got home for an
> occasional week-end.

Not many homes were, or are, much more isolated than those on
lighthouse stations but one of the caring aspects of that efficient
service is recalled by John MacRae who was able to stay at home
until his apprenticeship days.

> When they were posting a keeper, they did consider his school-age
> family and put him to a suitable station to get his children to school.
> That might be ten or eleven miles away, but it was possible. But that was
> only up to compulsory school leaving age; after that you'd to make your
> own arrangements. My father was moved to Islay while we were at that
> stage, so we'd to work by correspondence course from Bennet College
> in London and go to Glasgow to sit our examinations.

When the great body of sturdy, independent and often intel-
ligent boys and girls with other than academic ambitions, were
finally riddled through to till the soil, fish the sea and run the
enterprises that in the end made it possible for the scholars to
follow their bents, those boys and girls were left, heads still down
into books, to the care of teachers who groomed them for college
and university ... teachers often remembered with affection and
respect.

It's a century now since the Beauly schoolmaster recalled by
Donald MacKintosh, was coping with his top pupils under

conditions that few would want to tolerate in the 1980s, but which seemed natural enough then.

> There was a big room where four classes were taught *and* the head-master had his senior pupils round his desk in the middle of the room for Latin, French and German.

Ten years later in the first decade of this century, John Leitch made an early decision that his future (for all the donkey-cart runs, the sails on the West Loch and the flashing beauty of the wild life round his home) lay elsewhere than Tarbert. A lady teacher, he remembers, played her part in getting the basics right for his studies.

> She was a stickler for good writing ... gave us Vere Foster copy books with the proverbs along the top of each page to copy, and four or five lines under that first one, to write the words out better and better. I often think on these copy books.

Whether it was that discipline that did it or some of the distilled wisdom of those Vere Foster proverbs ...

> I decided I didn't want to be a fisherman ... and I'd enough of the shovel on the croft, so I went to Glasgow to the University.

At a murmur that he must have been one of the 'lads of parts' there was a modest admission

> Well, I *was* the medallist at the School and that meant a lot to some of the folk in a wee place like Tarbert, but when you look at some of the big schools in Glasgow and think on the wee one at Tarbert I didnae need to be very proud of that. Our classes were small because most of the boys'd been gasping to be fourteen and start working at the jobs just waiting for them to jump into. Of the thirty-five to forty in any class, only about ten went on to do Highers.

And some thirty years after that rememberer's student days, Farquhar MacDonald found his way to the medical school at Edinburgh University after going through the hands of the progressive and thorough headmaster he encountered at Plockton ... a man who aimed to develop more than brainy heads.

> There were just about half a dozen of us going on for our Highers when the new headmaster arrived. And oh! he turned out to be well ahead of his time. He found that there were no gymnastics ... not much P.T. at

all and that the boys just hung about during breaks or at lunchtime or in
the periods they should have had P.T. Well he watched all this lounging
around for a while ... summed it all up, and then he took a field next the
school, and divided it off into patches, allotments y'know, and he put
each lad to a plot to grow vegetables and flowers. Two or three times a
week we worked.

On another strip he put a row of hives and had a bee expert come from
Inverness to teach us bee-keeping.

He'd a boat too, a small yacht, and he taught us to sail ... and to scrape
it and paint it too. He taught some of the local people ballroom dancing
too and the senior pupils went along to that sometimes as well. But
some of the village folk didn't like that so much ... didn't hold with the
ballroom dancing.

And just in case all the cabbage-growing, sailing and fox-trotting
took the pupils' minds off their studies he kept a watchful eye on
any backsliding there.

He'd us regularly at his house in an evening to go over any of the
subjects we weren't sure of. And we'd get juice and biscuits from his
wife. It was like having private tutoring. Oh yes, he was away ahead in all
sorts of ways.

Forty spans of lessons, all of them from village or small town
board-provided schools; forty sets of memories, wry, warm or
simply tolerant; forty people, most now elderly, having lived useful
and widely varying lives ... all enriched by what they learned in
these old schoolrooms ... a hundred years summed up by the oldest
of them all.

When I see 't my great-grandchildren are into in their lessons now, a'
the different studies, and think on us at the same age in a wee school ...
it's an affa different world. But, mind, I'm no sure that even the ones the
likes o' mysel' that werena topnotchers didna learn better about gettin'
down to a job and doin' it right. S'no easy now, mind, but it wasna easy
then either.

13
Arm-in-Arm in Partners

The sight of the demure bride standing drop-eyed before the altar, and shy of her nervous groom, has always been (or at least in times less brutally direct than now) small indication of the wiles and rituals employed before a couple finally confronts its priest. Traditional formulae have been laid out clearly for the meeting, the chase and the catch; and perhaps the most generally used activity for the first flaunting of charms has, in most places been 'the dancing'.

The dance with its attendant formalities must surely have been a mating rite since prehistoric times. No doubt new routines came with every boatload of Goths and Huns and Normans to formalise the old Pictish loups and flings into poussettes and eightsome birls. But, whatever the scholarly roots and the aura of art and culture sprayed on to its steps and figures, none of the rememberers for this book had any doubt about what it was really for. Certainly not Gena Robertson at St. Combs near Fraserburgh.

> We'd to go up to Lonmay for the dancing. That's where we met the boys. Accordeons it would've been, and fiddles. When I think on't, the girls stood on one side and the boys th'other. None of them sat. You couldna get up unless a boy lifted you. But I used to like 'th'excuse me'. Then you could get in.

And, on the west coast at Connel, Catherine Murray recalls similar venues and inhibitions in the late 'twenties.

> The boys would arrive with their patent shoes and the girls in pretty dresses. It was all quite formal in its own way. The big event of the night was the Ladies' choice. But that was kind of agony too because you might be too shy ... you might not *like* to ask the boy you fancied.

But a set of quadrilles or an eightsome reel later, blush had turned to flush, jackets were off, the boys sweated, the ladies glowed and the evening was well underway.

> The dancing at Latheronwheel, where all the boys and girls met, was in the village hall. It was reels, quadrilles, lancers and all that. And likely enough The Flowers of Edinburgh.

By the early 'twenties in the decadent south, at the likes of Jean Durnie's Ardrossan, the programme had less of the robust Schottische about it and more of the new American shimmy.

> We went to the dancing quite a bit at a place in Glasgow Street. It was foxtrots comin' in then, and the Charleston. That's where you met the boys ... at the dancin'.

But in at least two places the dancers needed neither a roof over their heads nor Slipperene for the floor.

> I remember in Lewis in the 'thirties there used to be what they called in the Gaelic *damhsa-rod*, in the summertime. That was road dancing. They would choose a flat area like a bridge, someone would turn up with a melodeon and then all the young folk gathered for a wee jig.

John Leitch has similar memories from many a long year before that, nearer to the turn of the century at Tarbert, Loch Fyne.

> Sometimes in the summer we'd a wee dance at the crossroads, just out in the open where the ground was flat. The roads werenae busy y'see and you could hear the traffic coming and move over to let it through. It was The Dashing White Sergeant and The Highland Schottische, and maybe The Grand Old Duke of York.

But those who had no music in their feet were not doomed in the contest for favours. Oh dear no! There was always the 'walk'. Sometimes it was the formal supervised progress to and from the kirk with the whole village as witness to a flowering of acquaintance made earlier at School.

> My mother and father were in the same class at school in Lewis. I remember him telling me that he used to pull her big, long, thick pigtail. But later they met up, coming and going on the kirk walk.

But more often the 'walk' was a regular weekly expedition of the young, on recognised ground and away from the sharp eyes and clashing tongues of parents and neighbours.

Boys and girls at Ardrossan used to go walking along the sea-front, back
and forward, back and forward, eyeing each other up. I mind it fine.
'Oh-here, *I* like him.' 'Och away! No' me, you can have'm.'

That was in the early 'twenties, and a mile or two down the coast in
Troon about the same time, and perhaps ten years before and after,
they had a similar sea-front beat. And in the summer there was the
additional 'talent' from Glasgow:

Up and down along the prom they used to go, the girls looking for boys,
the boys looking for girls. I used to hear the older girls in the shop where
I worked lamenting 'Another Glasgow Fair and nae sign o' a man!' That
was Greek to me when I was young.

The sizing-up walk was no west-coast phenomenon, for the same
safaris were well known in Fife and recalled first by Alex Archer.

On a Sunday night you used to go to Leven and walk up and down.
Seemed like there were hundreds of lassies (a lot of them from the
spinning factory) and it was a poor Sunday night you couldna get a girl
to walk wi' you.

And all their purposeful frivolity was after a long Sabbath spent like
bees at a honeycomb going in and out of churches and Sunday
Schools of various denominations (as well as their own!).

Aye, it was the church and Sunday School, then the Baptist kirk and the
service at night ... then after that a' the youngsters came from Crail and
St. Monance and Pittenweem to Shore Street in Anstruther and walked
along the Anstruther shore in such droves that no one could've got past
... all boys and girls trying to click with each other. It was great fun on a
Sunday night really, when you look back. That would be from quite
early in the century right up to maybe nearly the Second War.

Less energetic than either dancing or walking, but with the same
unspoken declaration of intent, was what you might call the 'lurk'.
Two of Connel's former young lurkers recall their early days
separately but with closely substantiating detail. Peter Sinclair
mentioned it first.

When I was young I remember hanging about the village at night
although the shop was shut, and from there all the boys and girls'd go up
to the station to wait for the five o'clock Glasgow train arriving about
nine. That was the big event of the day. Everybody went up to the late
train ... didn't matter if you knew anybody coming off it or not.

And Catherine Murray confirms that.

> The station in Connel was where the young folk met and went off with
> their boy-friend or their girl. It was a great meeting-place on a Saturday
> night. Connel was a wee junction y'see and trains would come from the
> south, from Oban, and from Ballachulish to the north. We all stood
> around there under the paraffin lights, then we walked down to the
> shop, hung about there and sat on the wall.

Seventy-five years ago Margaret Mackenzie was a lurker in
Inverness.

> My uncle, by then, had the Criterion Bar in Inverness and sometimes
> when I was young I used to take his tea down to him in a basket, if he was
> too busy to come home. I liked that because I could meet the other girls
> and boys and loiter on the road.

Demanding more nerve and sophistication was the ability to take
advantage of the 'chance encounter', for those who had more in
mind than a seat on the wall ... perhaps even a notion to settle
down.

> Up at the Faroes some of the girls would speak t'you and some
> wouldnae. They didn't have much English ... spoke Danish ... oh, but
> bonnie girls!

Language does not seem to have been an insuperable barrier and his
home-grown wife (bonnie herself) has to agree about the pretty
Faroese.

> There's four girls made their homes here, married to Cellardyke
> fishermen, 'Dykers' they call these fishermen. One of these 'girls' lives
> just up here ... a very handsome woman ... and she's real Dyker-spoken
> now.

Holidays brought chance encounters too, with the influx of the
visitors to seaside places ... and their entourages. Peter Sinclair's
mother was part of such a retinue.

> My mother came from Perthshire. She was in service y'see, and the
> people she was with came here to Connel every year and took a house, so
> she came wi'them. That's how she met my father. He was the crofter
> along the road.

And their little married home still stands on the same plot as Peter
Sinclair's own.

Girls in service did not always have to stir so far from home to be thrown together with likely suitors. James Still, now of Inverveddie near Peterhead remembers romance on the steading itself.

Sometimes the maids married the bothymen on the farms, or neighbouring farmers themselves. I remember two of our maids Polly and Siné, I don't know about Polly, but Siné married a farmer.

Some, like John Leitch, came visiting, all unsuspecting, to the town and were ensnared by the charms of city girls.

I came from Tarbert, seventy-odd years ago, to look after my sister's wee shop in Glasgow while she was on holiday and that's when I met this lady. So you see I married a Glasgow keelie.

And the bright-eyed, gentle-mannered little keelie, now ninety herself, just laughs at the uncomplimentary tag.

Would-be lighthouse keepers, too, were a breed who sometimes met their matches in the city.

Y'see before you went into the service you'd to learn a trade and so you'd to go to a town or city for your apprenticeship. Some keepers met their future wives then, while they were serving their time.

But for many of the keeper fraternity there was a whiff about their unions of what might once have been called the 'arranged' marriage or marriage of convenience, for convenient it certainly was.

Courting was kind of special in the Service. Take my father now ... he married the daughter of the other keeper's family. That's a good arrangement because the girl knows what she's letting herself in for.

Another coupling, that in the telling at least, had the same traces of the marriage-of-convenience about it, was Jenny McCrindle's. Though when there's a twinkle in the eye it doesn't do to take it all as gospel.

I left Girvan school at fourteen and I worked in a shop in Pinwherry. It was five miles to cycle there and five miles back. It was too long to cycle and I'd met this chap by then, so I just got married ... young y'see.

Not all chance meetings led to marriage but a party in Musselburgh settled Andrew Fairnie's fate for him early in the century.

A friend took me to this party and his sister was there. That's how I met my wife. She was in service in North High Street. Lots of the girls were in the mill, but that was rough work. Service was nicer. She worked hard with these people but I was allowed to 'call' on her . . . just certain nights in the week, mind, and in the kitchen.

The signals put out and answered that both parties wanted to pursue the relationship beyond first meeting, the rituals of court-ship began. Andrew Fairnie's regular calling on his young lady in the 'big house' kitchen was courtly and open. Others, among them his own friends, no doubt just as innocent, did their wooing more 'hindlin's'.

This couple I knew courted from they were at school. They went walking together right-enough, two places . . . up the Niddrie road and over the Haugh across by the bridge. But not always walking. The girl lived up a close and they stood long hours in that close.

A warm kitchen was surely a more comfortable place than that to convince a girl that you were her rightful jo.

And what of the progress of the light-house keeper's courtship with the other keeper's daughter?

While he was going with his girl my father was sent away to another posting at Hoy High lighthouse at Stromness, Orkney, and they'd to do their courting by letter. And y'know in these places the postman knew more about your business than you knew yourself. They'd say, 'Here's a postcard from so-and-so, I see they're away on holiday to Blackpool' or wherever. Well, a lot of women on the stations were very quick with morse-code and semaphore, so to beat the postman, my father used to send cards in morse code. Here's one . . . it's a bit tatty after all these years so I keep it in cellophane . . . it's a picture of his new lighthouse that she would be going to as keeper's wife.

It seems like an unromantic scene to have been cherished so long, since one lighthouse looks, to the uninitiated, pretty much like another . . . unless of course the romance was in the coded message. But now the postcard is back in its envelope and we can take our attention off south to Fife.

The men round here used to walk to Cellardyke from Pittenweem and St. Monance to do their courting; they went walking or to the pictures then took their girls home . . . maybe had a cup of tea if they were 'accepted' at the house. Then they took the long walk home. Y'got to

the pictures for thruppence then. Ah, these days and these picture halls are gone now, aren't they?

If they weren't 'accepted' yet by the girl's people they had perhaps to use the next best shelter for the good-night cheeper, as in Jim Buchan's Peterhead.

Boys and girls round us did their courting in the washing-house.

There was always that tentative period in the early days of the association when the two were shy of having outsiders put two and two together and making a couple of them, before they were ready. Catherine Murray remembers that sensitive time of her young life in Oban.

When you still didn't want anyone to know who you were seeing, you'd arrange to meet *inside* at the pictures. Then when you were settled in, you usually got a box of chocolates put on your knee.

And, no doubt, a shy hand along with it.

But it was in the north that there were the strangest traditions surrounding courtship. Lewis had its own special wooing pattern ... ways that seem bizarre to the outsider.

There was a kind of reticence about courting. In fact, until quite recently, you'd get folk who'd deny that they were about to be married. There was this quaint idea that you didn't talk about things like that. It was hard on some really, because they felt there'd be so much nudging and teasing, that if they were shy at all they wouldn't dare to go through with courting and marrying.

Where they were prepared to face the ordeal, ironically all this gave rise to behaviour that would have scandalised the supposedly more liberal south.

They didn't walk out much to do their courting. It was all very secret. Boys used to come to the girls' houses in the wee sma' hours of the morning ... kind of 'break-in' to see her. (Anywhere else and you'd have been calling the police!) Anyway she would be waiting to see him and have a wee 'chat' ... the parents would be away to bed. It was quite the 'done' thing ... no knocking on the door, he would just push open the door, or come through a barn into the kitchen.

These recollections of Ness in the 1930s and '40s are confirmed by Mrs. Pryde, brought up on Bernera some twenty-five years earlier.

I was the docile one, the youngest, and I didn't hear too much about the courting. They kept that very quiet. You weren't *seen* with a boy.

But however docile and shy, she too made it into marriage with her young man from Stornoway.

Surely the most curious tradition for a God-fearing community was the old custom in Lewis of 'bundling'. It had died out in Isobel Wales's young days but was still well-remembered.

In the bundling days there were maybe several of a family in a wall or box bed with the young girl at the front still dressed. The boy would let himself into the house and lie down fully clothed beside her and do a little courting there. Don't know whether the others were supposed to be sleeping or not!

It must have been an accepted arrangement or a vigilant father would surely not have dozed off when he saw his daughter climb into bed unstripped, and felt the chaff mattress slump when she was joined by her suitor.

When the wedding was finally in view all need for pretence and coyness vanished, the date was set and the arrangements began to roll. There may have been recognised pre-wedding conventions in the islands and west coast, but those were better remembered along the east coast ... furthest north around Fraserburgh.

They'd what they called the '*booking night*'. That was when you put in the banns. After that was done there was a party and their friends would blacken the boy's and girl's feet and then wash them together. Then they were ready for the next day.

Across the Moray Firth to the south there was another caper, what Jean Buchan in Peterhead called the '*cla'es carryin'*',

That was the night before the weddin'. All the presents y'see, had gone to the bride's home, and that night they'd all to be carried to the new home, by all the chums. Often the clae's carryin' was better'n the weddin' ... what a fun you got! Then when you got to the new house you all piled into the bed ... oh aye, the cla'es carryin' beat some of the weddings really. What a fun!

And there were less spirited but pleasant eve-of-wedding niceties in Anstruther.

When you took your present to the bride's house before the wedding, you got a piece of shortbread and a bun ... and a drink of wine or a cuppa tea, whatever you preferred. You still do get that here. It's not like a show of presents they have in the west, it's just when you deliver it, they serve up the shortbread and the bun.

Now it remains only to have the couple wed in earnest. The ceremony, a meal and celebration are common to all wedding memories. The service would be everywhere the same, according to the Book, but recollections of the journey to face the minister, and the junketings afterwards, are rich and vigorous in their variety and surely arise from the ancient isolation of communities in glen and firth, the spread of particular villages, and the talent available for the wedding reception. Peterhead was big enough to have a pool of musicians, and so was Shetland. Jim Buchan remembers both.

After the ceremony there'd be the party and the dancing. There was always an accordion and maybe a fiddle, and there were some real good bands here for the big do's. But by fa-ar the best bands were in the Toon Hall in Lerwick. Great place yon!

And inland a mile or two Jim Still speaks of the variety of instruments at the weddings around Forglen.

After the ceremony there'd be the meal ... catered likely enough by the hotel, and then the eightsome reels and other dances goin' on till late. There'd be fiddles and a cornet maybe and accordeons, but mostly fiddles wi' us really.

There was less sophistication in the music at smaller villages like Latheronwheel but dancing feet raised just as much stoor on a steading as they did in hotel or village hall ... and there were other compensations.

A wedding was always a big 'do'. The minister would come t'the house then, after, they'd have the piper and maybe an accordeon in the barn that had been cleared for the dancing. They'd wedding cakes and drams and the whole thing went on and on till morning.

A light touch with bow or melodeon wasn't the only talent in demand for remembered weddings in small places.

I remember when a Lismore girl was marrying a Spean Bridge man. She worked for the McCaig family that built the big tower at Oban. Well, she brought my mother a stone of flour to bake girdle scones and fancy things for the wedding ... besides the hampers that came over from Oban.

And Mary Macfadyen who recalled that wedding, along with David Henderson at Latheronwheel, were first to mention receptions where 'you danced till morning'. But all-night weddings were commonplace in Musselburgh in the days before Andrew Fairnie's nuptials there.

> We had the last all-night wedding in Musselburgh. That was a common thing up till then, but just before it was our marriage they put a stop to them. They'd to be finished after that by 11 o'clock. But I remember ours was arranged already and I'd to go and ask the Police Sergeant about it. And he says, 'Well, you're no' allowed it really but you've your plans all made so I'll mak' an exception for you' he says. So ours was the last all-night wedding in Musselburgh. We were married in Innes's Hall down near the Roman Bridge at 10 o'clock the Friday night (Friday nights were always the wedding nights). So the ones at our wedding worked all day the Friday, danced all through the night till 5 or 6 o'clock in the morning, then went home to get ready for their work on the Saturday.

Some have recalled ceremonies, some the meals and some the wild abandon of the dancing, but for the pictures of whole communities en wedding fete from start to finish we go to the memories of St. Combs in the north-east, to Orkney and the Hebrides.

> My sister here, had one of the last really traditional weddin's hereaboots. That's sixty years ago. They'd the feet-washing the night before 'bookin' night, then for the actual wedding a' the couples invited (and that was everyb'dy really) marched arm-in-arm in partners to the two houses, his and hers, then walked them to the local hall where the wedding was to be. After the ceremony the girl's guests ga'ed to her house and the boy's guests ga'ed to his in their procession through the village, and they'd their feasts in their own houses, the bride and groom separately. The butcher'd've made the steak pies. Then they started the jollifications separately, singing to a precentor and so on, until the bridegroom collected the bride, and they went together to their new home.

Hugh Craigie remembers the Rousay galravaitchings.

> These island weddings were really something. They started at 6 o'clock at night and went on till six in the morning ... all in the barn ...

ceremony, food, dancing ... everything. Everyb'dy on th'island would
be there, and they'd a bit of a job to seat them for the meal. So-many of
the older ones would sit down first and the young ones got sent for a
walk till it was time for the second sitting. Then there was dancing to
the fiddle. Later on it was accordeons but in the old days 'twas fiddles.

And Mary Macfadyen, although she didn't much enjoy it then,
recalls with more pleasure now, a Lismore wedding of her childhood.

I was about twelve and the bridegroom was my cousin. So because we
were related we went to collect him. As well as having a best man he had
a best maid. The three of them linking arms and, with a piper in front
and the rest of us at the back, we were piped to the wedding. The
ceremony I remember was outside. I had a white piqué dress with tartan
patch pockets and the bride and bridesmaid had pale blue silk.

   The meal was in the barn that was all decorated, and there were
chickens galore; then when that was over the place was cleared for the
dancing. I didn't like it at all, the din and all the people. They danced
and they sang and they drank several rounds. That all went on till six
o'clock in the morning.

But for sheer stamina Lewis and Shetland take first-equal place.

I can tell you about a typical Lewis wedding ... typical of Carloway
anyhow. This would be in the 1930s. We went to the Free Church for
the ceremony and the couple got a long solemn talking to. Then they
went with their guests in an old 'bus for a tour round the villages singing
and shouting, and came back to the bride's home for a meal. After that
there was an all-night ceilidh and dancing. Next night they had another
party and dinner for the older people who were past dancing, and the
third night there was a party for all the children.

Weddings in Shetland, say in Halsay, were great marathons that would
last three or four days.

It's maybe a relief, after all that, to finish with the quiet wedding
of John MacRae's father that ended the morse-code wooing of his
former neighbour in the light-house.

My parents got married on Pladda off Kildonan, Arran. The minister
came to the lighthouse, because they couldn't get ashore, y'see, when
they were on a tour of duty, so he'd to come to them. They'd bunting
hung from the tower and all that, and the company was just the other
keeper's family.

And that's the meet, the chase and the pinning-down for you. Maybe the postscript could be the honeymoon, although so few mentioned such a thing round the northern half of the coast that it may have been a lowland indulgence. From the east, only Andrew Fairnie spoke of the honeymoon after 'the last all-night wedding in Musselburgh', a seemly visit by train to Glasgow after a seemly courtship.

But it was Jean Kane's honeymoon with her 'bus driver that took the breath away as a sheer improbable high-hearted adventure for one of eleven weans from an Ardrossan tenement in the 1920s. And if the minister had not been alert she might not have been the one to go at all. She summed up wedding, reception and afters, without waste of words.

> Here was me in my kind of pink tulle dress wi' the brown velvet bows and a big puff sleeve, standing wi' my twin sister for bridesmaid. The minister had to be careful no' to marry the wrong one. We'd a nice cake and Murchie did the purvey. We went in an aeroplane to London for our honeymoon. I was scared stiff. But–here, it was a very romantic honeymoon.

With a man of that brave imagination it must have been.

There are those who despise such memories as nostalgia, but maybe that's because they had sour grapes and registries (or even just what they call 'bidey-ins' in the north) instead of pipers, and fiddlers, cla'es carryin's, 'bus runs, purveys and girdle scones.

And a postscript ... a chance remark thrown away by a ninety-year-old who never entered that married state at all.

> No, I was never wed ... but, she says with a wicked twinkle, 'I'll no' die wonderin' ...

14
None of Your Dye or That

Elsewhere we've seen men leave home for the fishing, and then find safe haven again ashore. We've followed them as they followed the shoals and as they brought back their catch for some of the women to gut and pack into barrels for a pittance from the merchants. But there was that other special, sturdy breed of women, glimpsed already, who saw to it that some of the earnings from the fishing came straight from the consumer into their own hands.

There may have been far-seeing thrifty fishermen able and willing and disciplined enough to leave their womenfolk well-provided and with the perhaps seven or eight weeks of their fishing absence covered by a sum to lay out weekly for their house-keeping. But they were not all like that ... not in Andrew Fairnie's memory of his childhood ninety years ago.

> My mother went out with the creel. She provided the living for the family at home a lot of the time. Some of the men went away and left nothing in the house till they got back and if it hadna been for my mother and others the same, there would've been no money ... and most families were big ... seven or eight the usual.

Before the fisherwomen set out there was the task of filling their creels.

> My mother and my granny (she went out, too, w'the creel) got the fish at the wee market at the Fisherrow harbour.

Customers waiting along the coast and in the hinterland villages for their fish had to have a choice of fare, not only of a small variety of kinds of fish but whether to buy fresh or smoked. Mr. John Coghill remembers the procedure at Golspie.

> The fish were taken from the small market by the fisherwives themselves and then they smoked some of them over fir-cones ready for the

128

creel. There were no fish shops round Golspie at that time. It was just the women trudging round.

And there's an evocative memory from one who was young, long ago, in Macduff.

At night in Macduff when they were smoking the herring an' that, the town was just a haze of smoke, and on a still summer night ... the smell ... oh my word ... strong! But it was a good smell.

The creels packed, the family left provisioned for the day and the dawn grey, it was time for the fisherwife to be off ... not always on a short journey, and, unless she was in the face of the wind, with the waft of fish constantly in her nostrils.

They went from St. Comb's here or Fraserburgh, the sixteen miles or so in the train to Maude and went all round the countryside there, a whole day they'd be away.

Along the coast at Macduff another grandmother was hitching on her creel.

My grandmother walked the two mile from home, got the train at Macduff at six o'clock in the morning, got off at King Edward and then went to a' the different farms, walking all the time. Then she'd come back with the train at night. Sometimes instead of money she'd get fresh butter and bring that home to salt down for the winter. She enjoyed that life. She was a big strong woman, my granny.

And much need! But sure enough, since she lived 'active to ninety-six' the open air trudge can hardly have undermined her constitution.

Mind there were other fish-sellers forbye the creel-wives.

Some women found the day's darg easier if they could hurl their wares round on wheels. Alex Archer remembers the ones who left Largo to do their rounds when he was a boy in the 'twenties.

These women used to go away from here on an early morning train to Thornton wi' their barrows of fish. They went round Thornton and the country places there and came back by a train at tea-time. They pulled the barrow by a bit sea-rope looped round their back, and got their hands wi' the rope on to the handle of the barrow and that took the weight of it.

Across country in Ballantrae Helen McClung tells of one worthy
who made a real day out of her fish round with horse and cart, a
sociable progress round her clients ... a far cry from the sober,
thrifty and industrious Fisherrow or Macduff housewives with
their creels and their everlasting knitting. Let's call her Maggie
Diack, not to tell tales on that happy-go-lucky and harmless
wayfarer whose furrow, if not narrow, would no doubt seem hard
enough to those who smile at her, if they had to take her place.

> Maggie used to come round up the glen to the houses and farms with her
> fish-cart and horse, and we all bought fish from her. She got little
> enhancements on the way at different places and by the time she reached
> our place, well ... she was drunk really. But her horse knew its own way
> home.

For a period in the 'twenties and 'thirties in most of the
shoreland areas remembered, the old traditional round of the creel-
wife lingered on, along with the horse and hand-carts. But when
vans began to appear, their days were numbered. Old paths and
farm lanes, trodden so long, were widened to allow vans to make
quick, fresh deliveries from quayside to kitchens.

> It was sad to see the creels fade out when the motors came in. Mind, it
> must've been a hard road for the women right-enough, out on those
> hills in a' weathers, but it was a way of life and they were very sturdy
> w'it.

The new breed of ambitious young van salesmen didn't fritter away
their time either, and worked hard in a different way. After Alex
Archer's day's work out from Largo there was the next day's van
stock to prepare.

> At night we filleted and put the fish into trays. Th' used to be a lorry
> that brought big chunks of ice and you put that round the fish. Then
> you'd to stack the cold trays in the vans ready to take out early in the
> morning.

There were local village customers too, of course, who enjoyed
their fish and didn't have to wait for sellers to come round their
doors. Peter Sinclair remembers how they bought their herring and
haddock at Oban.

> There were two or three women who got fish at the pier and trundled it
> in barrows to their various sales pitches about Oban.

So some fished, some gutted and packed, some sold. But there were others so dedicated to the whole industry that they ran the whole fish gamut themselves. There was one such in Lochgilphead.

I mind Mr. MacTavish that had a wee shop selling fish. He went out in his own boat and caught them himself. He used to do kippers too. I used to get sent for his kippers. He had them hung in this black shed he had, over the shavings ... used to open the top half of the shed door and draw them out with a cleek-thing that had a hook on the end, to see if they were ready ... real kippers they were ... none of your dye or that. He used to look at them and say, 'Ach, they're no ready yet, you'll need to come back in the afternoon.' And then he would push them back in for a bit more smoking. I remember they were next-to-nothing cheap, penny a pair maybe.

The able Mr. MacTavish had more than rows of kippers to his credit.

I can remember all the wee MacTavishes in their fisher-ganzies at the school in Lochgilphead.

So where better to close. The awesome doggedness of the fisherwives and the barrow-trailers, the cheerful clatter on country lanes of fish-carts, and the versatile activities of Mr. MacTavish to put warm ganzies on his own Lochgilphead tiddlers, all are chronicled, however briefly. The white and smoked fish and the herrings-in-oatmeal lie steaming on plates, and the whole high-hearted and dangerous exercise to provide them is fulfilled.

15
All Kinds of Wee Penny Geggies

Long working days at sea or on land, the sheer complexity of producing heat, food, decent cleanliness, fitly maintained homes and spiritual wholeness, would seem to us to have left little time for leisure and pleasure at the turn of the century. But perhaps it was just the very scantiness of their free time that made both young and old wring the last drop from whatever of entertainment was available laid on, and, when that was exhausted, to provide their own.

Itinerant companies from the towns bringing slick, foot-lit shows to village halls were, at first, the real magic and it was a benighted community that never saw a Penny Geggie or a concert party doing a one-night stand.

> There were travelling players came and brought maybe 'Uncle Tom's Cabin' to the Unionist Hall. The teacher told you about it at the school before you went. It'd been about a penny to get in ... and I remember Graham Moffat came with 'Bunty Pulls the Strings'.

Jenny McCrindle, straight from the down-to-earth round of life on a lonely farmhouse was near-enough overwhelmed by a presentation she saw on the boards during her out-lodging schooldays in Girvan.

> It was a travelling company, and in the story on the stage th' was this man died and got brought back to life. My! But I'd nightmares after that.

It was surely the tricks of the cine-camera that inspired the earliest films, rather than the idea that this was a new medium for telling stories. When Andrew Fairnie was a boy it was more than he and his friends could fathom, to understand how the obviously impossible was made to seem quite natural.

We didna ken about cutting and editing films when I was fourteen. It was a real mystery how the very first film that ever I saw was done. The chap that showed it wound the machine just by the handle. It was about a man going to the dentist to get his teeth pulled. The dentist got him sat down with a big cloth round, pinning his arms, then he took a huge pair of shears and the man started kicking when the dentist came to cut off his head. The next thing the dentist had the head under his arm and was pulling out the teeth. Then he stuck the head back on. We couldna believe it.

The cinema memories progress after that to the weekly serial.

They'd knocked down two cottages in Portland Street in Troon to build a picture-house and we went there ... a penny on a Saturday afternoon it was. I remember Pearl White ... she'd be left lying on a railway line with the train coming. We used to think she lay there all week till the next Saturday ... And I remember 'Rebecca of Sunnybrook Farm' and the bit where she blacked her heel through a hole in her stocking so it wouldn't show. We cheered and clapped and the manager would go up and down with his stick thumping the floor to keep us quiet. That was the Saturday matinee.

The islands were later in discovering the delights of moving pictures, partly from kirky distaste for such wordly pleasure and partly for lack of access and facilities. But by the first months of the Second War regular diets of films had reached such fastnesses as the settlements of Ness, making its innocence one of the casualties of war.

Ah yes, the pictures came to the R.A.F. camp at Ness. Mind you, the airmen wouldn't let you in unless you were old enough, and I used to envy my sister Ina. She was that bit older and she could put on a wee bit make-up and pretend she was older than fourteen. Och it was all getting to be positively decadent ... *make-up* and films! And of course we used to sneak up to the side-door and try to see what the film was about.

But in most places there were well-established twice-weekly changes of programme long before that; and the young had discovered that there were other concurrent pleasures to be had from a visit to the picture-hall, which were not available at concerts in a well-lit village hall.

You could meet boys *inside* at the pictures, and hold hands in the dark. The sorta wilder ones even *kissed* in the back row and liked to tell you

that they didnae see the picture at all. But mostly you just sat wi' your boy and ate sweeties.

Sometimes there was just a chance meeting.

You got in for thruppence. I was there one night with my friends and *he* happened to come in wi' his chums and sit beside us. Then they walked us home. That's how it started.

And 'he' nodded and, to judge from his smile, seemed to think that in that long-ago encounter they had both done pretty well for themselves.

There were places like the one Jim Buchan recalls in Peterhead where, though it cost a penny less to get in, the company was a lot less congenial.

There was just the one picture-house and 't was *alive*, so we ca'ed it the 'scratcher'. Tuppence downstairs you paid at that flea-pit. It was fourpence upstairs but it was just as bad there.

If you had more in your pocket than the bare tuppence for your ticket you could stretch the pleasure ... make a whole evening of it as Gena Buchan did on her Saturday night excursions from St. Combs.

> On a Saturday night you went to the pictures at Fraserburgh, and when you came out you'd your chips or your fish supper before you'd to catch the half-past nine 'boozer' home. That was the train 't left just after the pubs came out.

Sometimes you had to make a choice between catching that conveyance home, or having the chips and facing the wrath of an outraged father, waiting at home. For a lass of spirit in Ardrossan there was that added spice once in a while to a night out, in running that risk.

> There was what they called the 'Here y'are' in Ardrossan. It was a big high carriage-thing and you went up two steps at the back into it and there were seats all round.
> 'Here-y'-are for Saltcoats.' That's what the man used to call out, so that's how it got its name ... we often had tuppence-worth on the 'Here y'are'. Anyway there was no pictures in Ardrossan and we'd to go to Saltcoats and you'd to get the last 'Here y'are' home, or else walk. Well sometimes we went for chips and lemonade ... spent the fare on them and didnae catch the 'Here y'are'. Father would think we'd been away kee-hoying somewhere and threaten to shut us out for the night. He did lock the door one night on Sadie ... left her kicking her heels in the close.

No word, though of whether Sadie's sin was late home-coming from the pictures or some other folly, but, no doubt, if one of the brood of half-a-dozen sisters had not unsnibbed the back window for her, Father would eventually have drawn the bolt on the front door and saved her from white slavers doing their press-rounds from the harbour.

Even the most intrepid of travelling theatre companies did not venture to far-flung thinly populated places, girdled by isolating seas or hills. And facilities for bringing Pearl White or Snub Pollard were not available there either, so there was more call on local talent. Performances recalled in Cromarty and Rousay were more or less formal programmes held in village halls.

They'd concerts in the Victoria Hall in Cromarty with fiddlers, melodeons and singers.

Now and again on Rousay they'd a Scottish concert with music and dramatics and fiddlers. There was one public hall on the island, but it was blown away in a bad storm many years ago now.

Over towards the west in places like John Coghill's Tongue, or Stornoway, or in Connel where Catherine Murray was a likely lass in the 'thirties, they threw in a bite to eat, a drink and a whirl or two of the dancing, and called them ceilidhs.

We'd Gaelic ceilidhs in the public hall here at Connel ... songs and dances to the fiddler. You got your entertainment with a dance in between, and a cup of tea and a cake.

According to Mrs. Pryde they were short on fiddlers at Bernera but managed their ceilidhs all the same.

Oh yes, we'd ceilidhs that all the boys and girls came to. Singing and melodeons mainly, not so much fiddles ... that was more in Stornoway. But 't was grand. The dancing was Eightsomes and Schottisches and Dashing White Sergeants ... all the dizzy dances.

Several rememberers boasted their own musical skills at blowing and bowing and squeezing, to help along the social life of Edwardian or even Victorian times. Others told of families who specialised in particular instruments. In Musselburgh Andrew Fairnie was an exponent himself.

I played the fiddle, mostly Scottish music. I'd a friend knew a man that was well-up in fiddles and I bought my violin from him for fifteen shillings. Sometimes I take it out yet and give it a wee tune, then put it back in its box again. I like to hear the Fiddlers' Rallies now, they're affie good aren't they?

And Farquhar MacDonald had a musical mother.

As a young girl she and her father ran a wee band. He played the fiddle and she played the piano and there was maybe an accordeon. They went out with that quite a lot. My Mother was one of the finest at playing Highland music that I ever heard ... really good!

On Hugh Craigie's Rousay in the Orkneys there was family dance-music-making that was almost hereditary.

> Some places th' were families that were bands in themselves ... fathers, sons, daughters, and grandchildren. They played for the dances, and that.

The Turriff blacksmith and his brothers formed another band.

> My father and his two brothers played their violins with a blind pianist and a man with a big base fiddle. They went out playing till the wee sma' hours at the dances ... then my father came home, changed to his working clothes and away into the smiddy. When we were young, maybe in 1906 or '7 we used to listen to them from outside the hall.

There was a will and a way to hold ceilidhs, even when there was no hall, as John Leitch remembers of Tarbert village over eighty years ago.

> Och yes, we'd ceilidh sort of things ... people meeting in each other's houses with their fiddles and melodeons. I used to play the melodeon myself at those.

And further south, in the quiet valley of Glenapp, Helen McClung recalls how it was with them.

> There wasn't much what-you'd-say 'entertainment' but the father at the farm where we got our milk was a fiddler and we'd go down there on a Saturday night; and others from farther down the glen would come up and we'd a sort of get-together in the farmhouse.

There were places where a tradition of music-making was fostered by a real enthusiast. One of these established an interest well over a century ago that is still flourishing around Connel and Oban.

> I remember mother telling me about a teacher here when she was young, that was a fiddler and played for the children marching into school ... following him like the Pied Piper. He taught a lot of youngsters fiddling and that's why there's so many still around here that play. There was a family of MacCallums turned out to be very good. One became the leader of an orchestra.

And Peter Sinclair confirms that the Firth of Lorn area is still rich in fiddlers a century and a half after Mendelssohn brooded there over 'Fingal's Cave'.

> ... lot of fiddlers hereabouts. There's the 'Reel and Strathspey Fiddlers' in Oban are very good.

Closer to home than Oban, or even the village outside his door, is the proof of the musical pudding in the sturdy shape of Peter Sinclair Junior, just come in at the door.

> This is my son. He's a really good accordeon-player ... played at The Pavilion theatre in Glasgow two or three times ... then there's my other boy, he sings. They do a lot of shows together in the summertime in the Corran Hall in Oban or one of the hotels.

The young crofter-musician smiles.

> Aye, I sing in Oban at dances and concerts and weddings. I get to all the weddings.

We've looked at dancing's most basic *raison d'être* as a kind of mating rite, but that was, and is, only part of the story. For young people it was also a large measure of their entertainment. Alex Archer in Fife was no slouch at the foxtrot and suchlike when he was a bachelor lad-about-Largo.

> It was all dancing when I was young. I was a really good dancer ... slow foxtrots, quicksteps, waltzes ... great! Y'see th' was three changes of programme a week at the pictures, then Friday night, ten o'clock till two, was the Late Night Dancing. Then th' was halls in other places, two at Leven. This was before I was married ... never went to the dancin' *after*. But *before* ... och before, I was at the dancin' every night of the week.

But even just along the road at Anstruther there was more to dancing than just 'the jiggin'.

> We went to the Old Tyme in the Town Hall ... y'know, Strip the Willie, and that. And the Lancers and Quadrilles.

The wild abandon of Strip-the-Willow and the Lancers might have been safe enough in the gas-lit halls of villages within hoochin-distance of Edinburgh, but up in the wilds of the north there were hazards. James Still remembers that.

> We used to go five or six miles to Aberchirder or Cuminestown for the dancing. That was after we'd learned to dance, of course ... w'an old chap 't played the fiddle. It was a job to get the girls and boys to dance together ... the boys stood 't one end and th' girls at th' other, then when the music started you made a bee-line for the one you fancied. It was paraffin lamps 't that time and sometimes these hefty lads that we

were, stomped so hard in the likes of an eightsome reel that we put out
the lamps ... wasna very popular w' the hall-keeper.

Stornoway was different. There were quite a few real social occasions,
dress affairs ... with some men in kilts, some in dinner-jackets, and the
ladies all dolled up. And then, Sir James Matheson had *the* ball at Lewis
Castle.

It might not have been easy to rate an invitation to Sir James' posh
'do', but it was probably easier than for Jenny McCrindle to get a
sampling of the pleasure at much simpler hops in south Ayrshire.

There was no entertainment in our home ... never! Th' only way I got
to a dance was skip out without the uncle knowing ... when he was away
early to sleep at night. Then I'd maybe slip off and away the three miles
to Barr. My mother would have the back door unbarred for me getting
back. Mind, the uncle really cared about me ... he was good. It was just
he was that strict.

Not all of the talents offered to the community as entertainment
were musical. As well as the ceilidhs, concerts and dances, there
was, in most places, an odd dinner or Burns' Supper and when a
local chiel, like this Fife fisherman, was found to be knowledgeable
about the poet, and willing, he was in great demand.

Aye, Burns was a great man w' a marvellous mind. I went out for years
and years to recite at different suppers round here in Anstruther,
Pittenweem and so on. I've Addressed the Haggis ... y'know, 'fair fa'
your honest sonsy face' ... I've done 'The Twa Dugs' and 'Tam O
Shanter', 'Death and Doctor Hornbrook'.

The young, of course, had their special activities laid on for them
with the dual purpose, in most well-founded organisations, of
entertaining them and setting their feet firmly in worthy directions.
And, although it is the social joys of Band of Hope and Sunday
School that are recalled with chuckling pleasure, to a man and
woman they are quite clear about what were the moral precepts.
Catherine Murray was a member of the Band of Hope in Connel.

Oh yes, we liked the Band of Hope. We always had a concert that we
took part in, where the songs were all about strong drink,
   'Dule and Care away we fling
   Dancing round a merry ring
   And this is the chorus we will sing
   Never drink Whisky or Brand-*y*'

We'd to sign the pledge too and we got a medal for that...that was the first year. The next we'd get a bar to it, and through the years we'd get four or five bars and then a ribbon brooch. And that was us 'Ribboners'.

The lighter side of things came with the swarry and the concert.

We'd a bag at the swarry with a sugar bun. Maybe there'd be a magic lantern, then an orange for going home. And we were in the concert, of course. We'd a percussion band with tambourines and cymbals, and we got all dressed up in our newly-washed and starched white dresses with pinafores over the top and white petticoats. I did 'The Laird o' Cockpen' once, with my friend.

There is, of course, 'more joy over one that repenteth' and even little Margaret MacKenzie from The Cromarty Arms was welcomed in the village Band of Hope, perhaps the more warmly for the peril of her home surroundings.

Oh yes, I went to the Band of Hope...lovely magic lantern slides at the Band of Hope.

A little later, down south in Troon, youngsters were being carefully bolstered on all sides against temptation, and having a hectic social life at the same time.

There was the Band of Hope, yes; but there was the Good Templars and the Rechabites too ... all temperance organisations. We were in them all at one time or another ... and went to all the swarries.

Two sisters, who were charming the Mammas and Papas of the day with their solo spots, can still rattle out their 'pieces', word perfect.

I can remember one of mine.

'This is the shop of Miss Louise
Now step-in here, Madam, if you please.
All our confections are sweet and new
The latest from London and Paris too.
We greet all with smiles, give no one a frown
For 'Louise' is the hat-shop best known in the town.

Mine was,
'Here's an old friend the handkerchief, in every shade and hue
It's wondrous possibilities we will display to you.

As you're aware, this little square, is sometimes edged with roses,
But plain or fine, it's chiefest use, is wiping little noses.'
Then you went
'Tra la la, Tra la la'
and wafted the hankies about. We got an orange to go home with.

As well as aiming for bars and ribbons at the Connel Band of
Hope, the youngsters there were kept busy preparing for the Junior
Mods, held in Oban and other centres within reasonable travelling
distance. Although the prospect kept the young contestants in a
fever, competition was hardly fierce.

I was in the choir and I remember going to Fort William once and we
came in *third*. There was great excitement. Everyone came to meet us
coming home, to congratulate us ... even the Lady from Dunstaffnage.
Actually, there were only three choirs in it, but 'third' sounded better
than 'worst'.

But while there were extrovert or earnest young entertainers on
the platforms of little halls and schoolrooms right round Scotland
doing their bit, there were those like Jenny McCrindle who found
the limelight too much for them.

When I stayed in Girvan for school in the wintertime the old landlady 't
I lived with, took me to the Band of Hope and the Y.W.C.A. and all
kinds of wee Penny Geggies in the hall behind the pub. Y'know, wee
slide-shows or concerts with turns, and you got a cuppa tea and a bun. I
didn't sing or do anything. I was too terrified ... too 'country' me!

Funny that though ... for she has a way of telling a tale now that
betrays no such crippling shyness.

So that was how spirited people in bleak, dark winters above
grey seas or deep in brackeny glens enjoyed their small leisure ...
welcoming travellers come to amuse them; or honing their own do-
it-yourself talents to offer their neighbours as entertainment. What
there was for them outdoors, when the sea sparkled and the sand
was warm, belongs to another chapter.

16

I Always Mind My Mother in Black

In other chapters we've put away the bairns' Sunday bests into 'good' room or lobby kists, and sent these sprigs of the family to school in their pinafores and chafing trousers. But what about these occasions when neither serge frocks nor school ganzies were fitting attire for the activity in hand ... the swarrees or the picnics or even the months of mourning for a grandmother? And what about their elders' cladding, their work-clothes or their braws? What do the elderly of today recall of their mothers' working attire, of the way their fathers and brothers were happed up, on their way to the fishing or the ploughing?

City folk can jouk their shivering timbers into closes or shop-doors for a respite from bleak winds or to keep flimsy fashions from a soaking, and they can clatter their silly peerie heels along puddled pavements to catch the shelter of buses or cabs. But it's always been a more serious matter on coast or croft to be clad warm enough against dour weather to work long hours without taking harm from chilling or wet.

One of David Henderson's abiding memories is of the sight of the ladies of Latheronwheel sweeping their shawls round their shoulders.

A' the women wore shawls over their shoulders, which is a very warm thing. My mother always wore one.

He has a very clear picture of that mother and the smeddum with which she attacked her chores.

And d'you know, other than at the kirk, I've never seen my mother with

143

her sleeves down ... Sunday, Saturday ... any day, her sleeves were up and her arms as brown as nuts.

Mattie Gordon has clear memories too, from her childhood at the turn of the century, of her Buchan grandmother swinging a swey to and fro, over an open fire.

I mind she wore a affa rough, dark skirt, a pair o' that clogs the women had then ... and she'd a thick bumphly buttonin' bodice over a coarse shirt. When she went out the house, maybe to a neighbour or that, I always mind the way she used to kin' fling a shawl, y'ken, over her head.

On the other side of the country too, some twenty years later, George MacGregor looks back at the grandmothers of Harris.

The very old ladies of Harris were still wearing coarse blouses and skirts with heavy cross-over shawls, and mutches on their heads.

And Meg Jack at harvest days on the Black Isle of pre-First War days, when the women wore loose, collarless working-dresses they called carsackies, and the men waistcoats or high-buttoning jackets over shirts with stud-fastened neckbands, and always flat bunnets and nicky-tams ...

All these were for working round croft or fisher-cot and over open fires. What Rose Baker remembers better, were women whose work took them from home for hours on end and demanded clothing for all weathers.

I mind fine the fisherwives about Newhaven, Leith and Granton wearin' their blue and white strippit petticoats and carrying their creels on their shoulders.

So characteristic and kenspeckle indeed was the fisherwife costume that it was standard wear for the choir formed by the Newhaven fisherwomen.

Many a time I heard that choir ... used to go to the Usher Hall ... I'd friends in it. They wore their shawls and bunched-up skirts an' that.

But Andrew Fairnie's mother wore that garb for her real and earnest working-life, when he was a child ninety years ago. And lest he should forget its details as he sits, spare and still handsome, in his Musselburgh home, he proudly points out the two china figurines on the mantel above his fire, brought by his own bride to their first married home.

When my mother went out w' the creel around the 1890s she was dressed like that ... like the figures there on the mantel ... a light-coloured shirt and a dark-striped skirt like that, with a pinny kirtled up over it and wide petticoats. She'd warm stockings too and, over the top of everything else, a dark blue overall. And the creel w' the lid on it there, she carried that on her shoulders at the back.

Such dauntless women were still in their traditional costume, still carrying their creels thirty-five years later when other fashions had gone through bustles, leg o' muttons and the shingle. Joyce Paton recalls one from Arbroath.

When I was young in Carnoustie she used to come round regularly selling her fish from a creel. Her name was Rebecca but she was always called 'Baikie'. I can just see her yet ... her weather-beaten face, and black, snapping, merry sort of eyes. She'd grey hair pulled back in a bun and she wore a very dark blue or black serge skirt with pale blue-and-white striped petticoats and a kind of kirtle or panniers. There was a cross-over warm shawl with black stockings and shoes ... oh yes, and she'd a bag for money.

That childhood memory of the panniers wasn't far out. Andrew Fairnie brings to mind his mother's two 'pooches'.

My mother and th' other women carried a wee bag in front of them ... what they ca'ed a 'pooch'. They'd two pooches really, tied round their waists, one for their money and one for their knitting. Y'ken a' the men wore jerseys. My mother knitted all our jerseys. Many a time I was sent to the ship's chandler's for a hank of three-ply navy wool. Wherever the women of Fisherrow went they had the knitting w' them. When they went for the train in the morning, the minute they sat down at the station waiting for it to come in, out came the knitting. Then *on* the train till it reached its destination they were clicking away. Then it went into their pooches while they went off to their rounds w' the fish. Whenever they were sitting or standing around for a wee while the knitting was never out their hands. Every man and laddie wore a jersey that the mother had knitted ... and stockings.

Across the Forth in Fife they were just as busy with the pins and many a mile was in-over-through-offed around the fisher-cots there. It was an integral part of a life that needed the jerseys, needed to provide them as economically as possible, needed the occupation for lonely evenings, and expressed itself in the creation of original

designs. There was imagination and craft and maybe a strand or two
of one-upmanship about it.

> The women in Anstruther a' knitted the men's and boys' jerseys them-
> selves. They sat at night when the men were away and did a' the
> different patterns. My cousin was a great one for knitting the jerseys.
> She used to make up patterns and her man drew them out on squared
> paper, and she followed the design from there.

For some with no menfolk of their own left to knit for, the work
was an even more dire necessity, in the days before compensation
and pension.

> My aunt lost her husband, and her son at fourteen, both just off
> Cellardyke there ... boat went down full o' herring. So she'd to work
> the jerseys after that to make a living for herself and the three bairns
> that were left. One big jersey could take her near three weeks and she
> got five shillings for that.

Not a very fat living for four mouths, but perhaps there was a
vicarious pride in seeing someone else's man well-clad for her
industry. For, of course, a braw new jersey and clean trousers were
for more than hauling in nets or lines or wiping fishy hands on. A
man rightly considered himself dressed ship-shape and trim when
he changed into those for a night off.

> When we went ashore we'd on a jersey and trousers for the likes of the
> dancing on Britannia pier, or maybe the pictures in a big place ... Mind,
> wherever we were we'd a' our navy blue suit for Sunday, for going to the
> kirk.

So speaks a Fifer, but the convention of the blue suit was so
widespread around the coast among fishers and crofters as to be
almost universal ... a navy or dark suit was *de rigeur* and that, with a
supply of jerseys and hard-wearing trousers covered all occasions.

> The Orkney men all had a dark suit ... their only suit ... for the church
> or for funerals. The shops in Kirkwall would send round a man with
> samples ... in a case ... and you ordered what you wanted. They might
> measure you up for a suit if you couldnae go to Kirkwall yourself.

The women too had their rules and Jean Durnie recalls her
mother's unvarying preference in the Ardrossan of the early 1900s.

> My mother always wore a black skirt and a black blouse, and yon kinda

satinette or sateen apron . . . always a fresh one for the afternoon when her work was done . . . so's if anyone came to the door everything was right, the house clean and the apron fresh.

And it didn't do for a mother to break the rules. That could be as shocking to the young as it would have been to the parent to spawn a dissolute teenager, had there been such a breed in Edwardian times.

I always remember my mother in black . . . only once I saw her in a light colour and that was a kind of mauvey coat she got in Colthart's. I couldn't believe my eyes! I didnae like it at all but *she* was fair made-up with it!

A Troon granny was more like the thing.

My grandmother wore very nice hats, and she always wore a black ribbon round her throat.

None of your flights of fancy there, into modes unbecoming her age.

Down the age-scale and into the years of the First War, Margaret Ritchie has vivid, if wry, memories of what was inflicted on the well-dressed Moray Firth twenty-year-old, and its consequences.

I remember getting a costume made for me. It was grey flannel and I didn't like it at all. I had a leghorn hat to go with it and woollen stockings. My auntie thought I was a right swell. But the American sailors there thought we were awfu' Hie'lan'. No wonder they got the girls to go with them with the silk stockings they got from home . . . and their boxes of candy.

The girls in Fife seemed more contented with their lot.

When we went to the dances it was a short dress, and if it was a posh 'do' we got a long one. My sister was an awful good sew-er and she used to get a bit material, mebbe a shilling a yard, and just put 't on the floor to cut up and make an evening dress.

A nimble-fingered mother could do a lot to brighten up the wardrobes of small girls otherwise doomed to the tussore and drab available 'bought'.

They were great sew-ers in St. Combs, sixty, seventy years ago. We'd white kilties and we'd jumpers, maybe green and grey diamonds and shepherd tartan skirts and sailor collars. In the summer mother used to buy gingham and we'd red-and-white or blue-and-white dreses with knickers and a hankie, a' the same, matching. That ginghams would be maybe only sixpence or a shilling a yard.

And the boys were not to be outdone when they were got up to kill; there's a photograph to prove the well-set-up grandeur of a douce-looking pair of four and five-year-olds, obviously from 'up the brae'.

Here's the minister's two boys in boaters and sailor-suits with frilly ankle-length pantaloons ... wild Turks they were too!

On the whole, the young Camerons of Lochgilphead were more practically attired.

We'd long, big, cotton kind of sark dresses for playing. They'd loose belts and we wore rope-soled shoes with them, that my mother sent away for, mail order. And we'd cotton bonnet-things, as well, that were called mad-caps.

Children were not exempt from marks of respect when their elders' dark suits came out to mourn a bereavement. It was so, from far north to deep south.

At Girvan when my grandfather died and we were all about seven and ten, we'd all wee bowler hats for the funeral and we wore armbands quite a long time after.

And Gena Robertson remembers at St. Combs ...

When my father died I was wee, and a while after I mind going to the Sunday School swarree in a white voile dress with black ribbons through it, and I'd a white bow in my black hair.
    And you'd a black diamond sewn on your coat sleeve. I d'na think that was good for bairns ... a' that black things minded me of my father. I d'na think that was good.

No doubt it wasn't. But was there a trace of wistfulness that grandpa's death is now so briskly faced and quickly forgotten, in her final comment?

They d'na go into black at all now ... or even wear the patch.

17
Up to the Neck in the Dolly Barrel

We'd a good scrub once a week and I think we were as clean then as we are now with our baths and showers and fancy toilet lotions.

It's been a long long time since even thoroughly decent people consoled themselves with the old Scottish idea that 'clarty was cosy'. The sheer doggedness with which mothers of the last hundred years pursued cleanliness for their young, rings clearly through every rememberer's recollection of bath night and the careful hunt for nits, or worse, in the hair. It was no small task to dunk, dry and toothcomb a whole tribe of youngsters once a week and retain enough energy after that for their own ablutions, without a hot tap to twirl or a bung to let the used water gurgle away without effort. Friday night in most homes was the evening for the series of jobs leading to the set-scene of the weekly tubbing. Some had even to start with bringing in the water from outside.

We'd to bring all our water from the well in stoups, fill the kettle with zinc ladles and swing it in over a good red fire. Then we got out the big zinc bath, filled it with the hot water and got bathed in front of the peat fire. What a job to empty it!

Even if there was a cold tap in the house, few claimed a hot one, and every Friday night all over Scotland black kettles were boiling up thousands of gallons of bath water; and thousands of zinc tubs were brought out from under beds and down off wall hooks.

Everybody our way had a big zinc bath that was brought to the kitchen for washing. Ours was kept in the lavatory and brought out for bath night.

Perhaps everyone in Musselburgh did have a zinc bath but in most other places it was a wooden tub ... certainly at the McCrindle farm of Merkland near Ballantrae.

For bathing it was a wooden tub 't you filled with kettles of boiling water off the chain. After you were done and dressed again you'd to cart the whole thing outside and empty it. My! what a weight it was!

When there were five weans and Mother *and* Father, kettles could barely cope. Helen McClung remembers the system for the seven in their family.

Our water was heated in the wash boiler and pailed out into a big wooden tub in front of the kitchen fire. It was a clothes-tub right-enough but one that was kept specially for the baths ... seven of them ... five children and Mother and Father ... seven, getting a good scrub every week.

When there were the thirteen modest souls of the Kane household in the Ardrossan room-and-kitchen, ways had to be found to preserve the niceties on bath night.

> There was no bathroom but every Friday night we were all bathed in front of the fire with a screen round us. My mother saw to the bathing and did all our hair as well. The wee-est were done first ... then us. Then after all that we'd get our piece ... never put to bed without a piece. It was all carbolic soap.

An afterthought, that last remark, surely ... not an old-tyme pâté for inner cleanliness.

Jean Buchan's mother was sensitive on the question of clean hair too.

> When we were young we weren't allowed to play with bairns 't the teacher sent home wi' nits in their hair. And every Friday night the tooth-comb came out ... right into your scalp ... and she used Derbac soap to make sure.

It was kitchen-tubbing like that in most places in the Western Isles and the far north, in Buchan and parts of Fife. But elsewhere there was a modicum of privacy in the bath place, and, however cold it was crossing the yard to get there, once inside the wash-house they could get as hot and steamy a fug up as in any Turkish bath ...

> For baths you just had to go to the sheddie at the back, where the clothes-washing was done, and lock yourself in. Then you'd get out the big barrel with the top half cut off, heat the water in the big boiler till 't was just right and pour it into the barrel, and you got into that.

That was in Macduff and there was much the same ceremony at Anstruther.

> We lived on the East Green for thirty years and we'd no bathroom, so we bathed in the wash-house in the dolly barrel. That took you right up to the neck and it was a grand bath y'got like that.

Indeed it was ... a treat looked forward to all week by fishermen trawling and lining in cold North Sea winds and with the smell of fish about everything they touched while they were at sea. And the children 'following' were part of the ritual too, to make it a family occasion.

> You were away at sea all week and then straight home and into the

dolly-barrel. And the family'd just go in after you, one after the other
... or maybe two getting done at once.

Down at Troon they were nothing if not frugal ... 'never-ever
anything wasted' ... not even, it seems, the hot sapple that two or
three grimy youngsters would soon 'lay'.

> There was no hot water in the house, of course, so sometimes after the
> washing was done and there was still hot water, you'd go out to the
> wash-house and get your bath there.

One of the heaviest, sloppiest chores remembered was the
emptying of these great vessels of sudsy water, so the arrangements
for Catherine Murray's family at Connel eliminated at least that
task.

> The bath we had in the wash-house wasn't plumbed in for water. It just
> sat under the tap from the boiler and when you'd heated the water just
> right in the boiler, you filled the bath from that tap and then afterwards
> there was a plug you pulled out to let the water drain.

In some places a concerned council or corporation provided
facilities for older youngsters who were perhaps outgrowing the
frolics of the kitchen bath. The idea was good but in Peterhead at
least, the provision nowhere near satisfied the demand.

> When I was young you went down to what they called the Corporation
> Slipper baths, beside the lifeboat shed, at maybe ten o'clock in the
> morning and you'd be lucky if you got your bath before four.

But no doubt the passing show at the bustling harbour entertained
the lads while they waited.

If John Leitch's memory serves him aright, for him and his
community it was neither family nor local authority that provided
bathing facilities but Nature itself.

> We'd no water in the house so mostly our baths were in the sea. You
> could walk quarter of a mile out into the loch and just splash yourself
> clean, and have a swim after you'd done.

One feels sure, though, that unless the Tarbert lads were fiercely
Spartan, or the Gulf Stream warmer than it feels to the modern toe,
there must have been winter washing arrangements too.

As late as the 1920s in many places even the efficient Lighthouse
Service fell short a little on its plumbing.

On most stations like Turnberry and Rhuvaal you'd no bathroom. Just the zinc tub in the outhouse where the wash-boiler was.

And John MacRae was the first to mention the W.C. arrangements current then, and earlier.

It was just the dry closet, in an outside hut.

Indeed it was dry closets most places and a call to it was often something of an adventure ... certainly at Carlock hamlet in Glenapp where Helen McClung lived.

We'd dry closets at Carlock and in the wintertime when it was kind of dark, two of us had to go together. We got a candle and matches and went round the side of the house, and lit the candle once you were inside. It could be quite frightening really if the candle blew out and you were left in the dark in there.

One of my chores was week-about with the sister next to me, scrubbing out our toilet and then doing the one for old Mistress Ferguson that lived in the next cottage.

Another who doesn't much miss the toilet facilities of her young days is Jenny Stewart of Ballantrae.

It was a dry closet at Merkland ... no' very dry though! It was just a wee hut with a seat built over the running burn, so at night or in the wintertime when you'd to go outside it was *most* uncomfortable. You would be sitting there and the draughts wheeching right through.

It was 'a' dry lav'tries' in St. Combs too, apparently all part of life's rich tapestry, along with fireside tubs, septic tanks and butts of rainwater.

But surely the most poignant scene on a cold day (sadder even than finding a laddie on a Victorian street with his bare feet in his bunnet to keep them warm) was the picture drawn by Jim Buchan of the dire straits of life in old Peterhead.

They'd no toilets in houses here at one time and folk had just to go down to the shore. Th' was the woman's side and a men's side. And sometime you went to a little pier at the back of Peterhead even on a cold day and just put your bum over the open sea.

Well, well! The 'Sanitary' has long-since pulled the chain on such desperate ongoings and left those poor blae buttocks as only an anecdote to chuckle over in better serviced days.

18
I Remember the Telegrams

The last battle on Scottish soil (indeed on British soil) was of course in 1746; and marked the disintegration of the old highland tribal system, for what was left of it after the decimation at Culloden was quickly emasculated by nervous Governments in London. There had been constant inter-clan fighting of course for centuries, but by 1746 that had dwindled, and indeed the last real clan battle had been fought in 1678. A story about *it*, passed on to David Henderson in his early days at Latheronwheel can stand as preface to memories of later wars that made naive boys into seasoned, disillusioned men.

> I used to hear my father say that it wasn't so long since they found a Highlander buried in the moss up by the Wick River, really well-preserved, clothes and all. That would've been the clay below the peat did that. Even now you can find wood and sticks still new-looking and crisp in there, after years and years. They said that Highlander was a soldier from the Battle of Allt-na-marloch between the Sinclairs and the Campbells, fighting for the land of Caithness.

Tin-type soldiers in scarlet tunics, dreams of flashing swords, plunging horses and medals for gallant glory ... that was the vision of battle in Donald MacKintosh's childhood in the 1880s and it persisted into the South African fighting until the remnant of those who had marched out in brave and piping splendour trailed home again bringing the tattered truth about war.

> I remember the men going off to the South African war, singing and rejoicing and waving flags. The great song then was 'Good-bye Dolly, I must leave you' and they sang that as they marched out of Beauly. That was the first time I ever saw soldiers in khaki. It was always red before that. But the khaki was for camouflage on the South African veldt. Oh, but they didn't know what war was then.

154

But they did by 1914 and from her Cromarty days Margaret Ritchie recalls a tragedy that took the hooray out of war for the shocked inhabitants along the coast of the Firth a year later.

> Part of the British fleet had come in and it was lying in the bay at Nigg across the water from Cromarty. One of the ships was H.M.S.Natal and the sailors in her gave a party for some women and children from ashore. And-here there was this big explosion in the ship and a lot of people ... hundreds ... were lost. They didn't lift that Natal for years and we saw the mast sticking up for a long-long time after.*

By now the war was taking men from the tiniest row of fisher houses and the most isolated crofts and showing them a world few had even imagined. Donald MacKintosh was soldier-age himself by then.

> I was off quite early to the 1914-18 war, and I can tell you there was no great flag-waving or cheering or hullabaloo in Beauly when the men marched off to that.

John Leitch at Tarbert was another who was not glammered by tunes of glory.

> I wasn't very long started teaching when I went into the army, to train first in Edinburgh. When they asked me what I wanted to join, I thought 'Well, the sight of a bayonet would put the fear of death into me so I'd better go for the artillery'. I went to Mesopotamia not France. That's probably why I'm still here. I was in some of the fighting there but well back.

Coming as the rememberers do from the sea-selvedge of the country most of those who joined up, naturally went to sea. David Henderson, some years younger than the canny, modest John Leitch, rushed headlong to his country's rescue.

> I ran away at fifteen to join the navy ... went to Wick without telling them at home. They sent me back for my father's permission, and then I

---

* At ninety-one Mrs. Ritchie has a remarkable memory. The Naval History Library at the Ministry of Defence confirmed her story in almost every particular. On the afternoon of December 30th H.M.S.Natal lay in the Cromarty Firth with her squadron. The crew was entertaining some guests to a film show and some light music from a Royal Marine band, on board. There was a series of explosions and in five minutes the ship was a mass of flames and sinking fast. Official figures gave the death toll as over three hundred and fifty men of the Natal's company along with seven women and three children.

went into the Boys' Service. First place I went was five changes of train
away ... to Devonport. One of my first memories of Devonport was
seeing Shackleton leaving there to go to South Georgia on his ship. I
think it was the 'Endeavour'. She had yard-arms on her ... carried sails
as well.

It was still too soon in the war for the irony to seep into young
naval minds of one particular ritual the training sailors were put
through from time to time.

We sometimes got the order 'Cheer Ship!' That meant ... 'go and man
the rigging and cheer the troopships' ... as they sailed off to France.
What a travesty ... cheering!'

Another who was off early to the navy was Andrew Fairnie.

I went away as soon's the war broke out to be a stoker. I was sent out to
the Mediterranean, minesweeping. We swept the Aegean Sea, the Sea of
Marmora and the Black Sea. I was doing that the whole war, and for
another year after it ended ... till the whole place was clear. We'd a
balloon on our ship and two officers used to go up six hundred feet to
see the minefields from there and direct the skipper by 'phone.
    We swept these mines up with a wire rope, till you could see them and
then every man that wasn't at some other necessary job, was issued with
a rifle and ordered to try and hit the knob of a mine, puncture the air
chamber and send the mine to the bottom. It was quite dangerous.

It was a far cry from Fisherrow for Andrew Fairnie's brother too,
and his war, whether or not equally dangerous, had a sadder end.

He was a wireless telegrapher on a seaplane and during the war, when
my father was down fishing out of Yarmouth, he saw a seaplane not far
out and in some sort of difficulty. He didn't know until later that my
brother was on it and, being the telegrapher, had sent a message to his
base that he'd be back in thirty-five minutes. But he wasn't, and we
never saw him again.

Meantime David Henderson was adding to his memories of
glimpses of the famous when he arrived at Scapa Flow for his next
stint of service.

When I reached Scapa Flow, just about the first person I saw there was
Admiral Beattie with the jaunty cap and the hand tucked in his pocket. I
was on the 'Barham' first and then on an old coal cruiser.

Ineptly or humorously called 'Blanche',

Then near the end, we were sent south to meet the German fleet when it surrendered at May Island in the Forth. We escorted them up to Scapa Flow. One of our jobs up there was to bring in their mail to the German prisoners-of-war, from a German cruiser the 'Konisberg'. It wasn't allowed near, we'd just to rendez-vous with them out at sea. Then there was *Der Tag*. That was the big day when they scuttled their fleet.

Meantime on the Home Front, taut and anxious families were trying to live as near normally as possible with shatteringly long lists of casualties appearing in newspapers, and hapless telegram boys becoming as feared as the lists themselves. It's hard for generations used to 'phone, radio and television links to imagine the slow transmission of news to such as the Macfadyen household in Lismore.

My brother Donald was in the navy and his ship was struck by a mine in the Baltic. Of course there were no radio news bulletins and it was a while before we heard of it. He'd been on the bridge and they'd just fifteen minutes to get to the boats, then they rowed to one of the islands. My father heard news in Glasgow that he was safe.

Then my brother John, that had worked on our boat with my father, had to go to the navy too.

Meantime Father had to do his best without his 'mate' on his own small cargo boat.

My father traded during war in his wee boat to Tiree. There weren't regular boats so he did a lot of the carrying . . . different things and other runs to what he had in peacetime.

Another man who made his own contribution to the war effort was one recalled by Jim Buchan.

There was this man in Peterhead used to run horses in big boats from Canada to France . . . he was a great horse-man . . . had been a horse-drawn mail coach driver.

Whatever the routine of life at home it was constantly punctuated by bad news.

I was about ten in Troon when the First War started. The school was commandeered and we used the church halls. But I can remember better, the telegrams coming with word of deaths and woundings, and the newspaper lists. We knew a lot of the names because the 17th H.L.I. was billeted in Troon houses before they went to France. I remember

them marching through the town in their khaki. And what a slaughtering they went to ... and they were mainly just office-boys from Glasgow.

But there were activities and interests too that were pleasanter by-products of the war ... never-to-be-forgotten memories laid down in young minds like Isobel Cameron's.

I've clear recollections of the early days of the First War at Lochgilphead, and the boat bringing the newspapers not being in until the afternoon, with the day-before's news. But folk were anxious to have it the same day and so the Post Office started to get a telegram with the latest news and put it up in the window at seven, every evening. My father used to take me down there with him to read it. I loved that walk ... with me skipping beside him down the brae, because on the way he used to tell me the names of all the stars ... The Plough and The Pleiades (that's the Seven Sisters) and The Milky Way ... lovely names to a small child. To me, it wasn't really so much the telegram as the *going* to see it. You could *see* all the stars in country or sea-shore places without smoke or lights to distract you.

It was none of your intangible heavenly bodies that thrilled young James Pryde during his wartime boyhood.

During the war there was part of the Seaforth Highlanders in Lewis, called the Ross Mountain Battery. They were an artillery battery and they carried guns and ammunition on groups of three horses ... Highland garrons, they were, smaller than ordinary horses but bigger than Shetland ponies. There were lots of garrons on the islands that were taken into this Ross Battery along with the local boys. The garrons had special saddles. One of the three carried the gun, one the gun wheels and the third the ammunition. When they went to Gallipoli they could climb the mountains. I remember as a boy seeing them on exercises.

One of the skills the womenfolk had to contribute had the bonus of earning them at least a pittance, at the same time as whiling away days of anxious waiting.

In the days of the 'milishy' at Muir of Ord market, there used to be great piles of knitting wool for handing out to the Beauly and other local women to knit stockings without feet, for the milishy hose-tops. They were paid ninepence a pair and the wool was in 'cuts', not ounces like it is now. All the women knitted as busily as they could, to do two or three pairs between markets to make a few pennies.

The older men too had their wartime tasks to help eke out rations. Some kept hens, others 'dug for victory'.

> In the war the Polo Park in Troon was made into 'plots' ... vegetable allotments, y'know. A lot had plots there ... Father did and so did the schoolmaster.

So that was the stars, the garrons, the knitting and the turnips to occupy the very young, the lads not old enough for service but passionately interested in its trappings, the mothers waiting for news and the fathers fretting for their sons. But what of the girls, whose natural village companions for the pictures, the dancing or the wooing, were far away? Some pined dutifully. Others did not. Margaret Ritchie speaks with a ring of frank recollection in her voice.

> I was at school in Inverness during the First War and my girl-friends' older sisters had a rare time with the soldiers training in the town, that they met at dances. But the local boys were away. Then after a while the Americans came over and the girls went daft for them. There were American sailors too, based at the Caledonian Canal and of course when our own boys came home on leave they found a lot of girls off with the Americans. I remember there was a big fight over that and the Americans were confined to barracks after it. Oh these Inverness boys were angry! My own friend's sister married an American and when he came back on leave to Inverness he'd to change from his own uniform into her brother's suit to disguise himself ... but he still had yon American roll when he walked.

But the end was in sight and, when the 11th November 1918 dawned, windows in the cities were flung open ready for the ringing of bells and the eruption into the streets. But the news was slower and quieter reaching outland places. Mrs. Pryde remembers how it was in her part of Lewis.

> There was no telegraph in Bernera in those days. All the war news would've come by Morse Code and I remember that's how word of the Armistice came to the Post Office.

Even in a small town, like Troon ...

> When the Armistice came I remember being taken to see the notice at the Post Office.

But whether the news was slow in trickling through or not, the celebrations were just as heartfelt.

> We'd a great bonfire, and seeing that going up is one of the most vivid things I mind best from all my life. Folk were laughing and crying at the same time.

Tragedy had a last fling before the decade was out and John Leitch was one who was almost part of another toll.

> When I got back from my years in the army I took yon bad 'flu that hit Britain just immediately after the war. Thousands died in that. I remember the doctor standing at the foot of the bed and warning me in Latin 'Festina lente' he said. So that was me. I 'hastened slowly' and I'm still here.

At ninety-five.

If there was little flagwaving hullabaloo in Beauly when the First War came in 1914 there was absolutely none in 1939. The veteran survivors of Passchendale and the Somme had scarcely seen their children grow up when the great maw of war yawned again to devour their sons.

But, like their fathers, they were, for the most part, willing to do what was required of them, with even those who conscientiously objected to taking life, prepared to risk their own. As in the First War most of the men who went away from coastal and marginally inland areas went to sea ... like Jim Buchan from Peterhead.

> I spent the war at sea. Two and a half years of it in a tanker going between Freetown, Lagos and Durban, fuelling at sea.

Not an occupation that seemed likely to have the crew face to face with the enemy.

> But when we were off Africa, there was a crowd of German P.O.Ws to be brought back to Britain from Durban on our ship, and we all got issued with revolvers. 'If any of them start giving trouble or running about, shoot them in the head'. Nobody did. They were nice enough fellows, but it fairly brought 't home to us what shooting 't kill was.

James Pryde was at sea too.

> I went through the war in the Merchant Navy. Funny when you look back, it's mostly the good times you remember, although a lot of it was

dull routine. I was in Haifa in Palestine for months and in that time I'd just four trips away, to Port Said and Alexandria and back, carrying supplies. We just sat most of the rest of the time waiting for word to go. You couldn't do anything ... go anywhere, explore Palestine or improve your general knowledge of the areas. But I suppose it's better to have memories of boredom than have bad ones.

Even the coast people at home saw and heard more of naval action than that. Peter Sinclair recalls an incident in Benderloch Bay, north of Oban, that has gone into local annals.

There were a lot of ships congregated there to go out into the Atlantic in convoy. Well, this ship was loaded with goods for India, and horses; and there was a bombing raid. It escaped into Benderloch Bay, but it sank there and the horses got loose and started to swim ashore. A lady, a Mistress MacNiven, lived in a cottage at Dunstaffnage Castle and she went out quite a depth into the water to lead them in safely. She got an award for that.

At that time too, Farquhar MacDonald was living in a sensitive area where there were naval manoevres.

We were in Kyle of Lochalsh then, and that area round Loch Alsh was what they called a Number One Protected Area. If you lived there you'd to have a pass as well as your ordinary Identity Card, to get in and out by sea or road or train ... right through the war that was. I remember in Lochalsh too there were four or five big Merchant Navy ships converted to mine-layers and they went out into the Atlantic. The base H.M.S. Trelawney was on shore, but 't was H.M.S. all the same. I remember, when we were in school one day, one of these mine-layers blew up and we heard the explosion from the classroom. That ship went down with hundreds of mines on board ... lay there for many years before it was salvaged.

Another time the siren went off and everyone thought a U-boat had got through the boom defence at the lighthouse. The very idea of a U-boat in Loch Alsh ... well! It was a false alarm of course.

Of course it was. The Lighthouse Service was surely more alert than that. The light-towers were, in their way, a front line bastion of defence as look-outs. They even had their own uniforms for the 'duration', as John MacRae recalls.

During wartime the lighthouses were painted black. The Scapa Flow one and the ones on the Outer Hebrides were particularly important

and the lights were lit only when the Admiralty told you, and that'd be for a convoy going by. Even in the dead of winter it was total black-out but for that. Then, as well as the normal peace-time work, you'd to look out for enemy shipping and so on.

It was very eerie in the light-room with no light on, and you'd still your regular turns of going out to check from the balcony. That was in the dark too, and so quiet ... so eerie.

Small backwaters like those where the lights were planted and villages on far points of land, took on a new importance because of their strategic positions. Even the Home Guard which, perhaps unfairly, provoked mirth in suburban or city locations, had a serious purpose when it was close to quiet, deserted beaches and bays.

It was quite important at Ness, the Home Guard; because it was a kind of outer point of Britain and landings for invasion could maybe have been made there.

And Jim Still reports that in the north-east, too, being in the Home Guard was a serious business.

I had to stay working on the farm in the war, but I was in the Local Defence Volunteers when that started up after Dunkirk (the L.D.V.). It came to be the Home Guard after a whilie. Right-enough we trained w' wooden rifles but we were good 't it. The Head Forester on the estate was automatically the Sergeant. He'd been in the 1914-18 war. We learned a lot really and some 't were military-minded were real keen. Th' was map-reading and various war exercises, y'know ... away for a week or two to do a stint of training ... all over the north.

There were good reasons to think that their area might be vulnerable.

There was quite a bit of bombing round Peterhead ... two or three killed and various buildings blown up. Of course a lot of convoys came past, and they used to say if the German pilots missed the ships, they didnae want to go home w' their bombs and just dropped them on the town.

The Peterhead folk did get something of their own back when a German submarine sank just off-shore.

How it sank was quite funny. In a submarine when the crew 'do their business, y'know' they put a lid on the toilet, screw it down and open a valve so everything blows out. Well, the story was that at the time this submarine was here, the Germans were getting down to manning them with quite raw crews. And this inexperienced Jerry opened the wrong valve so 't everything blew *in* ... sea and all ... and the sub sank. That was the story anyway. They were taken prisoner and one of the local

men, Farquhie Slessor, said he would've hung that sailor there and then
for the nuisance of that sub lying so near to shore.

There could be danger as well as nuisance in what lurked around the
shore or in the sea.

A lot of the Fife men carried on with the fishing as what they called a
Reserved Occupation or Essential Work. And a lot of them were a wee
bit older, too, than go for soldiers. They didna take me so I went fishing
off the Isle of Man, Ayr, Girvan, Ballantrae and Dunoon. I s'pose it was
dangerous but we didna think.

Although the navy and merchant service absorbed most of the
seabound conscripts and volunteers, some did go into other
branches.

I went to the army and was in France and Belgium after D-Day and the
Far East, but sometimes it's the funny things you remember. When we
were training we used to get hard tack biscuits once a week ... I suppose
to get us used to the idea that food might not always come the way
you'd think of as a meal. Anyway, when they came round with those, all
the men would start barking.

I went into the R.A.F. and I was posted for a time near Oban. That was
the first time I'd ever lived in the country or at the sea-side, but I went
back to stay there after.

He was one of the friendly invasion of airmen well-remembered
around the town and in Connel village. Peter Sinclair recalls them
there.

The R.A.F. was over the other side of the bridge between South and
North Connel. There is still a wee air-strip there. And the Sunderland
flying-boats were based at Oban ... flew on missions to Norway from
there.
    Actually the village that's Dunbeg now, was started in the war when
the airmen were stationed there. It developed from some of the men
staying on and from the ones that came to work at the floating dock ...
and from local people moving in, after the war.

As the presence of those floating-dock workmen indicates, not
everyone who was posted away from home was in the services. In
1939 in Largo, Alex Archer had just finished his apprenticeship as a
joiner.

I got called up and sent to London to live in a hostel in Kensington w'

hundreds of others from the north and the south, and Devon and
Cornwall, all-over, really. And that was me for the war, doing emer-
gency repairs to bombed houses during the blitz ... east-end mostly. It
was bombs first, then the rockets ... saw some terrible damage. You
went to streets where the people were still living with no windows and
maybe not much roof. We worked in squads and each squad'd get
maybe a street or two streets to see to. What a mess! Some were only
half-streets when we got there ... and half-rubble.

When the flying bombs came over you used to hear them up there ...
then they'd cut out and you'd wait for the big bang and hope it wasnae
for you! We got a week-end leave about every eight weeks. For the rest
of the time, Saturdays and Sundays, a' day ... every day ... you were
kept at it all the time.

But not too incessantly to stop him doing his courting.

I met my wife in London. We courted there during the war and got
married. Then she came here and liked it fine. She was a person 't could
adapt herself verra well.

His girl was posted away too, for a time.

She worked at the Royal Mint where they were making coins and bank
notes. They were evacuated from London to get on with the job where
it was safer.

Nurses, too, found themselves in unlikely places transformed into
wartime hospitals.

I had trained in Edinburgh and worked in Glasgow, then during the war
I nursed in the Turnberry Hotel that had been taken over as a hospital.

Even the children found themselves uprooted and in very uncon-
genial countryside and seaside surroundings that compared ill with
their own cobbled grey stamping grounds and the grim tenements
that were home. Who wanted fox-gloves and seathrift and the eerie
sobbing of oyster-catchers, when their peever beds and back-courts
were waiting empty in the city? The Tuesday Club at Ballantrae
recalls the sorry little travellers arriving at Ballantrae.

Oh yes, we'd evacuees here, but they didn't last long ... wanted home. I
can remember going to see to them at the school when they arrived.
Some were fine ... spotless, but others ... well! *They*'d just to be
cleaned up. But there just wasn't enough for them here ... no fish and
chip shops or pictures. They wanted home, and you couldnae blame
them.

It wasn't only the Glasgow weans that found themselves trans-
planted and confused. Another batch who were posted to strange
surroundings was the vanguard of American servicemen stationed
at Troon, and writing their first letters home to the New World,
not yet thoroughly understanding the Old.

> We'd Americans billeted in Troon and there was one boy sent to a
> cottage up the road there at Loans village (there's just a few houses
> there). Anyway this cottage had the building date over the door ...
> 1830, and when he wrote home he gave his billet address as,

> 1830, Main Street,
> Loans, Troon.

> And mind you there were only a few dozen people in Loans altogether.

Those, then, were the folk who were in, or near, the stir of action;
or training ready for it. But there were all those stay-at-home
people, the great back-up, not only to maintain ordinary life but to
take on special wartime tasks that fell to citizens not uprooted from
home. Farquhar MacDonald recalls a mammoth task in Kyle of
Lochalsh and a war hero well up to handling it.

> There was just the one policeman in Kyle of Lochalsh during the war,
> when it was crowded with servicemen. One policeman ... to keep them
> in some sort of order in the village, round the pubs and bars. There were
> so many they'd to stand outside in groups of twenty or thirty. And the
> one sergeant tamed the whole lot.

Maybe the sight of three stripes was enough.

And that's a glimpse of their war, their watershed ... the people
of machar villages and near-shore crofts. Some who went away
never came back, there or anywhere; some stayed away finding their
future in places they'd never have known but for war ... some came
back to go a-fishing again or carry on the other traditions of their
forefathers. But even there the world was no longer the same.
Fishing-boats were powered, and faster, so that long weeks at sea
were over.

And Jim Still sums up the changes on the land.

> It was the war really, put farming on its feet. During that time the
> Agriculture people went round all the farms advising about ploughing
> and different new farming ways that were better. Yes, it was the war. It's
> a shame to say that ... but I think it was.

19
Dry Whins in the Chimney

Not many city folk, with switches to flick for everything, pine now for the demanding days of home-life up the close, seventy or eighty years ago, with long washing and cleaning over a black range, or rising in a frosty dawn to light the fire under the wash-house boiler. But, in comparison with the rigours of life for their contemporaries on the sea-rims of Scotland and in the croft and farm country, they lived the life of Reilly in towns, with coal tipped into their very kitchens and water pouring from tap to jawbox.

Take the fire ... it's not just a couthy term of folklore that, in much older days than those remembered here, they called it the 'need' fire, for it was the essential heart of home, and its keeping, in the various exactly required states, of prime importance.

> My mother cooked on an ordinary fire with a chain for the soup or porridge pot. She baked too, and there was a lot of footering about with the fire to get it red, or low, or roaring, or slow-slow ... whatever way she needed it to make that partic'lar thing.

The earliest remembered cooking-places were open fires with various kinds of gadgetry to make the most of them ... certainly some kind of bars in front like a basket, to contain them. The hearth recalled by Andrew Fairnie in the three-roomed cottage at Fisherrow was like that, and its tending was a family craft.

> When my mother went out with the creel and my father was away at the fishing, I was the eldest and in charge of the five of us, and the fire. It was a high fire with bars across the front. You raked the burnt coals through into a big ash-can under it, that was emptied every day. But the fire was kept going. After Mother was away, we'd get up and get our breakfast ... a roll and a cup of tea, and away to school. Mother would've left something for our dinner, stovies or mince y'ken, or something like

168

that, for heating up on the open fire. There was what we called a 'gethering coal'. H'you ever heard o'a gethering coal? A lump in the fire that kept a bit heat in it during the day, then when you came in you just gave it a wee chop up and the flames burst through. We put the pot on that.

That 'raking-through' with poker on ribs was called 'riping' in Ayrshire and Jean Durnie 'minds her granny fine' at a similar hearth in Ardrossan, that she had worked over since her marriage in the 1870s.

I loved going to my granny's to get a tea-biscuit and butter with carroway seeds, carvey y'ken, and sitting at her grate. It was just two white slabs and a few wee bars; with a swee over the open fire that she drew in and out.

And it's not so long since that kind of arrangement was still to be seen at Peter Sinclair's croft above Loch Etive where the old byre that had been his grandfather's cottage still had a square chimney hole at each gable and, at one, a chain and hook still hanging there.

Small wonder the Granny's Hielan' Hame-and-Bannock images of Scotland still flicker so persistently for exiles or their offspring. Because even at home, those who have eye-level ovens and split-height hobs, and the micro-wave pinging that their pizzas are done to a turn, have sharp childhood memories of grannies in rural hamlets everywhere, stooping and stoking and cooking at peat fires under thatch roofs. These deft-handed women were swinging hobs and swees in and out, stirring broths, flapping girdle scones and curling oatcakes in ten thousand such homes in Harris, Orkney, the North-east and all over the South, even as late in some places as the 'thirties and 'forties.

I remember my Granny Campbell (this would be in the 1900s) at Kishorn cooking at her peat fire in their thatched cottage. It had a swinging hook and she baked scones and pancakes and oatcakes over that.

The scones were no genteel tea-time luxury. It was bread itself that was that.

Once a week, just, we got bought bread. A slice of that was quite a treat to us.

And Isobel Wales describes their open fire from the 'thirties.

> At Ness we had this fireplace with irons that we blackleaded, between
> pillars that we used to whitewash. It had what people call a 'swee', but
> we said a 'cran', with the hook for the black three-legged pot. I
> remember the broth coming out of that, and the clootie dumplings, and
> the black pudding made from the innards of a sheep.

There were other utensils for producing particular local dishes to a
succulent nicety. There's the memory from Macduff of something
they called a 'brander' in the days before the First War.

> D'you ken what a brander was? It was for roasting fish. It was
> something like a carpet beater but woven w' wire instead of cane. When
> I was wee I canna remember ever a frying-pan being in our house. When
> the fire was just right ... red, with no flames, the fish w' a wee dab of
> butter in it was laid on this brander and you held that over the fire to get
> roasted fish. My, that was good! There was a toaster too that cleeked to
> the ribs in front of the fire and you sat your slice of bread against it and it
> was lovely.

It all sounds couthy and homely ... satisfying somehow in the
hindsight of those who never experienced it ... very ethnic. But
Hugh Craigie's real memories are not so cosy.

> The kitchens in some Orkney houses could be as black's soot, for there
> was the big open fireplace so high that the chimney, such as it was,
> wouldn't draw. The smoke curled round the room and the roof beams
> were a' blackened. There was a house we used to go to and you could
> hardly see the family, the room was so full of smoke. And the whole lot
> o' them had bad eyesight. I used to think it was maybe w' that smoke.
> Your eyes smarted in't anyway.

But furnaces were blazing on the River Carron and the Cavalry
was on its way to rescue the luckier ones from their slavery, with the
ingenious delights of the kitchen range and its various amazing
devices. They should surely have reached Merkland farm near
Ballantrae by the 'twenties but Jenny Stewart shakes a rueful head
and we can pause to take a last look with her at the open fire for
cooking.

> Everyone else had a range by them and our landlord would've put one in
> for us, no bother. But my old uncle was so bigoted he wouldn't hear of
> such a thing, such a luxury ... too easy wi' yourself, that was.

Well, too easy for his hardpressed womenfolk anyway. And yet it's a proud and shrewd picture Jenny Stewart draws of the art her mother made of such drudgery, already out of date by the 'teens of the century.

> It was a very old-fashioned upbringing, in a very old-fashioned farm-house.
>
> The fireplace was the two jambs, big stones each side, that the ribs were set into and they would all be black-leaded ... ribs *and* jambs. Then swinging across you'd the arm and hook. All the cooking was done on that, and the baking. You'd a girdle and you'd to let the fire die down till it was consistent red all over, then she baked pancakes and oatmeal tattie scones an' that.

And just to show that young Jenny McCrindle was much too sensible to kick over all the traces of a hard rearing, she adds,

> I still make oatmeal tattie scones. It's a kind of speciality. When there's a 'do' on here in Ballantrae, they just say 'Mrs. Stewart'll make oatmeal tattie scones'.

And she went on to describe another contraption that her mother used for 'oven' as distinct from 'girdle' baking.

> We'd what she called an oven pot. It was a huge great big pot that went on the swee ... maybe seven-eight inches deep with a lid that protruded for about four inches all round. In that you put your cake or your shortbread. Then you took away half of the fire, put the pot on what was left, then shovelled the other half of the hot coals on to the pot lid ... so you'd fire on top and fire under, but not round the sides. The pot had a huge handle and we'd a pair of long, long tongs to lift the lid and see how it was doing ... quite a feat to do that and keep the fire on the lid. It was *beautiful*, gorgeous baking, that.

There was nothing so scientific, either, as the *sweep* to clean that much used chimney when it was hanging with soot.

> We never had the sweep ... just put the chimney on fire ... stuck papers or a bundle o' dry whins in the chimney and up it went!

But even if the great-uncle at Merkland did not tolerate such decadence, elsewhere the range, either small and simple or big and versatile, was the new 'in' thing.

> There was the fire in the middle of the range in a well behind the bars and there was a hot plate on the top. There was a lever to open or shut

the fire that heated the oven at the side and there was a wee hot water tank at the other side wi' a tap to it to fill your jug or whatever. There was no other hot water in the house.

The old chores were out, but the range brought a new batch and a new demand for elbow smeddum. Andrew Fairnie remembers an early range they had in Musselburgh.

> A Saturday was my mother's morning for black-leading the grate and emerying the steel trimmings. Then she pipe-clayed the hearth to make it white and clean.

And Isobel Craigie remembers another way of polishing the steel parts at Turriff.

> I mind being sent up the hill road to get fine sand to clean the steel bit on the range.

After years of the open fire with the steel fender round it, Mary Macfadyen recalls that her father put in a small range at their croft on Lismore.

> That made the baking easier but I remember my mother sweating over her emery-rubbing and bath-brick. And she'd still the same rule for us all about the kettle.
> 'Now when any of you take hot water out that kettle remember and put the same back in cold'. So that we'd always hot water, for that was all there was ... no hot running water.

At Oban, Thurso, Girvan, Fife, the Moray Firth and all points between, over the years from 1880 to the 1920s, contractors and plumbers built in ranges of whatever sophistication. And there were reasons besides cost for the choice of size. The Stills had a big one at Forglen.

> The reason it was big was that when the laird had a shoot on, the beaters and shooters used to meet in the house for their meal. The beaters an' that, ate in the kitchen and the laird and gentry through the house in the room. I remember my mother in her long skirt w' the apron over 't, serving soup out the big pot for them. I remember that big range had hobs at the side and I can still see the maid sitting (like Polly Flinders) on one of the hobs warming herself at the fire ... like on a stool. And there was a great big kettle. One of my earliest recollections is the sore toe 't I got when it fell on my foot. I'll not forget that kettle easily.

Another big kettle was remembered in Troon, but this time on another popular advance over the open fire.

> My mother spent a lot of time and effort on baking and cooking. Besides scones and pancakes there was gingerbread and treacle scones. Then there was the pan-haggis, hough and suet puddings, and the porridge every day. On birthdays you got your favourite dinner and a clootie dumpling. She cooked all that on a big American stove that could take four pots as well as the kettle. I remember that the kettle had marbles in it to keep it from furring up.

There were American stoves too, recalled and described in memories of Buchan and Lewis.

> It was a great thing, the American stove. It stood out from the wall on small legs, free-standing, and it had hotplates and a double oven at the sides. Ours in Bernera burned peats. It was like a range really, but not built-in.

> 'Ours at Turriff was black and it had round plates that you levered out to feed the fire inside.

Let's leave them there, then, before we lose the 'feel' of those heart-warming kitchens with the open fires ... or those glowing black monsters of stoves that welcomed the clutches of children shivering in from school of a winter afternoon ... and sent menfolk out to first-light labours well-lined with brose. Let's leave them before the coming of the prissy little gas cookers that were as cold as charity the moment the taps were turned off after meals.

> 'Away wi' you!' says the voice of a liberated owner, 'That first gas ring we had in the 1930s was the greatest thing ever and I wasnae sorry to see the back of yon old range.'

20
I'm H-A-P-P-Y

Now 'the winter is past', school books are snapping shut 'the voice of the turtle is heard in the land' and entertainment has come from halls and parlours to the great outdoors.

For the young of eighty years ago one of the season's early highlights was the Sunday School trip. The small Buchans, Mima and Gena, went on theirs from St. Combs.

> We went on a horse-drawn lorry. The horse a' dressed up, its mane decorated w' rosettes and ribbons ... and there's us sittin' up the back of the lorry on straw, w' our legs danglin' over the side.

Shoreland bairns knew more about the logistics of Sunday School trips than most, because, not only did they go *on* them, they also saw the tinnied hordes arrive from the towns and knew how they were fed, sheltered in rain or deployed along the foreshore in each school's allocated stretch.

> The last two Saturdays in May, and all of June there were invasions of Sunday School trips, catered by local bakers with bags of hot pies or sausage rolls, buns and cakes and urns of tea for the teachers, all delivered at a certain time to the right picnic. The visitors 'd always a church hall booked for fear of rain. They paddled in the sea and had their races on the beach. And when we saw the first of these trips coming we began to itch for our own.

Since it was all local 'hands on deck' to cope with the incomers on all the available Saturdays, the Troon youngsters had a day off school to go for theirs, mid-week.

> It was always the third Wednesday in June and all the shops were shut. All the Troon Sunday Schools went the same day on special trains with streamers at the windows, so teachers had a job of it to see the children didn't get mixed up. We'd all our new tinnies round our necks (or if times were a wee bit hard we'd at least new tapes on last year's tinnies!)

A farmer in our church gave the milk for the tinnies. We usually went to
Culzean or Montgreenan and we ran races. The prizes used to be
thruppence, tuppence and a penny, but-here some worthy soul got the
notion that you shouldn't run for money and after that it was sweeties
... but that wasnae the same at all!

At the end of the trip you were sent to clear the field ... not a scrap of
rubbish to be left, and if it was an estate you were at, you all stood in
front of the big house, maybe Lord and Lady Glenarthur's, and gave
three cheers (mind you, p'raps they weren't even at home).

So although the trip might not have been a very sophisticated
outing it was certainly a civilised one; and, give or take a teachers'
race or some dire mislaying of the eggs-and-spoons, each was a
carbon copy of all others ... miracles, mostly, of timing, feeding,
programming and rounding up.

When I hear folk say somethin's a dawdle ... as easy as organizing a
Sunday School trip ... I have to laugh and wonder if they've ever tried
it.

As summer wore on there were family picnics and outings.

I remember going on picnics away up the back of Connel here. We'd a
fire for boiling the kettle and we went to the farmhouse for milk. They
were lovely picnics, up there among the hills. We used to go in and see
the cows being milked and get a glass of warm milk after. I liked the *idea*
but I wasn't so keen on the warm milk.

I remember once, too, learning a wee lesson at Benderloch, and me
gathering beautiful heather on an outing there and bringing this lovely
heather home, then finding that the heather here at Connel, that I'd
never noticed before, was just as good.

The Archers from Largo went on interesting family excursions
that were a perk of Father's job.

My father worked on the railway and got free passes. So we used to go
on what was called 'Number 5 tour' up Loch Lomond. You went on the
boat where th'was a wee band playing and they came round with velvet
collecting bags ... just the day away. For real holidays I went to
Polmont to see m' other granny.

It wouldn't really have much mattered to young Alex Archer where
the boat was going or whether the tour was Number 5, 6 or 7.

You spent most of your time downstairs watching the engines and
paddles working, big, polished, bright, clean engines. I mind the man

smokin' his pipe and waiting for the ping-ping-ping! That was the order from the bridge to shift the levers, SLOW...REVERSE...BACK... FORWARD. Th' was wee wee gangways the men went up and down w' the oilcans, aye seein' to the moving-parts. Every time the big part of the engine came scooshing down it passed across this cloth that was all oily ... I remember that quite plain ... and hearing the paddles swishing round. Oh aye, downstairs on the 'Jeanie Deans' was the best.

Not all fathers had access to trains and paddle steamers but there was something to be said for fathers like Jim Still's who had their own transport, even if it wasn't a hundred percent reliable.

He didna bother about social life but they both liked runs in the car, up Loch Ness maybe. Their first car was a 'Galloway' w' running boards and big lamps, but it was always breaking down.

Where there were small resorts summer visitors brought a bonus to the locals with the arrival of seaside entertainers. Alex Archer recalls other thrills than the engines of the 'Jeanie Deans'.

The 'shows' came to Blacketyside, and aeroplanes for pleasure flips. I can remember seeing a man standing, his arms spread out to hold on, y'know ... no' verra high, mind.

But high enough.

The shows at Saltcoats offered Jean Kane and her friends various other opportunities as well as a sight of the Big Wheel or the Waltzer.

We'd a great carry-on. We'd never any money, but we liked the hurdy-gurdy music. And then sometimes you met someb'dy and you got treated ... a fella, y'know.

When the circus arrived at Connel it wasn't quite the Big Top but it was thrill enough.

We'd a circus came to Connel every year. It was just a small travelling circus in a tent but I remember the horses and ponies and performing dogs ... and the boards put down for us to sit on.

At a query about elephants there was a kindly laugh.

Oh there was no elephant or anything. It's a long way to bring an elephant!

Well, Ben Cruachan is hardly the Alps but, no, it wouldn't be easy to bring an elephant to Connel.

But there used to be one at Troon.

The circus came once a year to Troon ... and the animals, the horses and elephants, the man on stilts and the clowns, all paraded through the street to music. That was to advertise themselves.

And as long ago as the 1880s that Netta Ross remembered, the circus came to Beauly.

Beauly Square was just common ground when I was young in the 1880s. Menageries came and the circus, giraffes, camels, elephants and everything.

It's not easy to imagine exotic animals in placid, douce little Beauly Square. And there were even more unlikely sinful things going on around the village, but there's a recollection or two of more innocent pleasures to uncover, from other places, before we look at Beauly's more dramatic secrets.

Back down in Ayrshire communities had their fairs with side-shows and produce booths, toffee pulling, cheese and fruit stalls and the exchange of arling money.

There was the Marymas Fair at Irvine in September, and in Kilmarnock, the Curd Fair with all the cheeses in May, and then the Grosset Fair in July.

Concerts in cold halls on winter nights had their charms but they did not compare with the thrill of seeing beautiful artistes in performance on makeshift stages out-of-doors and then catching glimpses of such stars in the flesh on the streets, between shows.

We had Madam Campbell's Concert Party came to the sand to enter-tain, and you all went there ... the trick was to skedaddle before they came round with the collecting bag.

Then there was the Pierrot show at the Ballas' Bank in Troon here, down at the front. (D'you know about the Ballas' Bank? It's a bank of ground that's supposed to have soil on it from all over the world, that boats coming into Troon brought as ballast in their holds). Well, there were pierrots there for the season, just a wee show under canvas.

There were concert parties wherever summer holidaymakers were part of the local economy, and what boy or girl would not have envied the young Archers their intimacy with the great and glamorous?

There used to be pierries in Largo at the harbour and-here these pierries

lodged with this friend of my father's and we got to know them and got
to dress up in their fancy clo'es along at his house.

Even the pierries' landlord himself was worth a passing mention for
providing unrehearsed entertainment for the Archers.

Yon man that had the pierries lodging, he made elderberry wine, I
remember, and kept nanny goats. He used to put the elderberry wine
bottles under the bed to mature and ferment. And-here once they all
burst and the corks got blown out and the wine shot everywhere.

Quite what part, if any, the nanny goat played in the drama was not
revealed.

In the mornings and when there wasn't a matinée from a concert
party, a rollicking hour could be had on the beach.

I thought the summer mission was better'n the pierries.

And Margaret Kirk in Ballantrae says 'Amen' to that.

Oh yes, the summer missions were rare.

In Troon too.

There was the Albatross Mission here, and you played games and
learned choruses and action songs:-
   'I'm H-A-P-P-Y, I'm H-A-P-P-Y,
   I know I am,
   I'm sure I am,
   I'm H-A-P-P-Y.'
Yes, the Albatros was a kind of forerunner of the seaside missions they
have now.

Between 'houses' of the concert-parties there were donkeys and
rowing-boats; and penniless local boys earned a copper or two, and
tasted a little power into the bargain, as they helped the boat-
keepers to push out their clients or signal-in dilatory hirers with
angry elbow gestures and threatening shouts 'Come in the "Mary
Jane".'

And if the local brass band was up to an outing, the young of the
village trooped with the rest to whatever served as a bandstand.

But what was that hint about the nefarious occupations that
fascinated the Beauly of a century ago ... and much less?

George Sutherland was first to let dab about those.

In the glens that open out at Beauly it's not so long since illicit distilling was very common and there was great ongoings between the distillers (smugglers they called them) and the excisemen. There used to be 'holes' where they'd their stills and hid their casks. I've been in one ... away underground, and you wouldn't credit how beaut'fully it was built ... like a beehive, ten feet high and about twenty across and there was a small burn running alongside. That 'still' ran for about twenty years. Another man ran one very near here for years, and when he finished up he sold the fittings to the plumber at Muir of Ord ... told me so himself.

The truth of his recollections was confirmed by his friend Donald MacKintosh.

There used to be quite a bit of that smuggling in the village here itself ... as well as up Strathglass way ... *in a certain house.*

and the sense that this was no 'once upon a time' tale was heightened by the wheeshting warning from the third party to the conversation, Netta Ross.

Mentioning no names ...

When the liquor was brewed to their satisfaction the smugglers hid it in dips and crannies, old bothies, in thatching, under beds and in bunkers.

They said that some of th'excisemen kept a few pots hidden themselves, planked here and there because if there came times when they couldn't produce some illicit whisky they'd taken from a smuggler, they might lose their jobs. So they'd always a planking, for if they were having a lean time.

If Jim Buchan ever attended the equivalent of the Albatross Mission at Peterhead its message didn't stop him from falling into one small temptation.

When I was a loonie, where we're sittin' now was a' fields that seemed miles away from the town and the sea. It isna, of course, but it was a' crofts then and I used to come up and steal peas.

On an odd occasion in most places there was a one-off spectacular that entertained briefly and was never forgotten. Ella Sutherland remembers one of those from her very early years at the beginning of the century.

I left Beauly when I was about three, so it was before that, and it was one of my very first memories ... a big fire at the Priory Hotel near our house. My brother and sister and I were taken out of our beds and I can remember seeing the flames and hearing the cracking of the bottles when they burst with the heat. I'll never forget that.

Perhaps more than 'one-off' were occasional entertainments provided where there was a boat-yard.

A launch was a great sight and we used to rush down to watch the boat sliding off the stocks into the water.

But an hour or two spent with a ball was as universal a pastime within sound of the sea as elsewhere.

I d'na ken aboot other places but th' was an affa lot o' games, football, hockey an' that, there in yon field behind the sea-wall.

When it came to sports, team against team or simply man against nature, there were year-round pursuits from Orkney to Portpatrick, Ness to Berwick-on-Tweed ... football certainly in all of them. Hugh Craigie played on Rousay.

I was mad on footb'll, played in the Rousay team ... we played against teams from the other islands.

And the local teams were well supported in their day by those at the Ballantrae Tuesday Club.

Th' was three football teams hereaboots ... a Laggan team, a Glenapp team and a Ballantrae team, and th' were great competition between them.

Sometimes there was an excursion from Connel to the Big Time footb'll.

We used to go to Glasgow, sometimes, when I was a small boy ... to see the Rangers at Ibrox. We went across the Clyde on the Erskine ferry, and that was a great thing.

And those three rememberers, from north, south and halfway 'up', say it all for football. But then there was shinty. The laddies who went whistling down the brae with their boy-size shinty sticks grew up to play in man-size teams.

I played shinty for the village team as a young man ... played against Benderloch and Oban-Camanachd. Camadh means a bend in Gaelic, so they call a shinty stick a caman.

A team game, whose devotees had to bear their souls in patience for right weather, was curling, though the discipline of waiting for the frost to oblige was lost on Catherine Murray when she was young Miss MacSwan.

> The weather in those days was somehow always right for whatever you wanted to do ... freezing in the winter and sunshine in the summer for swimming. We never thought of it being just folk fitting in with what the weather did. Anyway my father was a keen curler and there was a wee pond over the other side of the loch. So they'd to row their stones across in the boats. A lot of men here curled.

And her brother Mr. MacSwan remembers the same pond.

> You didn't get to skate on the curlers' pond over the loch there. They would've chased you for that. But there was another wee pond 't we skated on in the winter. Then, like my father that was a great curler, I curled myself later.

And no doubt chased the next generation of skaters.

Perhaps the most spectacular team challenge of all (it was more of a crowd contest really) came many Ericssons ago with the seafaring Norsemen, and lodged at Kirkwall in Orkney.

> That's the Ba' Game ... purely a Kirkwall thing, still do't, of course, but I know of it from long ago. It was between the Uppies and the Doonies ... that's the Harbour end and the Laverock and Victoria Street end. Hordes of laddies played in the morning and the men later. The idea was to get the ball either in't the harbour, or to a mark at th' old castle. It's a long tussle really, up streets and down lanes. They can throw it, but mostly they smuggled it about and hid it ... went on for hours ... still does ... and th' don't stop for anything but maybe a drink.

In country or small village surroundings even more than team or mass games, there was abundant scope for loner sports, the pitting of individual wills and skills. There was the hill-walking and climbing the MacSwans tackled round Loch Etive.

> I've been to the top of Ben Lora and I've climbed Cruachan.

> I've climbed Cruachan too. I did that with some friends the day I left Connel Post Office. It was the month of May and so hot at the top we all got burned with the sun.

> You can go up Cruachan by car now. There's the track for the hydro power station.

Those who didn't earn their bread at the fishing enjoyed it more comfortably as a sport. Hugh Craigie fished for young saith or coal-fish.

We used to go catching sellags, about four inches long and very sweet. We took them home to Mother to cook. If you didn't get two-score't wasn't much worth going.

Catherine Murray's father, behind his counter most of the week, took to Loch Etive on his boat of an evening.

He used to go out fishing in the Loch, just a recreation y'know. There was a boat to most houses in Connel and we all used to go out with bamboo rods and bring in lots of cuddins (that was the name we had for coal-fish or saith). In no time we'd have a pailful that we'd take round the old folk in the village. We'd neighbours used to dry the cuddins on a string. I can just see that string of cuddins yet. Sometimes we salted them for the winter.

Loch Etive had a well-defined swimming season too.

We bathed in Loch Etive every day all summer but we always stopped after the day of the Oban Games in September. They're in August now to attract the visitors but it used to be that the Games was the end of the season.

The River Deveron flowing towards Banff was a happy hunting ground on summer days for James Still.

You used to go swimming in the Deveron. It was a wee bit dangerous in places and you'd to swim in the shallows, just. We fished for trout there too.

There were few memories of swimming among the fisher families. There was, perhaps still is, a vaguely fatalistic and super- stitious idea that, in serious accident at sea, a non-swimmer would struggle less than a swimmer to survive, and have an easier passage to drowning. But the rest plashed happily in the North Sea, Atlantic, Pentland Firth, on the Clyde coast and in the Forth; and played like seal pups off every Hebridean shore.

Those Oban Games, that marked the end of Catherine Murray's swimming season, were another social highlight, with Porage Oats wights heaving hammers about, and with small, perspiring dancing girls in kilts and velvet jackets dangling and jangling with medals.

The Oban Games was the big *thing* (still is) with the shops all closed and everyone on holiday. Mother always took a basket with sandwiches and plums and we'd sit up on the hill over Oban and watch the games. Mind you, we were more interested in the picnic and the 'shows' that we went to after ... better than the tossing the caber or the wee girls dancing.

Apart from packing the picnics and the thrill of gutting and frying the sellags and cuddins that the family trailed home, there wasn't much social life for mothers in the plethora of fisher-rows and croft-touns remembered for this book.

Hardly any recreation for the likes of my mother.

So says David Henderson of Latheronwheel.

She'd maybe just the cattle-show or the ploughing match.

What her pleasure at these 'festivals' could have been, is lost in his own warm memories of them.

The ploughing matches were all horses, of course, and that was a great competition. There was a contest for the best-dressed man and the best-dressed horse, and och ... all kind of prizes. They were usually held at the Home Farm. They'd big fields for the match ... They got their ground turned over for them, of course.

Outside social life was scant for the women of the lighthouses too.

If it was possible at all, it would just be they went away with their storm lanterns to the W.R.I. .... take maybe an hour and a half to get there for the sake of seeing some other women for an hour or so, then all the way back again. Going to the Rural was just about all there was till the wireless came. The wireless was a great thing at the lighthouses.

There was the Rural in most places. And *visiting* was a more practised art in the early decades of the century than now. Isobel Wales saw it in Lewis as a regular activity.

Recreation at Ness was really 'visiting'. That was the great social thing ... dropping in on people ... any time ... and always a cup of tea and biscuits and scones ... whatever was going.

And Hugh Craigie saw it in Orkney.

Visiting was a very big part of social life. You'd set your bike to the wall and just push open the door and walk in't another croft-house and have an hour or so's chat. The old man would just go on sitting at the fireside supping his porridge.

On the lighthouses it wasn't only the women who had to be self-reliant and find their interest close at hand during long evenings at isolated lights. John MacRae looks back to his younger days.

> The keepers themselves were mostly readers, and of course they were provided at each station with a first class tool kit ... for joinery and so on. I knew keepers who could make anything ... tables, display cabinets ... all sorts. They could take two or three years to a big intricate piece ... but then they'd all the time in the world when they were off watch. They made rag rugs, or did cross-stitch and tapestries. And outside, they fished. You'd to be very self-contained and resourceful really as a keeper.

John Leitch too remembers his father's handiwork in his Tarbert days.

> He used to spend what little spare time he had, carving sticks ... shepherd crooks. I've one here I did myself but it's just simple. His were elaborate with fine curly bits at the head ... very fine. He'd work at one of those for a long time. There were a lot of shepherds round Tarbert then.

And, his wife jogging his memory, John Leitch recalls pastimes of his sisters.

> The ladies enjoyed their sewing and handwork. His sister did that filet-lace ... did it for big families ... place mats and dressing-table sets. It was a kind of embroidery done by darning in and out of prepared squares. And d'you remember your sister Annie used to give you a penny for each square you got ready for her? That would be the easy bit ... then all the squares were put together.

Those, then, were the recreations of two or three generations ago, with perhaps bowls or a passing craze for shooting, billiards or badminton. But sometimes hobbies, sports or laid-on happenings palled, the brass band was silent, the pierrots sunbathing, the handwork laid aside. Helen McClung can see herself swinging dejectedly on the gate.

> Sometimes you wearied and didn't know what to be at, and then you went to the little burn at the back and made leaves and petals of marsh marigolds act as boats to sail down the stream. Or you gathered spawn or tadpoles in jam jars, and watched them over the next week or so till they turned into frogs.

And Ella Sutherland, now in Avoch, remembers even simpler pleasures.

> I remember long hot days in summer, walking over the warm stubble in bare feet.

The word 'bored' is not in the vocabulary of seventy and eighty-year-olds. There were interests to be found in their green years where a generation now more sated with choice, might not even look for them.

> When I worked in the Post Office and lived on Iona, there was no entertainment, no concerts, no cinema, and not many people. I spent hours on the shore, quite content, just watching the sea and the waves.

A good apprenticeship, surely, for enjoying the quiet kaleidoscope of changing light and mood Catherine Murray sees now from her window view over Loch Etive in Argyll.

21
When a Cough was Called a Host

For most folk of the days before the 1930s the first of life's dangerous confrontations was with birth itself, and for the most part survival depended on the normal presentation of the baby or the old-wife skill of an experienced, if often untrained, midwife. Most mainland communities had a home-grown 'woman' to call in and the routine was well-established from early pang to 'wetting the baby's head'. Sometimes it was the doctor who delivered the infant.

> This incident happened on the mainland of Wester Ross when the doctor went to a house to deliver a baby and he was working with the woman till the early hours of the morning. Well the baby came fine and the delighted father went to get the doctor a dram from the cupboard. It was the middle of the night by then and pretty dark. But he got out the bottle and poured out a glass each for himself and the doctor. Well, after the first taste the doctor spat it out.
> 'Whatever's this? Are you tryin' to poison me?'
> 'Och man, I'm sorry, I've given you from the bottle of seal oil.'

There was always help available on the mainland at childbirth but often islanders had to depend on boat and tide or hoof, and in the 'nineties and early days of this century, on sail, to fetch midwife or doctor. And while, no doubt, all the players in these dramas were suitably fraught at the time there's many a re-telling of them relished in hindsight, certainly by Hugh Craigie who was at the eye of this storm.

> I was born on the island of Rousay on a wild night in 1917 and there's a story of how my father went for the doctor. He'd to set off in the middle of the night with the pony and gig for six miles to catch a post-boat to Evie on the mainland of Orkney. T'would've been a sailing boat ... no motors then. He'd to get hold of the doctor, bring him back

across on the boat and then just let the pony have his head to go flat out
these six miles in the darkness to the house.

Before that there had been a midwife on Rousay; (but my birth was
wartime and there was none then) anyway there's a tale about a birth on
the neighbouring island of Egilsay where there was no midwife or
doctor. There was this farm there, with a lot of men working and the
farmer's wife the only woman, and she was expecting a baby. When the
baby was nearly coming the farmer interrupted the men's breakfast to
send them to take the boat and come to Rousay for the midwife. All the
men ran except one kinda simple chap who still sat on at his breakfast.
But the farmer chased him off after the others. As they pushed off they
discovered that the bung was missing from the boat and the water was
coming in, so they made this chap sit with his fingers in the bung-hole all
the way to Rousay and when his fingers got cold and he took them out
they shouted at him to get them back in.

As with most eventualities there were well-thought-out pro-
cedures for birth in the lighthouse service, although there may have
been little surprises at the climax of the delivery.

When there was a lighthouse birth, if the station was accessible a nurse
came in and lived with the family. It was four or five weeks when I was
born because my brother Lewis and I were twins. He was called Lewis
because he was born on Lewis.

That was birth, but at the other end of the scale there were
kenspeckle, long-lived folk who were something of a novelty in the
community.

There were a few old people in Harris. It was an airy, healthy sort of
place and there were even one or two very old ladies, over ninety, used
to help at the hay-making in their coarse blouses and cross-over shawls.

That's one of George MacGregor's abiding memories from his
young days in Harris. But old age was not the common lot of the
contemporaries of most of this book's rememberers.

I was in a graveyard not long ago and I couldna help noticing on the
headstones what a lot of youngsters died of scarlet fever and diptheria,
at one and two-year old and not much older ... and of whooping cough
... these three troubles.

Andrew Fairnie mentions only three in Musselburgh's past, all of
them killers of the very young. But except for the sturdy, destined
to live unscathed into ripe years, coming into the world at all was a

gamble, before the mycins and moulds that now preserve even the frail into aspic old age.

When a smit struck, the authorities did their best, with commonsense, isolation and purge; if not to cure at least to minimise the spread.

> There was a bad epidemic of scarlet fever in Lochgilphead, and the children who took it were sent up to the Fever Hospital, up the brae. They got their heads shaved and parents just got to see them through glass windows. And och aye, the school was closed up.

And in Largo another outbreak was of meningitis.

> One or two children at the school died. They called it fever on the brain then ... terrible in a small village ... closed the school of course.

Parents, as well as authorities, were sensitive to the dire effects insanitary play-places could have and Father Kane must have shuddered at the prospect of serious infection running through his cut-dozen offspring at Ardrossan, of whom young Jean was one.

> When I was wee th'were a lot of illnesses that you don't hear much about now. Th' was the scarlet fever and the measles and the diptheria. My father was very very strict about which part of the shore we played on ... never the south beach.

And with good reason, for beaches were not always innocent paradises. That stricture to the young Kanes was in the west, but there were taboos in the east too, and the risk was not only to children. Contaminated shores or shallows could strike indirectly, with unwary humans as vicarious victims.

> I remember when my Dad was fishing out in the Forth once and they picked up one or two oysters in their trawl and ate them. My Dad ended up ill with typhoid ... must have been infected ... raw oysters, too near sewage likely-enough. He was six weeks in hospital, isolated.

But one by one such scourges were being tamed, as Peter Sinclair remembers from a case in Connel.

> There was a tuberculosis hospital here and ever so many people in it from the country round about. And that was pretty grim because there wasn't much cure. If folk went in there ... well you could be sure ... But-here there was one Connel boy went in ... oh, about the war time ... and he made an amazing recovery when nob'dy thought he would.

So that particular litany of death-dealing infections, fevers and dwynes was tamed. But there were other things, then and since, which demanded the call-out of the doctor, and some of these one-time medics of village or island are still well remembered characters, some after seventy or eighty years, the earliest by David Henderson.

> The way I remember the doctor in the district around Latheronwheel at the beginning of the century, was riding his Arab mare. If folk wanted him he would ride that mare through anything, cornfields, hedges, ditches ... didnae matter, the Arab mare could take it. After that he got what they called a Red Indian motorbike. My! you should've seen him going round corners on that, bent over nearly level. Then he went bang! Broke both legs ... after that he got a car. That was the doctor that went up to the crash where the Duke of Kent was killed in the Second War, flying from Dunrobin to Scapa. The doctor was an old man by then and he trekked six miles up through the snow to try and help.

Another long-ago doctor is recalled by Andrew Fairnie.

> Talking of illness puts me in mind of an uncle of mine 't went to the doctor with a cough. At that time, this'd be maybe the 1890s, a cough was called a 'host' and he went for a bottle for this host and the doctor made up the bottle as they did in those days.
> 'You know, Doctor,' says my uncle, 'I would be a'right if it wasnae for my legs.'
> 'Your legs?'
> 'Aye.'
> 'How long've you had them?'
> 'Ninety year.'
> 'Well, when I've had mine ninety years I'll no' be grumblin'.'

To the north west again, twenty or thirty years later. There was a larger-than-life character striding about the hills, attending, between his other pursuits, to the health of Harris. George MacGregor lodged at his home.

> The doctor was from Nethy Bridge originally, and he was a great outdoor man, fishing, shooting, walking ... and he was a piper. Fond of a dram too ... but he was a rare doctor. I lost touch with him after that for a time and then when the National Health came in, they said he left Harris with two cases, one for his pipes and one for his whisky. He went to South Georgia after that as Medical Officer so I suppose the bleakness there would suit him just as well.

In some of the fey places of the north-west 'doctors' were not always orthodoxly degreed or registered for the task, even in Isobel Wales's days there as a child less than fifty years ago.

I can remember in Ness having what they called a King's Evil ... a big boil on my neck. My aunt sent for a seventh-son-of-a-seventh-son to come and put his hands on it, to try and heal it. He was just a man in the village and I remember thinking,
     'Here, what's this man doing touching me like that?'
     Anyway nothing happened, so they sent for another seventh-son-of-a-seventh-son, two villages away. He was too old to come so he washed his hands in a bowl of water and they brought that to me and dabbed my boil. The local doctor saw me too but the King's Evil just took its own good time to go away.

The chance of a doctor or the seventh-son-of-a-seventh-son taking to the Lighthouse Service and being on hand for illness or accident was as remote as the job itself. And so it was no such straightforward matter to take poorly there. But, efficient as ever, the officers had arrangements for calling help. John MacRae remembers those early days.

Near every lighthouse there was always a local man that was called an 'occasional keeper' and if there was trouble at the lighthouse with one of the regular men ill, he would come and act as a kind of locum. But of course you'd to get word ashore that there was something wrong and th'were some quite interesting ways of doing that. Take Ailsa Craig. At one time there were three keeper families there, and it was the job of keepers at other stations like Turnberry and Stranraer to keep an eye on Ailsa Craig, because if there was illness, there was a place on the Craig where they lit a bonfire so the smoke would be seen ashore and the Girvan life-boat with a doctor went out.

     There was another way too ... sometimes they would send a homeing pigeon with a message tied to its leg to say what the trouble was.

But new, less romantic or adventurous ways of responding were at hand and even where the S.O.S. still went out by smoke-signal and bird it was not always answered by small boat.

My father had an illness when we were stationed at Esha Ness in Shetland and he was one of the first patients to be lifted in the Renfrew Air Ambulance Service and flown from Shetland to Edinburgh.

Sometimes the call went out for help over greater sea disasters than the illness of a keeper.

I remember a Norwegian ship going down and about three days afterwards the bodies beginning to be washed in around the lighthouse. We'd to get in touch with the coast-guard and the police . . . And there was a strange kind of postscript to that. Just shortly afterwards when it was the other keeper's turn to be on watch he signalled to me.

'John there's a noise down there on the rocks like a person in distress, best go and check.'

Well, I thought on the Norwegians again and away I went out. And here's me in my sou'wester and oilskins with my storm lantern out in a wild-wild night scared stiff of this wailing and sobbing't I could hear. But-here, it was a big bull seal that had been thrown against the rocks and ripped itself open. All I could do was go for my gun and come back and shoot it.

Illness, pain and accident, all are bad enough for those in towns who are snug in modern homes a stone's throw from doctor or clinic, and only the nearest chemist's shop away from pill or potion. But in isolated villages sixty, seventy, eighty years ago, perhaps a six-mile ride away from help, there could be a dour fight to keep going until it came. And for those on islands or rock stations the whole miserable experience could be compounded by the difficulty of signalling distress to begin with, and by surly seas that could drag out the waiting time interminably.

But you'd just to dree your weerd, for that was your life, away like that fae the town.

22
Five or Six Men to Get Pieces

It's been a long time since townspeople saw the menfolk among them as trappers, hunters, woodcutters and tillers of the soil, bringing in rabbit and hare, as of need for the pot, or broadcasting their own seed to make bread. But there's still a lingering echo of all that in the memories of outlanders ... in the complications of getting necessities into their stores and girnals when they were far from centres of supply. Many were self-sufficient, but with a grimmer kind of satisfaction than the 'good-lifers' of modern cult. David Henderson stoically recalls one of his early chores.

We'd four cows so we'd good fresh milk ... and we kept a pig for our own use. It used to follow Mother about, even came into the kitchen for biscuits ... tame as anything ... until it was killed. That was a big day. I'd to hold the dish for the blood to make the puddings ... black puddings y'know. Then they 'leeped' the pig ... that was putting it in boiling water before they scraped the birse off it. Birse is the bristle the shoemaker uses to stitch boots with ... so stiff it doesn't need a needle.

The womenfolk at Hugh Craigie's boyhood croft made black puddings too, and he recalls them better at a later stage, matured, seasoned and stored in the girnal-kist.

At night we used to go out and cut a piece of pudding and cook it at the fire.

The ladies salted down mutton too, hung up hams and split and dried fish for the months ahead.

As well as the rearing of pigs and cattle for their own consumption the Hendersons grew the corn which would eventually reach their own table.

The corn went to the watermill a couple of miles away. You didn't pay the miller, he took his payment by keeping a quantity of your meal.

There was no money changed hands. It was payment in what you call 'kind' (or kain). When that meal came home it went into the kist and when we were young we used to get the job of tramping it down to pack it tight so it would keep better. We got lifted in to do that and we loved it. We washed our feet first, mind.

They only washed their feet, but the Craigie youngsters had special clothing. Hugh Craigie recalls every stage of their crop from seed to table.

It was bere 't we grew. That's an old Scottish crop that can grow on poor land. Ordin'ry barley has two rows of grain up the heads, bere has the rows right round and it's much rougher. We grew it and then took it to the miller to grind. My grandfather wasn't a big man but he'd carry ten stones of it over a mile home up the valley. At home it was packed into one of the big girnals, wooden boxes like bunkers, y'know. It was very light and fine when it was milled, so soft that we'd to pull on special white stockings to tramp it down hard. It had to be hard to keep it fresh and that's why it'd to be scraped off with a plate when it was to be used. That kept the rest firm. Then Mother made bere bannocks of that.

That need to tramp down the meal to keep it fresh was confirmed by Jim Still's memory of Forglen.

We took the corn to the miller and got our own meal back. We'd get a bow and a firlot of meal at a time for the girnal, that's about a hunnerweight and a half. It had to be well firmed down to keep it in good condition.

Some went further afield and less legitimately to add a little variety to their usual home bred fare and bring a spice of life and adventure to an austere and demanding existence.

When we were at one island lighthouse we used to go deer-hunting to another island, myself and another keeper, Macleod of Skye, who was a butcher to trade (all keepers had some other trade). Anyway we went over in a small boat and when you caught sight of a deer you'd to get leeward of it ... they've a very strong sense of smell y'know, and shoot from there. With the kind of gun we had it wouldn't be killed outright, but Macleod killed it immediately after. Then he would skin it and when we got out into the water again towing the deer behind us, we dumped the skin over the side with a boulder to sink it. After two or three miles in the sea the carcase was washed clean. After we got it home it was kept in the cellar till it was ready to eat. It was poaching of course, but islanders are good at the poaching and venison was a luxury beside the fish and rabbit that we usually ate.

They kept hens almost everywhere, Ballantrae, Tarbert, Connel, Lismore, Bernera, Skye, Tongue, Latheronwheel and Fife ... for their own use and sometimes as part of the barter system that persisted for centuries in rural areas.

> When my mother had too many of the prints of fresh butter she made, and of her eggs, she used to pack them in a basket with cabbage leaves round them and between them, to keep them cool. She would send me up to the village shop with it and the grocer would send back half a stone of maybe sugar and anything else Mother needed to the value of the butter and eggs, and a wee bit money perhaps, to make up any difference. I remember it was a heavy basket for a wee lad.

Sometimes among certain of the Bernera islanders the hens and eggs were exchanged for services rendered ... but that was not so in the Macleod household when they were handed over.

> We kept hens, for ourselves really, but you may be sure the doctor and minister got the best of these when they called ... gifts they'd be though ... not payment ... but certainly some did that.

But the saddest little vision of hens as family fare is Isobel Wales's minding of herself being sent with one of the hens she had fed from her pinny, to have its neck screwed.

> My aunt would say, 'Take this over to Tammy and get its neck wrung.' I remember one escaping from my arms once. But yes, I'd to carry a hen over to this Tammy, alive, ... and bring it back dead ... Well I ask you, and me just a wee Glasgow person!'

One who was well prepared for life on a farm by a watchful and far-sighted father was Miss Hilda Reid the blacksmith's daughter, soon to wed Farmer Strachan near Turriff.

> Father sent me to Craibstone, a bittie out of Aberdeen, before I was married. That was a centre where you learned to be a farmer's wife. We were taught housekeeping, milking, looking after the hens, bee-keeping and cheese-making and I did all of these things. We'd grand honey from the bees (though I was a bit frightened of them at first). We made a lot of cheese on the farm, cutting the curds and turning them over then pressing out the moisture in chessels. I had zinc chessels ... some had wooden ones.

Jim Still, too, remembers the cheese and butter-making at his home.

Mother made butter and we used to like drinking the buttermilk. And she made cheese in a kind of wooden tub in a cloth, and there was this stone press to squeeze out the moisture. Good cheese that was.

It was cows that obliged with the milk for all that cheesemaking in Buchan, but cows round lighthouses were thin on the ground.

No cow's milk for us. I was brought up on goat's milk. Every keeper at all the stations had three goats that we milked night and morning. We made butter in jam jars off goat's milk and a good cheese-crowdie as well.

The croft communities, of course, included the bothy men who shared the tenant farmer's store, since they ate in the house, but the married workers in their own cots had their supplies allocated to them by right.

The married men at Ribera farm got half-a-ton of dressed potatoes when the crop was in. And they got their allowance of meal ... their oatmeal y'ken, ... och, and they'd other perks.

And no doubt they went berry-picking around the lanes and hedgerows and met scores of others from the crofts and fishercots on the same happy hunting grounds.

We used to go gathering fruit on the Bramble Brae. They hung thick there. We picked pounds of that brambles. Then we'd our own raspberries and gooseberries for making jam. They made a lot of jam in our kitchen, because there were five or six men to get pieces.

Even in a small town like Troon, where there was a good string of small, well-stocked shops, no self-respecting housewife would have touched or countenanced 'bought' jam. A woman could be branded nearly scarlet for such decadence.

Oh yes, Mother made jam, rhubarb and ginger, rhubarb and apricot, and jelly. I can see the walking-stick yet, pushed through the spars of two back-to-back chairs, and the jelly-bag with the juice dripping through into the ewer-basin of the wash-stand set. My father went brambling in the Fullarton Woods so the brambles were free and the jelly just cost the sugar. My mother used to sit totting-up how much it all was a pot!

There weren't many fruit bushes round lighthouses but the MacRaes did a fair bit of what you might call organic or environmental gardening.

We'd quite a lot of our own produce and we'd rare vegetables because we'd used the seaweed from the rocks for manure in our wee bit gardens ... yes, grand vegetables.

Many of the fisherfolk had homes opening straight on to the street with tiny yards at the back with space only for nets and creels. Others cultivated small gardens.

> We'd good soil for the patch we ca'ed a garden and it was a matter of pride to my father that my mother'd never to buy vegetables for soup. That was kinda funny, mind, for it was her did all the work!

But the award for thrift in making use of the most unlikely basis for a good meal, goes to that Troon mother who sent her man out brambling, and who did more than tot up the cost of her jam. Her motto was 'easy dinners are dear dinners' and her starting point for a pot of soup was neither a tin-opener nor a stock cube from her larder.

> It was one of the perks for cooks in the big houses to get the roast dripping in their kitchens and sell it to the grocers. Mother used to buy a bowl of that, turn it out and take the 'brown' off the bottom to make a sort of tasty stock for potato soup. Then she used the dripping to make meal haggis ... a sort of skirlie or pan haggis. We'd that with bread toasted at the fire.

What about that fire? How did they fuel fires and stoves and ranges twenty miles from nowhere on the coast or on the islands?

> Every winter th' were trees blown down in the woods and the forester 'd go round and mark them off to different ones among the tenants for fuel, and for planks or posts.

Then there was coal. There was often a benison for the people of the sea-shore in the sea-coal gathered by the children. And even ordinary coal was brought home sometimes as an unlikely perk of long distance fishermen like those from Peterhead.

> When the fishing out of Yarmouth was over for the season, a boat crew could take a load of coal at 4s.6d.-a-ton from Blyth to Peterhead ... maybe forty tons, and that was shared out among them. That was once a year and it lasted them six months.

There was a prodigal irony about the delivery of coal to the lighthouse people that would have made the good Troon lady and most of her contemporaries grue or swoon if they had known of it.

> You'd your open fire on the stations. Once a year the wee Para Handy boat came round with coal and the puffer man unloaded it and brought

it up to the station. We'd cellars and when you got word the puffer was coming you cleared the cellars ready. I've been on stations where we'd to throw out hundredweights of coal over the rocks to make room for the new load. It wasn't easy y'see to gauge exactly what you were using and you daren't run out of coal but you couldn't turn any back with the puffer. What a waste! ... It was always coal, never peat.

But it was peat, and peat only, in many places including the island of Bernera with the Macleods.

Our family dug and stacked our own peat. The working days at the peat were real occasions ... we'd picnics and och, it was grand!

They cut their own at Latheronwheel too, one man on the tusker with his foot on its step sinking the blade, the rest lifting and stacking. And it took five hours for the Craigies in Orkney to cart their year's supply home when it had dried out after the digging.

The storing of fuel for the winter was so essential a part of life for those in the peat areas that the whole months-long process was woven firmly into home and village life, the women no less involved than the men. The little Isobel Campbell evacuated far from Glasgow kitchen bunkers and city streets, carries memories of 'the peat' that have the very feel and smell of the Lewis bogs about them.

My aunts did the peat work. Every April when the better weather came they went out to the peat area with their cutting irons, 'tairsgean'. They wore old old clothes and boots because cutting peats was very messy especially early in the work in April. The peat was soggy and heavy with water. We used to go with the aunts when the weather was good. They worked and we played ... had picnics out on the peats. When they cut the peat they laid it on top of the peat bank. It was so heavy that they could barely lift it. They just heaved it aside and left it to let some of the water drain from it, so that it dried in the wind and any sun. After a week or two they would go out and turn it. That was the next operation. Then later they went out again to stack it in special piles to let the air through it again ... a few more weeks if they were lucky and the weather was right they might have it back at the house by about the end of June. That was the only fuel, so it had to last the whole year. One of the big difficult jobs was getting it from the peat banks to a made road good enough for the old lorry. Each household had a special day for the lorry and all the neighbours helped ... one day to one household so that everyone got back the same peat they'd dug. The men threw it on to the lorry and the women stacked it back at the house. The lorry might take five loads back and forward till all your peats were home.

Another necessity of life not always easily supplied was water, as witness those labours of washing day recollected elsewhere. But Isabel Cameron has a more mystical memory of going to the well for water than those sturdy youngsters whose only aim was to bring it back and tip it into the wash-boiler and who did not dawdle, in wonder, over the chore.

> We went to the well at my Seanair's house ... down the side of their field, and leaned over to scoop it up in a bucket. There was a spring deep in it that made the water *move* and I liked to hang over and watch it. I've often thought that was what the 'living' water in the Bible would be.

Even where there was a cold water tap indoors it was not always the best for the purpose. Isobel Craigie remembers a little chore of hers.

> I used to carry water in for the butter-making from the spring. It was fine cold water, colder than the tap water for washing the butter.

There were always household essentials not to be found locally and these had usually to be sent for. They came to their lighthouses in response to an order from John MacRae's mother.

> At certain lonely stations a relief-boat came out once a week, say from Port Askaig on Islay. Lighthouses were very early to have 'phones, y'know the old turn-the-handle 'phone; anyway my mother would've 'phoned an order and it would come by boat with the mail. She did clothes-shopping and that, from mail-order catalogues.

For the Orkney islands too, what couldn't be grown, gathered, culled from the sea, or bred as meat or poultry, had to come by boat.

> The steamer came to Rousay once a week with supplies, bread and that. The shop collected the bread packed in boxes at the pier and it would still be warm when you got it. After it had gone hard or even fusty-green you were on to your mother's baking, mostly bere bannocks and oatcakes.

The arrangements for island supplies to Lewis, half-a-century ago seems, even in patronising hindsight, to have been a highly efficient enterprise, at both ends, customer and warehouseman, and the link between the heart of the city and a village on the edge of the north Atlantic, away ahead of sail-cloth ceilings and baths in dolly barrels. It was almost a naval-type operation ... a rendezvous off Bernera.

Our groceries and other things came by boat when I was young. The supply boat came and my father and some of the others took their boat out to get their groceries that they'd ordered out of a catalogue from Coopers in Howard Street in Glasgow. It'd be stones of barley, stones of this, that and the next thing ... everything in bulk and loaded in tea-chests. This boat would be a MacBrayne's I think ... or maybe the *HEBRIDES*, MacCallum Orme's boat.

Where there was a town nearby there could be more regular forays to replenish larder and cupboard. And any town worthy of the name had its Store ... not just any store ... as Alex Archer of Largo recalls.

In the 'twenties, when I was a boy, my mother did her real shopping in Leven, not Largo. It was all the 'Store' there ... that's the Co'. It kept everything from food to clo'es, and paraffin for your lamps.

And from St. Combs they went north to Fraserburgh for shopping, just along with the hoi-polloi in the train but knowing that they had more genteel transport at home, for shorter trips.

We'd go to Fraserburgh for the main shopping ... in the train. Mind we'd a pony and trap too ... affa grand, a pony and trap!'

So that's the bere in the girnal, the cereals in the kist, hams on the rafters, everything squirrelled away and hunger staved off till the next Martinmas and pig-killing time. And we can leave the story of supply to the country's fringes with a glance at the important matter of the very young learning to lay out their income just as thriftily. When goods came by boat there was probably a poke or two of sweets, but that was nowhere as interesting as the real selection you got in a place like Ballantrae.

When we were young we got a ha'penny on a Monday and a penny on a Friday, and you could go to the shop and pick from a tray ... sherbet or sugarollie, ogie-pogie-eyes ... and there were wee bars of something that you'd to shut your eyes and pick, and if you picked the one w' the wee pink bit on it you got an extra thing.

... and a firm foundation for a canny future.

23
Clean Comfort and Plain Vittles

Talk of holidays to a city rememberer and you hear of whole excited families, bursting hampers, buckets and spades and pier entertainers ... even the novelty of a change of sink. Peep into the memories of a domiciled sea-sider and you hear of the joys of a successful letting, Rooms with Attendance, long hours at the catering, and caddying for golfers ... one man's leisure another man's labour.

Alex Archer recalls older days in Fife.

> Long ago when I was a boy folk used to come to a' the places here, Lundin Links, Largo, Crail an' that, and some brought their maid or their nanny.

And one of those maids,

> I was in service in them days and I mind when I heard we were goin' to St. Monance I bought a pair of speckled sannies, and my-here! Did I no' think I was something, slappin' about the pavements in St. Monance in them sandshoes!'

From late last century the business of letting was common to some extent in all the places remembered, but it was nowhere more 'the thing' than in Ballantrae.

> What you want to hear about is Ballantrae in its holiday heyday ... well that's no' now! But in the old days when the Glasgow Fair came roon', *everybody* prepared ... everybody in Ballantrae took in. If they'd only one spare bed in the house it was let to someb'dy that was lettin' to someb'dy else! They didnae always feed them but they let them beds ... even the schoolhouse and the manse *and* the council houses. Bigger houses had wee-er places at the back and the folk moved into them and let out the house. Glasgow merchants and ship owners came to these wi' their maids. There was golf for them then, mind.

It wasn't only in the lodgings that a living was made from the holiday-makers. Margaret Kirk of Ballantrae has unresentful memories of her summer labours.

My father was the butcher and I was up about half past three in the morning makin' sausages and black puddings.

Y'see a lot of visitors took in their own meat and the landlady cooked it for them. That's what they called Rooms with Attendance.

It was like that further north too, as Catherine Murray of Connel, Argyll, recalls.

There were always a lot of holiday visitors came to Connel and Oban, and took houses. The householders would have a wee bothy at the back for themselves in the summer. Some of the folk from Glasgow or Edinburgh brought their maids with them. We'd the General Shop and it was all good and busy for us. Rooms with Attendance was popular too. Folk came year after year. They went to Oban for a livelier sort of holiday and came to Connel if they liked it quieter.

Troon, within cheap reach of Glasgow, almost doubled its population every summer until shortly after the Second War. Ease of travelling to and from business for father was a consideration while the family paddled and pied on the beach or visited the teashops.

When the business men came from Glasgow, and brought their families and maids, Troon was packed. I worked in Kirkwood the Baker's here and y'know these merchants would run up their accounts for maybe two months and you sent the bill to Glasgow at the end of the summer and never *once* did we not get the money. Never was any doubt about it.

So the money poured as merrily into the wooden money-bowls of the time as it did into ringing cash registers thirty years later.

There was a shipyard in Troon which was the menfolks' main source of employment but when the hammers fell silent for the annual break there was a problem.

There was no holiday money for the men y'see, so the week or fortnight's money had to be found someway. Holidays were idle time. So from about the 1890s on until about the Second War letting was the other real town business. People were glad to let, to make up the pay. Lots let their rooms and stayed in their kitchen and all the houses early in the spring had tickets up in their windows 'JULY' or 'AUGUST' or maybe 'APARTMENTS'. That meant they'd vacancies.

The need for a full let to cover Father's unpaid work-leave was taken earnestly by even the youngest member of the family.

There was a wee boy in the Sunday School and he was very excited one day, just itching to say something.

Apart, presumably, from his Golden Text.

Well James, what is't you've to say?'
'Please Miss, we're LET for August!'

While young James rejoiced at that good fortune, his older brothers were caddying for the golf, getting out early in the morning to catch the handsomest tippers.

Though, mind you, golf wasn't a rich man's game in Troon.

Better heeled, or winded, folk took much longer journeys for their holidays, adventuring into almost Arctic unknown, the outposts of Empire. George MacGregor remembers one of them.

This man came to Thurso from England for the first time and after he'd been for a wee while he invited some friends from the south to join him. They weren't too keen to come to the back o' beyond like Thurso, but they came, and before they left they'd booked their holiday for the next year. They'd never seen such grand beaches as Thurso and all round the north. The real fine white beaches are in the Hebrides of course, the shell sand, but Thurso's are beautiful. There's the rivers too, for the rod salmon fishing.

Rose Baker has memories of as far and venturesome a journey, but to the south from Edinburgh.

My stepfather was English and he used to go down to see his mother, and I mind sailing wi' him from Leith to London in a cargo boat. Two nights, it took us, down the east coast. My stepfather had been a sailor, y'see and never *thought* on takin' the train to London.

Nor did Hugh Craigie's Orkney grandfather 'think on' taking the train to Edinburgh.

My grandfather went a lot to Edinburgh. He'd two daughters there. He was a great man for a boat and he went to Leith, sailing from Orkney.

There were what glossy brochures now call 'interest holidays' to draw people to the same haunts year after. When John Coghill was young ...

> Tongue was a very busy place. It was sea-loch fishing, of course that brought folk, and the hotel was absolutely full all the fishing season. It was a thriving thing, the hotel, always lots of what we called 'haw-haw' English voices and just *scores* of rods hung up or stacked against the fence in the evenings. Then the fishers would be up and away early in the morning.

> It was not just food for the body and relaxation for the mind that visitors sought, but peace for the soul too; and catering for the happy families was with more than black puddings from Mister Kirk the Butcher or cakes from Mistress Kirkwood the Baker's Wife ... 'Kirk' certainly though.

> In Lochgilphead the church would be packed on summer Sundays. You'd to hurry to get a seat. Some folk took cottages up the brae and some came to friends or boarding houses, but they *all* came to church.

So recalls the daughter-of-the-manse who was young Miss Cameron, the Minister's Daughter.

Some people have nostalgic memories of holidays barely a hop, skip and jump from home. Margaret Ritchie has of hers.

> We went our holidays from Inverness to North Kessock on the Black Isle ... got the 'bus at the market yonder ... then the ferry. That wasn't much more than two miles maybe altogether I suppose, but it was across the water and we were 'away our holidays'. It was a bit quiet for me, Kessock.

But what kind of throb of activity she would have fancied, the rememberer did not confess.

Rose Baker remembers hers from Musselburgh.

> We went to Burntisland, regular ... took the boat from Granton just across the Forth.

And another memory of a Black Isle holiday.

> We used to go to Avoch where the folk are called Avochy-dollies. I mind the postwoman on her bicycle and the man who went down to the shore every night and morning to see if there was a salmon in his net. A warren of fisher rows it was, Avoch. And they used to say that's what made it easy for smugglers to jouk in and out to hide from excise men ninety or a hundred years ago. We took a cottage next-door to a Mrs.

Mackay who gathered rainwater in crocks and zinc basins to wash her clothes. Her father had built that cottage himself with stones from the shore. Built it wi' the gavel-end to the sea. I mind the wee stair up the middle of that house ... tiny place it was ... and the ship in the bottle she had. 'It's a very old house this, and I've lived in it all my days,' she used to say.

But not as old, perhaps, as the Victorian one whose mistress said earnestly and proudly of it,

It's a verra verra old house this, I'm no' sure whether it's B.C. or A.D. but it's verra old.

Another short journey was from Ardrossan across to Arran and that took little Jean Kane to the real seaside.

A friend of my mother's stayed in Brodick and she was awfu' fond of us twins. My mother used to dress us up in cotton kilted skirts wi' sailor tops and collars ... aye and straw hats ... and did we no' think we were *toffs*? Well-here she used to take us like yon down to the harbour and say to the men on the Arran boat, 'Goin' to take them across and Miss Fullarton'll be at th' other side to get them?' Just the two of us went, and that was our summer holiday. Miss Fullarton let her house and slept in the wee place at the back. We used to go up Glen Rosa, and when it was goin' to rain there was yon mist over the Glen and you couldnae see Goat Fell at all.

There was another consequence of living at the seaside apart from the labours of bed-changing, 'between' cleanings and providing three meals a day for paying guests.

On a Glasgow holiday there was a fair invasion of all your cousins and aunties. Mother would make a big pot of soup or mince to feed them. They wouldn't always say they were coming, or sometimes they came 'for the day' wi' a week-end ticket!

And bang went the two-three days' respite from the paying visitors. That went on from Stranraer to Orkney, but sometimes there was two-way traffic and that was when the seasiders had their kind of break. Catherine Murray from Connel was part of that exchange.

The way we did for holidays was we went to the city for ours and our relatives came to us at the Glasgow Fair. Oh what a treat to go round the Glasgow shops, and then one year (that would be 1938) it was the Empire Exhibition.

It was like that too for others busy with holiday visitors.

We never went as a family, just singly or in twos and that would be to a relative. Or maybe we went to Edinburgh, to Marchmont, where the landladies had students through the winter. Oh, but we thought it was wonderful! Crawford's or McVitie's for coffee with a window seat overlooking Princes Street Gardens, or cheap day trips to Fife. And Jenner's ... oh Jenner's!

The lighthouse-keeping fraternity had its own peculiar problems.

Keepers seldom went away holidays themselves. They didn't sleep well when they were off like that.

There was gentle laughter at the sympathetic suggestion that that might be because they missed the lash of the sea or the sobbing of gulls.

No, no, no, just because, for a change, they were in bed all night ... not just the usual four hours on and four hours off. The routine was upset. But the bairns went. I remember as a nipper, (my father and my grandfather ... aye, and my great-grandfather, being keepers before me) we went to Glasgow for holidays to someone that would be retired from the service. I remember seeing the open trams. What always sticks in my mind is one going along Argyle Street past Lewis's (maybe it was the Polytechnic then) and here th' was this great big camel in one of the windows, made up of towels just! Funny the things that stick in your mind. I can see it yet, that camel, clear as clear, and the trams wi' the drivers out in the open cabins. That was our kick ... coming to the city.

There were those for whom holidays, even the two-mile-away sort, were just a dream.

My mother never got a holiday ... too big a family and too wee a pay-poke.

And one Fife lady was a grown woman before she had her first.

We couldna afford holidays really. The first one I ever had, I was about twenty, and that was back to Macduff to see my granny.

But it would have been a poor soul who never got a day away at least, from time time.

Troon people didn't go away much on holiday in the early years of the century, but Ayr Races week-end was *the* holiday time here. You didn't go away and stay, but you went to the Shows at Ayr. Some would go to the Races right enough, but *everybody* went to Ayr. A lot of people came for days-out to Troon as well, mind, if the weather was good. Then the tea-room belonging to the baker's shop would be packed wi' what we called 'saut-water folk' (city people coming to get a sniff of sea air). They came on Special Day Tickets.

So the story of holidays for the coast-dwellers was largely one of hard work to provide visitors with a good holiday and to eke out their makings over unpaid leave and the coming winter. They laboured long hours to supply hot water, clean comfort, plain vittles and a variety of recreations, not to mention the small services which made things run smoothly. The visitors needed the locals, and the locals needed the visitors. They watched, sharp-eyed, for the signs of an auspicious start to each new week of the season.

The boys used to hang around the station with their bogies (made of a box-on-wheels with long handles) to take the luggage to the holiday houses ... mind, Sammy Dykes, the man that was the real franchised porter, used to chase them ... Well anyway, we used to watch from the shop to count the hampers and see if it was to be a good week.

And it usually was, with landladies beavering away over wash-boilers and kitchen ranges, with 'weans' in the west, and 'bairns' in the east, trailing tin spades grittily along the prom, and mothers stuffing sandy, salty bathing-dresses into bags to take back to the lodgings and hang out from windows to dry ... the bunting of the seaside holiday.

24
A Hearse Was a Very Posh Funeral

One of the first things a fisherman got after he was married was a lum hat, a three-tail swallow-coat and dark trousers, an umbrella, a pair of gloves and elastic-sided boots ... kept that all their lives or, for some, until they got too fat. That was for funerals in my father's generation over a hundred years ago.

And, unlike the norm of the 1980s, an outfit more needed in their youth and middle age than in their sere and yellow years.

That was in and around Musselburgh but if there is one constant feature of funerals long ago it *is* that, almost to a man the mourners were in bowlers and dark suits, though not often the swallow tails. But in Ayrshire, Lismore, Oban, Lewis, Orkney, Peterhead, and Fife, with few exceptions the dark suit, white starched shirt-front and bowler were required symbols of respect, even on the very young.

When I sent to my grandfather's funeral with my two young brothers I was about twelve and they'd be ten and seven, and all three of us had wee bowler hats.

Standard dress defined, funeral rituals varied interestingly from place to place according to the quirks, traditions and whatever constituted seemliness and a decent send-off in that individual community. First was the announcement of a death where there was no local daily paper.

They used to put notices in shop windows to intimate a death. The printer would have big black-edged cards ready and then he would print in the details, y'know the sort of thing ...
MY FATHER CALUM MACLEOD DIED HERE TODAY 3rd MARCH 1900.
FUNERAL WILL BE ON 6th MARCH AT 11 A.M.
                                MALCOLM MACLEOD.

That was the way of things in Girvan, Ballantrae and in Lewis and the other islands, so that within an hour or two, the whole community was informed. Some would brush down their dark suits for the interment, others would do it sooner, for in some parts there was a wake to attend first.

I can tell you an example of a wake in Lismore I was at when I was young. This cousin of my mother's died. He'd been one of two bachelor brothers that stayed together. The first night after the death the close relatives came to keep the remaining brother company and when the second night came he asked me to come and help with the tea and that, for other neighbours and friends coming in. So I took two clean dish towels (they'd been just two bachelors y'see, so I didn't know about *their* towels) and sat there till about three or four in the morning with them all. We just sat and talked and maybe someone would read a passage from the Bible. It was just a kind of sitting-up with the dead and the bereaved. I remember my uncle was a good Gaelic reader of the Bible and he read a chapter. I made tea twice, and then about four o'clock Donald said I should go home. I always remember't was a beautiful moonlight night over the island when I walked home over the crofts.

The cups and saucers back at the bachelor home left decently and hygienically dried, Mary Macfadyen arrived home to what seemed like a chilling reception.

My sister was away so the house should have been empty but when I got home I heard a queer kind of panting and rasping ... like the cousin's breath that had been dying. I hardly dared to move, but I went into the kitchen and here it was only my brother-in-law home unexpectedly from the sea, pumping up a primus stove to make a cup of tea ... my, but that panting was an eerie noise.

Nothing like a west highland lyke-wake for putting you in the mood for a good mid-nightime haunting!

Not all wakes were entirely solemn, certainly not from start to finish in the kind remembered in Lewis by Isobel Wales.

There would be the wake before the funeral of course. People came to the house between the death and the burial and sang Psalms and had Bible readings. It was a watching over the dead, really, and a sort of keeping company with the family. Mind you it *could* turn into a bit of a carry-on, because it was often the younger folks who came later and stayed on till morning. I remember being vaguely appalled ... this

granny lying dead in the next room and the youngsters joking and laughing. It seemed terrible.

Or perhaps it was just the natural ability of the young in close and strict communities to find leavening even in solemn custom.

Next day it was the committal. In rural or island communities where good roads were rare the people held for a long time to the funeral custom of processing on foot to the graveyard, with mourners in relays carrying the coffin.

At Ness the coffin was carried on a big ladder-thing. It had handles front and back and the men held it by these. One team would carry it so far and then there was this ritual change-over. Those carrying would stop and the next group would've overtaken them and be alongside to

take over. Then when they'd got hold of it the first lot moved to the
side then fell back to the end of the procession. It was quite a long walk
to the graveyard. Only the men went, of course. The women stayed at
home. The men didn't go back to the bereaved home; certainly not at
the funerals I know about. They tended to get hospitality at any of the
homes they passed. Everything stopped in the village ... peat work,
croft work ... everything.

The 'ladder-thing' noted by the little Isobel Campbell at the Butt
of Lewis was a bier and it featured also in Farquhar MacDonald's
reminiscence of Skye.

When a funeral was setting off it was just a straggle of people formed up
outside the house ... no military precision about it. Then the coffin
would be carried out and this ragged column would follow the four or
six men carrying the coffin on a bier. Then, automatically, and quite
soon, without anyone giving orders, another six would move up and
take over the bier. So the coffin could be at the head, or the middle, or
the back of the procession. It would be a 'carry' of several miles to the
grave.

If the late lamented 'lyke' had had as much twinkle about him as
those who passed on this tale he would have been cheered that the
mourners at his funeral had something to smile about.

I'll tell you what happened at one house. This funeral column moved off
and went about a quarter of a mile up the road till't almost disappeared
over the horizon. Then as the women were watching from the sides of
their drawn blinds they saw about a dozen men hurrying back down the
hill and into the funeral house. Then they came out carrying the coffin.
They'd moved off without it, not realising y'know ... thinking, because
of this system of changing bearers and having the coffin sometimes at
the back and sometimes in the middle, that it was there somewhere
among the mourners.

Although it was a customary mark of respect, over the funeral
period, for all work to stop in the community there were those, like
the doctor on Skye who sometimes forgot, or cheated on that
courtesy, and who furtively hoed a drill or two of their croft
turnips. On one occasion the said doctor was so engrossed with his
neeps that he forgot the primary social duty of the day. As he was
probably the doctor who had lost the patient in question, then he
was surely adding insult to fatal injury.

The man who died had been very well-known in the community. All the denominations turned out for him, the Free Kirk minister, the Parish minister *and* the priest. He was to get a fine send-off this man . . . all of them in their dark suits and bowlers. The graveyard was right beside one of two croft houses with black hens scratching about there and into the graveyard. My father was standing there along with the chemist, and at the very last minute the doctor arrived. He'd obviously forgotten all about the funeral and was still in his muddy shoes and croft clothes. One of the men leans across my father, 'A'ach even the hens have turned up for this funeral' he says.

'Aye' says the chemist, 'and at least *they're* dressed for the occasion.'

The unspoken understanding of the bier-changing was choreographed into a very traditional ritual elsewhere in Lewis, recalled by Mr. and Mrs. James Pryde.

Around Stornoway there seemed to be a tradition grown up that every man attending the funeral had a turn in carrying the coffin part of the way . . . maybe only twenty or thirty yards, but you'd all to get your turn. The carrying was part of the ritual. Then when everyone had done it, the coffin was put into a horse-drawn hearse for the rest of the way. So, you see, the bigger the funeral the more had to carry and so the shorter the journey by hearse.

Perhaps that was a relic of a time before horse-drawn hearses. For that was the first mention of wheels and they were something of a wonder in places like Latheronwheel in spite of its name.

A hearse was a very posh funeral. It was usually a bier . . . just carried. The bier just lay in the churchyard from one funeral to the next. It was the joiner was the undertaker and jack-of-all trades and he ran the day. When it came to the coffining operation there was a party went to the joiner to collect the coffin. They coffined the body. Then the joiner walked along while the first four carried the bier then after so-many paces, he'd say, 'Right next four take over'. And the crofters took turns all the three miles to the churchyard.

When the days of the hearse came that was a big thing. The women never went, oh no, no, no!

Just as well for their feminine peace of mind, since the lad that was David Henderson at twelve years old, carried an unforgettable memory of an early burial he attended.

I was at my grandfather's funeral and they'd opened up the old family grave and I saw bones all lying there. I remember that.

For a time that combination of the walking column and the horse-drawn hearse continued in places all round the coast. Alex Archer remembers it in Largo.

> First funeral ever I was at, I would be about twelve. It was horse and cart-hearse wi' two black horses from Upper Largo pulling. The hearse had fancy glass sides like in show-folks' caravans w' fancy-work round it. And a' the men and boys walked behind that in bowlers ... oh aye, bowlers.

Tarbert didn't insist on the black horses.

> There was no motor hearse at Tarbert, of course, when I was young. The coffin went on the horse-drawn hearse ... not black horses necessarily. I don't think they specialised in colour.

But they did in the after-refreshments.

> Of course there was a lot of whisky at Tarbert funerals.

And at Latheronwheel too.

> They always had biscuits and a dram after the funeral.

But full marks for undertakers' style, formality and ceremonial goes to Peterhead in the heyday of the processional funeral there.

> They were very long-winded affairs here then. There was the procession and the horses w' their plumes ... it was a horse-drawn hearse. The local funeral contractor here had his horses groomed to perfection, black they were, shining and glossy and the man wi' the top hat and whip sat up in front. A' the men followed, but if 't was a public figure was getting buried his colleagues on the committee or council or trust, whatever it was, they followed right after the hearse, before even the family ... was a kind of tribute to his office. That contractor was an old man when I was young. He was a carter as well and when he died, for respect to his trade they took his coffin to the cemetery on a flat horse-cart.

Yes, they had it to a fine art in Peterhead in Jim Buchan's young days, and no doubt after all the pomp and circumstance of plumes and councillors, there would be the steak pie, or the dram ... or both. Indeed the dram was so thoroughly obligatory at funerals in certain areas that principle itself could fall before the demands of social nicety.

> My aunt in Skye disapproved of having drinks at funerals ... disapproved of drink altogether ... wouldn't have a bottle of whisky in the

house. But when it came to having a funeral in her own family they sent for *two crates* of it. Oh it was a strong custom that . . . two crates! It was poured into glasses and carried round on trays with wee squares of cheese to take with it.

Two crates! Well ... as the saying goes, 'if a thing's worth doing . . .'.

But the years were turning; even small villages started to see the odd 'motor' on their roads, and walking processions, as Peter Sinclair remembers them, began to become mere tokens of old forms.

By the 'twenties and 'thirties funerals here in Connel were followed on foot just till they were beyond the village, then the mourners would get on to the brake or whatever there was, and go the rest of the way on that. The blinds on all the houses in the village were still pulled down though.

Further north in Harris at about the same time, both coffin *and* closely-related mourners were conveyed together in an ancient 'bus. They travelled in the 'bus to the graveyard, seated on either side of the coffin ... *twice*, if they were not careful! And thereby hangs George MacGregor's macabre little tale.

This old lady died in her 'black' house and it was the custom for the relatives to do the coffining, not an undertaker. Well, when they got the coffin from the joiner, it was the job of the one relative to put the old soul in and lay the lid over the top, and another came in and screwed it down. They'd all their duties y'see. When the four or six men came to carry the coffin out, it was light, but the old lady had kind of dwindled away, and they were big men so they thought nothing of it. The funeral took place and they all came back home for their cup of tea or their dram. Then someone said, 'We'd best be opening up the curtains.' So they went round the windows and then one lady drew back the ones over the old box-bed and let out such a yell, for the old woman was still lying there. So they'd to go back to the churchyard, dig up the coffin and go through the whole thing again. Mind, the coffin hadn't been quite empty. There was the joiner's screw driver left inside it.

Except for undertakers and ministers, almost all the parties at funerals nowadays are older than the mourners of long ago. Few children attend, because the deceased (unless there's been a youthful tragedy) is often touching ninety and his mourners nearly contemporary.

In those days when you heard a man was seventy you wondered when his funeral was to be. I'm in my ninety-sixth year and I'm not wondering yet ... and this lady is over seventy. That would've been extraordinary in my young days.

And 'this lady' smiles at his gallantry, for she too is over ninety. He's right. It was extraordinary long ago to reach the nineties and so rare was such a specimen that one ancient on the shores of Loch Long made his very living out of it.

It was quite the thing for holiday-makers to go and just *look* at this old chap sitting outside his cottage selling *postcards* of himself.

So we can leave them now, lying quietly, in spite of mishaps, forgettings and unruly wakes, in peaceful kirkyards on hillsides and above the machars of island and firth, laid to rest long ago by their friends, 'in sure and certain hope ...'

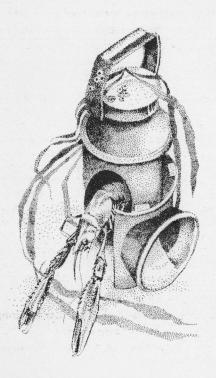

Glossary

a'	all	*ceilidh*	(G)* concert
affa, affa', affi	awful, awfully	*chap*	knock
arle	agree terms of work by exchange of coin.	*cheek-by-jowl*	close
		cheeper	kiss
		cheerie	chair
aye	yes, or always	*chessel*	cheese-press
		chink	space
bannock	oatmeal cake	*claes*	clothes
beadle	bellman, church officer	*clarty*	dirty
		cleek	hook or catch
bere	four-rowed barley	*clipe*	tell tales
bidey-in	live-in partner	*clootie*	cloth
bien	prosperous, comfortable	*conkers*	horse-chestnuts
		coo	cow
birse	bristle	*couter, cooter*	tidy, put to rights
blae	blue as with cold	*craik*	demand repeatedly
bonk	blow		
bools	marbles	*cran*	measure of fish
bothy	quarters for single men	*cratur*	creature or whisky
		creel	fish-basket
brander	cooking rack	*crock*	earthenware container
braws	best clothes		
breeks	trousers	*crowdie*	gruel, or cottage-cheese
brose	uncooked porridge		
bumbleerie	bottom	*cuddies, cudden*	young coal-fish
bumphly	crumpled, overclad	*cuddy*	horse
		cupach	(G)* cripple
bung	cork or stopper	*damsha-rod*	(G)* road dancing
buttie	sandwich or halibut	*darg*	set task
		dawdle	waste time
caller	fresh, cold	*derring-do*	boldness
canny	cautious	*dirle*	rattle
carsackie	loose working overdress or waistcoat	*douce*	quiet, well-behaved
		dour	sulky
cauld	cold	*douse*	extinguish
camanachd	(G)* shinty-playing	*drawers*	underpants
		dree one's weerd	bear one's situation
caw	turn in circle		

* Gaelic

220

drove	drive	*hinner end*	long-run
drystane-dyke	unmortared wall	*hinterland*	inshore land
dule	sorrow	*hoor*	hour
dulse	sea-weed	*host*	cough
dwyne, dwine	dwindling, decline	*hullarackit*	noisy and clumsy
dyke	wall	*hurl*	ride
		hussaurs	hussars
eke	make most of		
erle	agree terms of work by exchange of coin	*imperial*	mint pan-drop
		jambs	fireside uprights
		jannie	janitor
fankle	tangle	*jawbox*	sink, wash-tub
fash	bother	*jeely*	jelly
fey	strange, introspective	*jo*	sweetheart
		Jock Tamson's bairns	God's children
fite	white		
fleeing	flying	*jouk*	duck, evade
flukies	flounders		
footer	fuss	*kain*	(in) kind
footie	football	*kee-hoy*	hide and seek — mischief
forbye, forby	also		
forelan	herring-box	*keen*	blow sharply
fug	fog	*ken*	know
		ken-speckle	well-known
gaed	went	*Kirk*	national church
ganzie	jersey	*kirk*	local church
garron	small horse	*kist*	chest
gavel	gable	*kist o'whistles*	wind-box, organ
geggie	game or play		
gegie	article used in game	*lad o'parts*	clever boy
		leerie	lamplighter
gird	hoop	*loon, loonie*	lad
girdle	hotplate for scones or oatcakes	*loup*	leap
		lykewake	a watch-over the dead
girnal	meal chest		
glammered	bewitched		
guddle	fish by hand	*macher*	sandy tract by sea
graith	soapy lather	*mattie-full*	fat herring
grue	shiver, grit the teeth	*mim*	prim
		nae	no
hack	fissure in skin from cold	*neeps*	turnips
		nicht	night
ha'p'orth	halfpennyworth	*niffer*	barter
heidie	headmaster		
hidlins	secretly	*orra*	other, extra

paling	fence	*sonsy*	plump, comely
peelly-wally	sickly	*spigot*	tap
peerie	spinning-top	*stook*	stack
peever	hopscotch stone	*stoor*	dust
piece	bread-snack	*stoup*	container for liquid
plaid	shawl, blanket		
plank	hide something	*stovies*	potato-and-onion dish
poke	small paper bag		
poind	confiscate	*sugarollie*	liquorice
pooch	pouch, pocket	*swarry, swarree*	soiree, evening entertainment
potottie	potato		
purvey	catering	*swee, swey*	fire-chain to hang pot
qually	qualifying exam		
quare	queer	*tackets*	nail studs
queyt	oilskin overall	*tairsgean*	(G)* peat-cutter
		tattie	potato
riping	riddling	*teuchter*	highlander
		thirled	bound by habit or obligation
Sabaid	(G)* Sabbath, Sunday		
		thole	endure
saunnies	sandshoes, plimsolls	*ticking*	mattress cover
		tile (hat)	tall
sapple	soapy lather	*tim*	empty
sark	shirt	*toff*	well-dressed, genteel
saut	salt		
srcreeve	screech	*toon*	town
scrimle	scramble	*tot*	add
seanair	(G)* grandfather	*tottie*	potato
shielling	shelling, winnowing	*tulzie*	tussle, fracas
		Turk	harum-scarum
shift	change (of clothing)	*Turra'*	Turriff
shinty	a wilder version of hockey; used also of stick used in game	*vittles*	basic food
		wag-at-the-wa'	pendulum clock
		waur	worse
skedaddle	run away	*weel-aff*	well-off
skirlie	quickly made meal pudding	*weel-put-on*	well-dressed and spoken
sine	since	*wheech*	swiftly-passing
siller	money or silver	*wheesht!*	hush!
smeddum	mettle	*whin*	furze
smiddy	smithy	*wight*	strong man
smit	infection	*wir*	our
sneister	scorch		
snell	cold	*yon*	that, yonder